Foundering Fathers:
What Jefferson, Franklin, and Abigail Adams Saw in Modern D.C.!
2nd Edition

By Edward P. Moser

Moser Ink. Publications
La Puta Isle Projections

2116 Arlington Terrace
Suite 1
Alexandria, Virginia 22303-1500

www.wordsmithwizard.com
Savvyveteran@gmail.com

Foundering Fathers: What Jefferson, Franklin, and Abigail Adams Saw in Modern D.C.!

2nd Edition

Illustrations by Andy C. Ellis

Moser, Edward P.
Foundering Fathers: What Jefferson, Franklin, and Abigail Adams Saw in Modern D.C.! / Edward P. Moser
2nd Edition.

Edward P. Moser   Foundering Fathers

1. Humor—Politics. 2. Comedy—History. 3—Thomas
Jefferson. 4—Benjamin Franklin. 5—Abigail Adams.
6—Washington, D.C.

Produced in the United States of America

ISBN-10: 1492257923
ISBN-13: 978-1492257929

This book is dedicated to Ben Franklin, Thomas Jefferson, and John and Abigail Adams, whose notions of thrift, independence, self-reliance, civic virtue, and restraint in government are needed now more than ever.

"*A Republic—If they can keep it.*" – Ben Franklin

Contents

"Mysterious Undertakings at Famous Graves"

In the moonlight, the hooded men stepped warily past the grave stones and resting places. Past the grave of Robert Morris, the American Revolution's financier, past Dr. Benjamin Rush, a friend of John Adams. They ignored Commodore Bainbridge, the captain of the USS Constitution, a.k.a. "Old Ironsides," and also Philip Syng, supplier of the ink and quill with which the Declaration of Independence was signed, as well as John Dunlap, the Declaration's printer.

As they tiptoed along, cloaked in black, the men were thankful for the moonlight, which helped them pick their way through the sprawling urban graveyard, but worried that the light would let them be seen. Knots of tourists heading back from Independence Hall were occasionally glimpsed through the cemetery's iron gates. Fortunately, they seemed drunk and inattentive.

Philadelphia's Finest

The graves of honor, with their large resting stones, were easily found. They ignored the one for his wife, which was smaller and lay lower to the ground. They got to work, first with pick axes, their blows making tingling sounds from the pennies visitors had tossed onto the gravestone. They loosened the heavy, covering slab, and with effort lifted it and put it aside. The epitaph chiseled onto it read:

1

"Like the Cover of an old Book,
Its Contents torn out,
And stript of its Lettering and Gilding,
Lies here, Food for Worms.
But the Work shall not be wholly lost...

"For it will, as he believ'd, appear once more,
In a new & more perfect Edition,
Corrected and amended
By the Author of all."

They shone flashlights into the grave, then lowered and placed grappling hooks around the coffin. As feared, it crumbled too much to be lifted in one piece. So the scientist had the others tie the ropes to him. Then they slowly lowered him down.

The miner's light strapped to his head illuminated the crumbled remains of the coffin, which he brushed aside. Now he saw the mummified remains of the deceased; the outlines of the famous visage could still be discerned. Bits of hair hung from the skull, and bits of skin from the shoulders. The hollow eye sockets still held the eyeglasses with the fused double lenses, one for seeing near, and one for faraway.

The scientist signaled his helpers to lower him down to mere inches from the corpse. Taking out tiny scissors, he clipped off samples of bone, hair, spine, and flesh, placing them into a small plastic bag.

He motioned for the others to pull him up. Back on solid ground, he sealed the bag with care, placing it in a metal box. The others lowered back the gravestone, and they all slipped away, after erasing from the hallowed ground any tell-tale signs of their passage…

Massachusetts Machinations

…Two weeks later, in Quincy, Massachusetts, they had the benefit of a moonless night. They waited until three in the morning, when the streets were deserted, and the metro station across the way had long been shuttered. The street lights along the byway were few; the wires to the two nearest had been snipped. The normal police patrol along Hancock Street, their researchers and scouts had told them, wouldn't reappear for over an hour. They needed the time, given the multiple barriers to entry.

Furtively, the five men stepped to the locked door of the United First Parish Church. Minutes before, a computer expert on their team had hacked the place's security system, shutting down all alarms. The scientist pulled out a duplicate key, and slipped the lock.

Inside, their flashlights pierced the darkness, and they quickly reached the crypt. "Should we take off our miner's caps?" one of the men asked the scientist. "After all, it is a church."

"Don't be a dummy!" he shot back. He thought, 'You can't find good grave robbers anymore.' Then the duplicate key to the heavy iron door didn't work. The world-famous geneticist swore, then told himself not to worry, knowing they had worked out every eventuality. He nodded to his security chief, who took out a tiny bit of plastic explosive, and jammed it in the lock. They took cover down the hall, in the darkness, and the lock broke open with a mild bang.

The crypt contained four raised marble tombs, each crowned with a heavy slab, two of them with a wreath of flowers on top, signifying the wives of the deceased. They ignored the two dead presidents, and took up position around the flowered tomb nearest the back wall. They glanced at the brief biographical placard on the wall to ensure it was the right one. They hoisted the slab, lifted the lid off the coffin, and the scientist, easily this time, leaned into the vault to clip the precious bits of bone and nail and skin.

After gently replacing the lid, they placed an exact duplicate of the lock back into the door. They left the church, well ahead of the returning police patrol, and drove off in a SUV with phony plates…

Mountain-Top Manipulations

…A month earlier, again late at night, the same team had opened an ornate, wrought-iron gate, and stepped into a small cemetery atop a steep hill in rural Virginia. The security cameras trained on the main grave had been hacked to mask the current video feed with innocuous images from earlier in the evening.

The gate had been rather small, about six-foot high, with no barbed wire or metal spikes at its top. The security chief suggested merely hopping over, but the geneticist didn't want to risk injuries, so he ordered his men to pick the lock.

The grave robbers were surprised at the recent dates on several of the tombstones: their target's descendants still owned the property, and burials of family members still occurred there.

4

The excavation this time was more complicated. The grave they sought was easily identified, marked by a seven-foot obelisk and two base stones. But to reach it, they had to get past four surrounding graves, of the wife, daughters, and son-in-law, without damaging them. So they dug down, then across, then up to the prized coffin, leaving a tunnel just large enough for a man to crawl through.

The scientist wasn't squeamish, or claustrophobic, but his efficient style disliked the extra work and risks involved in this dig. Still, after months of labor, spectacular success was too close to give up now. His way lit by his miner's light, he crawled through the narrow passage, and bellied up to the underside of the coffin. Taking out a small mechanical saw, he cut through the rotting timber. His calculations had proven correct: he was located right underneath the back of the deceased's skull. He clipped the samples, put them safely away, and in the tunnel's darkness started back, thankful the workers had widened the passage there to permit him to turn around easily.

Once back on solid ground, he and his team took considerable time covering up their tracks, before exiting the quiet place, and heading down the steeply winding roadway of the little mountain in Albemarle County.

"High-Tech Hijinks at a Top-Secret Lab"

Deep within the Maryland firm's cavernous quarters, a bank of superdupercomputers churned out an endless array of data. On the display screens lining the walls, triplets of genetic letter code flashed by continuously, like news items in the Times Square electronic message board:

"...TTC TTA TGC CTA CCG CGA CCA GCT GAC GGA GGT GGC..."

Dr. Gregor Meddlesohm smiled, proud of his handiwork, of his achievements, and of the feats yet to come. His computers were the world's fastest, his biolabs the best-equipped, his scientists the highest-compensated, many of his thinkers grown wealthy from the stock proceeds of successful products. He pulled the keys out of his pocket to his Porsche Cayman roadster and, as was his habit, fingered the keys while he reflected.

He had been the first to map out the human proteome, the labyrinthine set of interactions among proteins and genes that produced all animals, all plants, every human. His team had devised a drug that rendered coronary bypass surgery unnecessary while curing female impotence. His researchers had banished cancer, at least many forms of it, as well as hangnails and nasal drip. But all of that was prelude, he was confident, to his next triumph.

On the Trail of Their Prey

Outside, the gold Mercedes-Benz 320 SUV pulled up to the lanes reserved for the highest-ranking officers and the most honored guests of reConstitution Biotek. The driver turned to his boss and nodded, feeling the Glock in his shoulder holster jiggle. His superior, known to the world as the head of his Middle Eastern nation's largest biomedical firm, and to the well-informed as its leading expert on biological warfare, stepped outside, and pushed his muscled, 6-ft, 2-in frame toward the entrance.

Originally of Afghan descent, he called himself Abdullah Abdullah Abdullah—many persons in that part of the world have the same first, last, and middle name. He left his own sidearm in the vehicle, while taking the heavy briefcase.

Nearby, the occupants of the battered 1965 flatbed Ford were in the "cheap seats," the parking lanes for the firm's rank and file. But they were handsomely compensated, not by Dr. Meddlesohm, but by a powerful Central Asian terrorist group. They watched Abdullah Abdullah Abdullah depart, then made their move, putting their secret weapon, Adriana, into play.

Adriana, a native of Rio and a fashion mag cover girl, unfastened another button on her silk blouse, and hitched up her leather skirt a notch. She stepped out of the passenger seat and, carrying a large Louis Vuitton purse, strolled toward the Mercedes on stiletto heels, the pickup truck slowly following. Sitting in the back was Jacque Carlos, a Columbian mercenary who'd fought against Gaddafi in southern Libya. He pushed down the rear door, and pulled a metal object out of a satchel.

The voluptuous Adriana stopped in front of the Mercedes, placed her handbag on the ground, and luxuriously stretched her finely tapered arms into the air. The SUV driver gave her his full attention. As he did, the Ford rolled slowly behind his vehicle, and stopped for a moment. Carlos dropped out and with swift movements placed the object on the undercarriage of the SUV, and just as smoothly got back onto the truck, which quietly rolled away.

Cloning on Demand

Meanwhile, inside the lab, Dr. Meddlesohm greeted his guest. "You can call me Abdullah for short," said Abdullah Abdullah Abdullah. "Though my friends call me Abdullah Cubed." Meddlesohm ushered him into the heart of his laboratory complex, and the two got right down to business.

On a computer workstation, the visitor opened his briefcase, and even Meddlesohm, though immensely wealthy, was impressed by the stacks of Ben Franklins and the fabulous trays of precious gems.

"Thank you for following our instructions," he told Abdullah. "I believe it's smart, at least at the beginning of our relationship, to use only untraceable cash and goods."

"I concur," said Abdullah tersely.

"Perhaps next time we can have you simply wire funds to one of our corporate accounts, and save you a trip halfway across the world."

He waved theatrically at the supercomputers' displays. "Early on, I had my scientists and my machines sequence my own genome and proteome," he boasted. "But now we're cracking the code to personages who may equal my own brainpower and creativity."

Abdullah asked, "So, you clone these personages, like they did with Dolly the Sheep?"

Meddlesohm sniffed, wondering if he'd overestimated the intelligence of his new customer.

"That's so 20th century! ReConstitution Biotek, and I thought you'd been briefed on this, has made a major new breakthrough over traditional cloning. Let me show you—let's go to our ReConstitution Room." If Abdullah felt offense at Dr. Meddlesohm's haughtiness, he remained stone-faced.

Meddlesohm led him through a vast warehouse of biolabs and computer rooms, at the end of which was a large lab with steel walls and armed guards at the entrance.

The scientist's security badge had a unique, thousand-letter strand of his genetic code embedded within it. He placed it on the door's scanner; the door slid open. "Let's go," he told his visitor.

Abdullah and Meddlesohm came to a square-shaped room, with a locked doorway, which the geneticist opened with his badge. Surrounding the chamber were chemistry labs and storage space for computer and biological gear.

As he entered the space with his host, Abdullah noticed three coffin-shaped containers, with see-through lids, placed on pedestals about waist-high, and holding what appeared to be mummies, or corpses wrapped in gauze. Near them was a smaller, transparent, coffin-like container, five feet long by three feet across. Attached to all the pods were tubes, wires, and relays of various kinds, many of which were attached directly to the mummies. From the sound and look of the connections, Abdullah could tell some were electronic links, while others transported fluids back and forth.

On second glance, Abdullah saw that the heads of the figures were uncovered, and appeared to have hair of different tints. 'It seems,' he thought, 'they are the recently deceased. Perhaps to have samples taken for this new kind of cloning.'

Meddlesohm spoke up. "In the traditional cloning process, we make a clone, or identical cell, from another cell, grow it for a time into a larger clump of cells, then implant it in a female of its species.

"Or," Meddlesohm smiled, rather wickedly, "sometimes in a female of another species. Or," he laughed, "in theory, we could even place it in a male. As long as the right hormones and other chemicals are applied to make the clone grow properly..."

Abdullah looked around the room. "Where are the female carriers used for your cloning?"

Meddlesohm, his respect for Abdullah's intellect falling fast, barely heard his guest, and kept speaking.

"...Some other, inferior labs have used artificial wombs to bring to term animals such as lambs. But we're the first to do it with humans. More importantly, with growth hormones and other means, we do it very rapidly, jumping ahead of messy and time-consuming things like childhood and adolescence."

The scientist preened, lowering himself up and down on his toes. "And all by artificial means, no mothers needed."

Though keeping a poker face, Abdullah was annoyed by Meddlesohm's cocksure attitude. And he doubted what he was hearing was true.

"Even if you were able to quickly bring clones to adulthood," he said, "wouldn't they be mental infants? From a lack of education, from the lack of basic human interaction and experiences?"

Meddlesohm chuckled. Most people were so behind the curve. The world was going to be astounded when it found out about his work.

"Quite the contrary," he responded. "We've found that the tissue and bone of deceased persons retain the DNA of not just physical attributes, but mental ones. Our biggest finding is that fossilized or mummified brain and nerve tissue contain 'memory genes'. Such portions of the genetic code contain the subject's adult memories—the full experience of a lifetime. And they can be fully restored!"

Abdullah, still dubious but impressed by his host's confidence, glanced at the glass boxes. Something about them made him uneasy.

"But again, even if true," he responded, "wouldn't they be useless in modern times? Today's technology would overwhelm them; they'd be unable to fit in with contemporary customs and habits."

Meddlesohm responded with head uplifted, arms folded, as if he were lecturing to himself.

"The opposite will be true. We're bringing back brilliant, dynamic persons who were hugely innovative, and wildly popular, in their time. They will be able, with the proper coaching and education we provide, to rapidly adapt to this time and place."

The visitor was persuaded that ReConstitution Biotek had made significant scientific advances. But he couldn't believe everything Meddlesohm was touting. He thought of the organization he was working for. Its hard-nosed leaders would be displeased to find they were being lied to, or swindled.

'But Meddlesohm is extremely wealthy,' he thought. 'He has no financial reason to lie. Perhaps his research still has a ways to go, and he's exaggerating the progress thus far out of vanity.'

A Convincing Demonstration

The geneticist paused in his exposition, and saw the doubt on his visitor's face. He went over to the small container, and pointed out a circular petri dish at its center.

"Watch closely," he said, "as I activate this device," and he tapped onto the virtual keyboard of his wireless phone. "Otherwise, you might miss something."

Abdullah went to the container and, bending over, peered through the glass at the petri dish, which contained nutrients and what appeared to be a clump of cell tissue. Next to the dish was a cup filled with biscuits. The tubes and relays attached to the container made a rising, rushing noise.

Surprised, he saw a whirling motion in the dish's contents, as if it had suddenly come alive. Then the contents expanded rapidly, like a sponge absorbing water. Within a minute or so, the contents had taken on a form, what was it, the form of a fetus! It looked like a human fetus for a few seconds, and then the whirling object, growing bigger, seemed to grow feathers, no, it was fur! The object next sprouted limbs: four legs, and its head became distinct. Abdullah instinctively jumped backward, afraid the creature, whatever it was, would burst through the container.

He looked with wonder inside the box. It was a standard poodle!

And it was fully formed. It moved its head, wiggled its tail and looked in his direction, and took a few halting steps forward and back.

Abdullah found he was sweating profusely, hyperventilating. He stared at the animal. It had finally seemed to stop growing. But it was a full-grown, adult standard poodle, and it seemed healthy and alert. All this had happened in just a few minutes!

The poodle, with a quick, smooth motion, scampered over to the cup of food. It began eating the biscuits like it had been doing that all its life. Abdullah realized with a shock that what Meddlesohm had said about genetic memories was true. The creature, in a very real sense, *had* been eating like that all its life. Its previous life! And it was starting its new one as if it had never left it.

"Perhaps you believe me now," said Meddlesohm.

"This, this is be—beyond astonishing," Abdullah stammered.

As they left the ReConstitution Room, Abdullah walked past the larger boxes, and stole a glance at the faces of two of them. Even in their quiescent state, he immediately recognized them from American coins and currencies.

'This lab will change the world!' he thought.

As if reading his mind, Meddlesohm said, "Our current projects are essentially 'beta tests' to prove the technology works. But still, we hope to make a small fortune in contracting out the world-class expertise of our first subjects in addressing political-military matters, and in creating new scientific breakthroughs. We're bringing several famous males from the past to full maturity, and a well-known female too, to make sure our technology works equally well with women subjects."

"You could apply your research subjects," ventured Abdullah, "to solve the world's problems."

"We could," said Meddlesohm, "and of course we've already thought of that. In next year's beta test, we hope to bring Edison, Einstein, and Aristotle back to life, as a trio of researchers. And maybe Newton." He rubbed his hands with glee, thinking, 'It'll be fun sneaking into Westminster Abbey at night to grab tissue samples from the tomb of the discoverer of gravity!'

The two were now nearing the end of the warehouse of labs, close to the firm's entrance.

"Some organizations," noted Abdullah, thinking of his organization back home, "could direct your know-how toward darker purposes."

"Yes," said the scientist, his eyes lighting up even more. "We could bring back armies of Caesars, Napoleons, and Hitlers, and conquer the world! Nations would pay me billions, trillions, for such knowledge! Or for protection money!"

"Well," he finished, "thank you for visiting. I trust your organization will be interested in what you've found."

Abdullah walked back to his Mercedes SUV deep in thought. He climbed into the passenger seat, and told his driver to take them back quickly to the hotel. He had a lot to tell his superiors. Or perhaps, given the value of the information he'd gleaned, he would start his own organization, and make himself fabulously rich.

As they pulled out, the occupants of the Ford flat-bed studied the display screen of their tracking device. The dot pinpointing the location of the SUV had started to move.

Now they could easily track Abdullah's vehicle. And Gregor Meddlesohm's, whose Porsche roadster they'd been tracking for weeks. Not to mention another vehicle that reConstitution Biotek was refurbishing to transport its most prized test subjects.

"The Founders' Flight to Freedom"

The three very valuable persons were sleepy from the pills their keepers had given them, and from the dim light of their confined space. In the metal capsule, the electrical lights were off, and the smoked window glass allowed little natural light to penetrate.

They awoke to find their legs shackled to the floor, and burly men watching them from the front of the long, rectangular container. Down a narrow corridor were twin rows of leather seats, on which the trio were seated near each other.

A Terrific Trio in Trouble

Abigail Adams spoke first. "Where are they taking us?"

Benjamin Franklin replied groggily, "I heard one of them say we'll be transported to an undisclosed location. To a more secure facility of the Corporation."

Thomas Jefferson shook himself awake. "We're being treated as slaves!" he groaned. "Two hundred years after my presidency abolished the importation of slaves!"

The three had been brought back in their well-known prime. Franklin in his sixties, when he was a world-renowned scientist and publisher. Jefferson in his fifties, when he'd attained the presidency. And Abigail Adams in her thirties, when she was rearing one of the most noted families in her nation's history.

Franklin looked at his shackles, and then the overseers. "It's like we've been kidnapped!"

"Is it kidnapping," replied Jefferson ruefully, "when the persons in question are officially deceased? Acknowledged by no one, without any identification?

"Gentlemen," said Abigail, trying to stay calm and practical, "let's not be legalistic, but focus on the problem at hand."

"I hate these pills they give us," said Jefferson, "they dull the mind, and we need our wits."

"Yes," replied Franklin, sarcastically, "the pills are supposed to *calm us*, to help us *adjust* to our new era." His own wits were returning. Franklin reached into the day back he'd taken to carrying around.

"Thomas, here, and Abigail, you too, take these," and he handed them two pills each. "I took them from one of their chemistry labs; they're supposed to lessen the sedatives' effect. Mr. Jefferson is right: we all need to be clear-headed, if we're to find our way out of this most unusual predicament."

"So, Dr. Franklin," replied Jefferson, "you intend to fight, and not submit?

"After all, their enterprise has made us what it terms a generous offer: a yearly stipend worth a fortune, exposure to the latest scientific advances, and living quarters any prince would envy."

"Chains of gold," said Franklin harshly, "and shackles of silver.

"They that give up essential liberty," he continued, rhetorically, "to obtain a little temporary safety, deserve neither safety nor liberty."

"I would rather be exposed," agreed Jefferson, "to the 'inconveniences' attending *too much* liberty."

"I would rather," stated Abigail, "die a free man than a slave."

"It's decided then," said Franklin.

16

Perhaps from Franklin's stimulant, perhaps from settling on a goal, they started to feel more clear-headed and determined.

"We make our escape," stated Jefferson, "on the first good opportunity."

"Yet what will we do, and where will be go," asked Abigail, "upon our escape?"

Franklin replied dryly, "We're all accustomed, Abigail, as revolutionaries, to beginning the world anew. I'm sure we'll think of something, when the time arrives."

Considering Their Situation

They turned their attention to the front of their capsule, which was better lit than where they sat, and to the men who were alternatively watching them and talking furtively among themselves. Straining to hear, the Founders were able to make out some of their intonations, but none of the words.

Franklin reached back into his day pack, and pulled out a hand-sized, pistol-like device, with a small dish antenna where a gun barrel might have been. He took out ear phones, slipped them on, and stealthily pointed the antenna gun at the watchmen.

"It's well they let us keep some personal and professional items," said Franklin, balancing the listening device on the top of the seat in front of him. "And that they let me tinker with the latest technical gadgets." Jefferson and Abigail looked at their friend and his gizmo in wonder.

"Our keepers," Franklin continued, "are encouraging my aptitude for scientific invention, which they would then employ for their own ends. In any event, this device amplifies the sound of the person's voice on which it is focused."

"Your instrument, Dr. Franklin," observed Jefferson, "would have proven useful, back in our time, in our diplomatic talks with France, as a means of eavesdropping upon the other negotiators, to ascertain their strategy."

"That would be a cunning application, Thomas," said Franklin, "though at this time I'm thinking more along the lines of a tool to assist the hard of hearing. In fact, I've contemplated starting a business line featuring my own enhanced version of this device."

"Gentlemen, please, back to business!" breathed Abigail. "What are the guardsmen saying?!" Franklin listened intently with his ear phones, while Jefferson stared at the men conversing.

Jefferson murmured aloud: "'The new foreigners, the foreign agents, they can examine them there. Where we're going, they can, could inspect our subjects, then they can, could make bids, the highest price wins out, and...'"

"Thomas!" Abigail nearly shouted. "How are you eavesdropping on Dr. Franklin's eavesdropping?!"

"Dr. Franklin may be more technically proficient," Jefferson replied, "but I'm rather skilled in languages—and in lip reading. In fact, I can lip-read in six languages. And yes, those fellows up there are talking about taking us to another guarded facility, and selling us to some foreign organization for the highest price."

Abigail was outraged. "Like a slave auction!" She forced herself to be calm, to think through the situation. She asked, "But why would they want *us*?"

"I wouldn't underestimate ourselves," Jefferson responded. "Dr. Franklin here was one of the most esteemed scientists", and Franklin began to object, but Jefferson waved him silent, "of his time, or any other time. And he's already shown," and Jefferson pointed to the listening tool, "a considerable facility for practical innovation in the present day."

"And you, Thomas," answered Franklin, "you were"—and Franklin shushed Jefferson's attempt at modesty—"you were at the zenith of the political and diplomatic professions, among others. And, based on the newscasts we've seen, such skills are in even higher demand today than they were in our own tumultuous era."

Jefferson reflected for a moment. "When my Administration first set up the Patent Office, it was to prevent the theft of inventions. But today we're witnessing the theft of inventive people.

"Which is why we're so closely guarded," he continued. "We're valuable commodities, far more than a prized slave, a stud horse, or a treasure chest."

"It's ironic," Franklin commented ruefully, "that the Scientific Revolution I helped champion has come to this. I've been hung on my own petard."

"But why *me*?" asked Abigail plaintively. "I understand why our captors would want to bring back to life you two gentlemen, both of you Renaissance Men—and please, Thomas, no false modesty—men of great accomplishment."

"Well," Jefferson attempted, "you were one of the most refined and erudite woman of that era, or I dare say any—"

"—Please spare me!" interrupted Abigail. "Honesty, please. Our lives may depend on our squarely facing the facts of the situation.

"Why *me*? Why not Mr. Adams? Or, say, Robert Fulton, if they wanted to pick another man of technical renown?

Franklin coughed softly. "Well, they may want, a woman, as part of the biological experiment."

"Dr. Franklin!" exclaimed Jefferson. "You don't mean—"

"—What I mean, Mr. Jefferson, is that, in conducting a biological experiment of this sort, the experimenters would want a wide test sample."

"'A wide test sample,'" repeated Abigail, confused.

"I've had some talks with the company scientists on their research methods," explained Franklin, fidgeting a bit. "To compare the different components of an experiment, they employ what they call a 'control subject', in this case a woman, to see how her 'results'—her health, her reactions, her ability to learn in this new setting—differ from those of the male subjects."

"So, I'm a 'control subject', eh?" Abigail Adams grimaced. "Let me tell you gentlemen something. I lived through a decade of war and bloody British occupation, and I will not be anyone's subject!"

At that, their metal capsule lurched forward, causing the Founders to rock in their seats.

"An odd sensation," remarked Jefferson. "Could we be in one of those modern conveyances for moving through the air?"

"From the moving pictures they've showed us," replied Franklin, "those air machines start their journey smoothly. This conveyance jerks about like a horse cart. And the sound of its engine"—and they all paused to listen to the loud, throttling noise—"doesn't have the whine of the air-borne craft I've heard, in the motion pictures and the electronic news. Its lower pitch suggests a motorized land vehicle."

"Who's driving it then?" asked Abigail. No driver could be seen.

"Is the driver," asked Jefferson, "one of those *robots* that we read about, in our remedial history and technology lessons at the Corporation?"

Franklin pointed to a tall black box at the front-left of the capsule. "I believe the driver is in that compartment. And likely a human, not mechanical driver. Even their technology hasn't advanced that far yet."

"I believe you're right," said Jefferson. "At times the watchmen direct their utterances to that box, as if there's someone inside it."

"The driver can undoubtedly see the road," replied Franklin, "unlike us," and he pointed to the opaque windows. "They've taken pains to ensure that no one can look in on us, and that we cannot look out."

The vehicle was now well underway. "The average speed of these motorized carts," remarked Dr. Franklin, who had bent over to examine his shackles, "is about 60 English miles an hour or, to use the more rational and accurate French system, 96.56 metric miles an hour.

Loosening the Bonds of Servitude

"That was very stupid of them," he continued.

"What?" asked Abigail. "To stick with the English system of measurement?"

"No, I'm referring to my leg irons, which have a digital lock, not a mechanical lock and key."

As Franklin pulled a square black device the size of a woman's hand out of his day pack, a laughing Jefferson remarked, "Your satchel, Dr. Franklin, is like a magician's bottomless bag of tricks."

"The essential concept," Franklin replied, again hunched over, "is the same as a combination lock. There are only a certain number of possible combinations, though admittedly a great many more with a digital device than a mechanical one. I would need a very powerful algorithm, a more powerful algorithm than I can recall, to break it."

"I think I've heard of him," said Abigail. "Al Gore: he was one of the recent vice presidents."

"Not Al Gore, but algor-ithm," corrected Franklin. "Although it's said he invented the Internet, so perhaps the term is named for him.

"But as I said, I can't unlock it that way. I'll try a simpler solution."

A wire with a plug ran out from Franklin's little gadget, which he inserted into a small socket on his leg iron.

"Dr. Franklin," said Abigail, "you seem quite current with the latest know-how."

"Our overseers," he replied, grinning, "are very, very interested in any insights I might have into electricity and electronics, given the modest success I had in those fields in my prior life. They've encouraged me to take a number of online courses on those subjects, as well as to acquire any paraphernalia that might help me to advance my studies."

"Now, the 'key' for a digital lock," he explained, "is simply a string of numbers and letters. The key is stored in the lock's digital memory. This device reads the key, then plays it back to the lock, and, *Voilà!*"— they all heard a soft clattering on the ground—"the locks falls off!" Franklin passed his lock buster to his friends, and in short order they were all free.

As they rubbed their ankles to restore circulation to their feet, the Founders noticed the vehicle slowing down.

"Are we reaching our destination?" asked Abigail.

"Possibly," replied Franklin, "though the immediate reason for our de-acceleration is the fact we are now in a close quarters of a city."

"How can you tell, Doctor?" asked Jefferson, always appreciative of his savvy friend's insights.

"Well," said Franklin, looking at the heavily tinted window glass, "we can't see much, but I have been able to make out the sun throughout our trip. From its position, I've calculated our direction, which from our Rockville, Maryland start has been to the southeast."

He pulled out a pocket watch he'd ordered from eBay. Although an antique in the current era, it had been a marvel of precision and portability in Franklin's own.

"And I've timed our journey. Accounting for an average speed on open roads of, say, 50 miles per hour, that puts us squarely in George Washington's namesake town, otherwise known as the District of Columbia."

"Dr. Franklin," said Abigail, "I can see why our captors prize you so highly."

The vehicle slowed to a crawl.

"I've been reading," said Jefferson, "that the District's byways are in a continual state of chaotic reconstruction, fueled by federal programs of economic 'stimulus.'"

"Yes," said Franklin. "I heard of it: the official name is the Economic Recovery and Reinvestment Act for New Transportation, or ERRANT."

"Perhaps it's the cause," reasoned Abigail, "of our slow progress."

"Maybe it will provide us," said the Sage of Monticello, "with an opportunity for escape."

In fact, a construction project had diverted their shuttle bus into downtown D.C., near the White House and Lafayette Square. A few drops of rain had begun falling, which had the usual effect of turning the city's normally choked traffic into complete gridlock.

Meantime, at the front of the bus, the driver complained to one of the overseers, "We'll never get to the other facility at this rate!"

Watching the Watchers

Just behind them, and following their journey with considerable interest, were four men in a Mercedes-Benz SUV: Abdullah, a driver, and two heavyset bodyguards.

"That lying Meddlesohm is reneging on our deal!" snarled Dr. Abdullah, recalling his visit to reConstitution Biotek. "We made a firm financial agreement to turn the three ancients over to our organization. Then we find out he's moving them to some secret location—probably to sell to someone else!"

"But look, boss," said the driver, pointing to the dashboard's directional display: "I got them on the GPS: they'll never escape us!"

24

"You idiot!" shouted Abdullah, smacking the driver on the head. "We'll hardly lose them in this kind of traffic. Turn that thing off!"

Abdullah angrily muttered to himself. "They think they can betray me, huh? Then it's time we took the fruits of their labors. No need to clone anyone— we'll just take the American legends for ourselves!"

In an alley just ahead, meanwhile, four men bunched in the front seat of a pickup truck were keenly watching their GPS displays, which showed reConstitution Biotek's slowly approaching shuttle bus, and Abdullah's SUV behind it. They had kept informed up to the instant of the Founders' whereabouts, and Abdullah's, and they were ready to strike.

"We've got them in our sights!" said the leader, Stan, a bearded fellow from Turkmenistan. "Allah be praised! And Krishna too: I wouldn't want to offend my infidel friends in India, after all."

"Where are all the cops and security?" asked the driver, Van, from Kyrkgibsonstan. "We're just a block from the White House, for God's sake. I mean Allah's sake. Or Krishna's."

"Congress is out of session," said Dan, from Younocanistan. "And the president is as usual out of town playing golf—God, Allah, Krishna, or Jehovah damn him—or we could try to kidnap him instead!"

"Also," said Stan, from Turkmenistan, "it rained a tenth of an inch this morning. So the government granted all its workers 'early leave' to go home."

"What a racket!" said Van, from Kyrkgibsonstan. "I'm voting Republican in the next election."

"The hell with that!" answered Dan, from Younocanistan. "I'm applying for a government job!"

"Hey," began Jan, from Pakistan. "Why don't we just attack the White House? Everyone's out of town and there's no one to defend it! I hear it's got an indoor pool, billiards, open bar, everything."

"Listen, Jan," said Stan, "stick to the plan, man.

"What a propaganda coup it'll be if we kidnap the Great Satan's very own Founding Fathers, and put them on YouTube as hostages. America will collapse!"

"Maybe you're right, Stan," said Jan. Squeezed together in the front seat with the others, he squirmed uncomfortably.

"Stan," asked the driver, Van, "should I pull out and cut them off?"

"You knucklehead!" came the reply. "They're hardly moving, we'll just walk over."

"It'll be nice to stretch our legs," said Dan. "Jesus Christ Almighty! We've been cooped up here too long."

"Hey, what about Abdullah?" asked Van, eyeing the GPS dot identifying his SUV.

"Don't worry about him and his men," said leader Stan, from Turkmenistan. "In all this traffic, he'll never find us."

Making a Break for It

In the bus, the three Founders, now freed of their restraints, watched the guards, and waited for an opening. Up front, the driver looked out the entrance door's window, and noticed a man knocking on it. He was garbed in a checkered headdress, baggy white pants, and a loose, pajama-like tunic, and was holding a big club with spikes in it. The man held up a sign, reading, "Directions, Please?"

"Look at that," the driver said to one of the overseers, as he pushed a button to open the door. "That's a tough break, getting lost in all this traffic."

Before the guard could stop him, four men with clubs and chains rushed into the bus.

"Terrorists!" the driver shouted.

"Who says we're terrorists?" said Stan, of Turkmenistan. "We're in this to make money. And maybe a little terror on the side." And they started pummeling the overseers.

The Founders saw this, and figured they had their chance.

"There's a way out the back!" shouted Abigail, eyeing the rear door. The three rushed in that direction.

Behind the shuttle bus, an alarmed Abdullah saw the armed men enter the vehicle. "Who the hell are they?!" he shouted. "They're going to take what's ours!" He and his thugs jumped out of their vehicle, and threaded their way through heavy traffic toward the bus.

Their driver, left behind, called out: "Do you want me to park the SUV?..."

As they rushed, guns drawn, past idling cars toward the bus, Abdullah told his men, "Let's surprise them; enter from the rear!" Reaching the vehicle, they pulled on the rear door, which was locked.

Abdullah got on one knee, his back turned to the bus, put down his gun and his cell phone, and began preparing some plastic explosive to blow out the lock.

Then the rear door flung open, and appearing in the doorway were a balding, older man, a tall, middle-aged man, and a younger woman. The tall

27

man eyed the men with guns, thought very fast, and cried, "Help us! They're trying to kidnap the test subjects. In there!"

As the Founders stepped out from the bus and started to run, the thugs climbed in, as Abdullah turned around to see his men entering, grabbed his gun—while forgetting his cell phone—and climbed in himself. Franklin, spotting the cell phone on the ground, suddenly stopped, grabbed it, and began running after his friends.

Abdullah's gang rushed up to the front of the bus. They saw that the terrorists and the overseers were in an all-out brawl. The newcomers were about to join in the fight, when Abdullah stopped cold. He could have kicked himself for having been so dumb.

He cried out, "The subjects have escaped!" The terrorists and the watchmen kept fighting. He raised his gun above his head, and fired off a shot. The terrorists and the overseers ceased fighting, and looked dumbly at Abdullah. Then they looked at the empty rear of the bus.

Stan from Turkmenistan had halted his club in mid-swing. "My God!" he cried. "I mean, Allah Almighty! What do we do now?"

It was Abdullah's turn to think fast. "I propose," he told the others, "that we form a temporary alliance, to capture the Founders. Later we can split any proceeds from their sale."

The overseers, anxious to get their charges back, nodded. Stan, anxious to pay off his new mortgage on a mosque, also agreed.

Down the road, the Founders, breathing heavily, paused in the middle of the street, stunned at the motorized carriages all around them. 'Their materials are so refined,' thought Franklin, 'compared to our wood and iron carriages.'

The Founders jumped when the cars inching toward them, their way blocked, made scary, honking noises. They scrambled onto the sidewalk: Abigail and Jefferson were astonished to recognize their surroundings.

Lafayette, We Have Returned

Apart from the cars, Lafayette Square looked much like it did during their time in Washington two centuries before. There were the twin rows of brick, federal-style town homes fronting the park-like square, and St. John's Church across the street to the north, and the White House and grounds, just across the south end of Pennsylvania Avenue. Newer were the statues of American heroes, like Andrew Jackson and Lafayette himself.

Long-dead memories swam through Jefferson's mind. Across the park was the house of Commodore Stephen Decatur, who had executed then-President Jefferson's order to destroy the Barbary pirates of Libya. Jefferson stole a glance at the statue of Baron von Steuben, the disciplinarian of Washington's army, who had harshly criticized then-Governor Jefferson for the poor state of Virginia's militia.

The three hurried down the square, away from the bus, and away from another grand statue, of Lafayette himself. Franklin and Adams were shaken by the image, remembering their meetings with the French officer in Paris in the 1780s, their dear friend now turned into a weathered statue.

Jefferson reeled from the flood of memories. One of his last public acts before his death in 1826 was to host a visit by the aged Lafayette at Monticello. One of his last thoughts before dying was a fond remembrance of America's Revolutionary War friend. Now this cold stone image, in this new life—it was too much.

"Thomas!" screamed Abigail, grabbing him by his shirt, pulling him back to reality, "they're coming for us!"

The terrorists, Abdullah's men, and the guards had poured out of the bus and had spotted the Founders. They were trotting down the Square toward them.

"Where can we go?" roared Franklin. "They're sure to catch us."

"After so soon attaining our liberty," groaned Abigail, "such agony to give it up again!"

Another distant memory struck Jefferson's mind. 'Could it be?' he thought. 'Could it still be, after all this time?' It was their only hope.

"Follow me!" the ex-President cried out. He rushed across the street, Abigail and Franklin at his heels, past the gridlocked cars, ignoring the blasts of horns. The pursuers saw this, and snaked their way through the crowded byway themselves. Franklin and Abigail ran behind Jefferson into a narrow alley between two of the town homes. A sign on one of the houses announced, "Historic home of First Lady Dolley Madison".

They arrived at a tiny yard in the back of the three-story dwelling, and ducked behind its fence. "Where is *it*!" Jefferson shouted to himself.

"Thomas, what is the matter?!" cried Abigail.

"This was Mrs. Madison's town home for many years, after she and James left the White House," said Jefferson, speaking in rapid-fire bursts. "The British torching of this city, while they were in office, scarred them indelibly. Dolley had an escape tunnel built underneath her house, in case another foreign invasion necessitated her flight."

Jefferson pulled at his long, reddish-brown locks. "At the time, I was shown the architectural sketches for the tunnel's entrance, but it's not here!"

Franklin eyed the yard, the old brick work of the house, the shed built next to it. "Has anything changed since that time?" he asked.

Meantime, Abigail peered down the alley. The gang of pursuers had entered it, and was striding, weapons at the ready, in their direction.

"Gentlemen, kindly hurry! We must resolve this matter—or return to captivity!"

Jefferson wracked his brains. It was hard to sort out memories so ancient, yet so new and vivid. Then it hit him. "The shed is an addition!" he cried. He grabbed a heavy shovel lying on the grass.

Six-foot, three-inches tall and lean, Jefferson was very strong: with two blows he shattered the door lock. They entered the dim place, and Abigail reflexively and futilely looked around for candles. Suddenly, the space was brightly illuminated. Franklin stood at the doorway, smiling, his fingers on a wall switch.

"Partly because of my earlier research into electricity," he said, "inducing artificial light is much, much easier now."

Casting about the shack, Jefferson tried to calculate from his memory of the home's design where the tunnel entrance might be. His eyes fell upon a sewer grate. He and Franklin tucked at both ends, and it pulled up, a dank smell emanating from a wide hole stretching deep below.

A Passage to Freedom

The three looked at each other. "Allow me," said Franklin, pulling a smart phone out of his pocket. "This actually makes for a serviceable torch, or flash light, as they call it these days."

"Where'd you get that?!" asked Jefferson. For reasons of security, the Founders were not allowed cell phones.

"Just something I picked up," Franklin answered.

Jefferson and Abigail watched the doughty oldster descend into the abyss. At the same time, outside they heard their pursuers arrive at the end of the alley.

Franklin called out from below: "Our escape path is quite serviceable. A bit dank, but I can spy a tunnel, big enough even for Mr. Jefferson, running far along in a southerly direction."

Abigail, then Jefferson, clambered after the good Doctor, with the former President carefully placing the grate back in place.

They walked slowly through the dim passage, Franklin holding up the smart phone like a torch, drops of water from the ceiling leaking down on them.

"Are we under the Potomac now?" asked Abigail.

"No," replied Franklin, staring at his cell, and the app he'd called up. "I estimate from our rate of speed, and from the latest Google maps of the area, that we're a good hundred yards, I should say meters, from the river."

"Thomas," said Abigail, "when did the Madisons tell you about this tunnel?"

"They didn't," he replied. "James Monroe, their Secretary of State—and my protégé—sent me the designs."

"Mr. Jefferson," responded Abigail in admiration, "is there anyone you didn't know back in the day?!?"

"Yes—and Dr. Franklin knew them."

The ceiling leaks increased, and took on a foul odor.

Laughing, Franklin looked at his display, and commented, "These 'wikis' provide good summaries on topics of all kinds. Though you'd be shocked, Thomas, to see the scandalous things they've published about our personal lives. Apparently there's no privacy in the modern world."

They arrived at a subterranean intersection. A larger tunnel, with a running stream filled with sewage, cut in front of them.

"This wiki on the District of Columbia," said Franklin, "says the city, in 1871, built this sewer, under the canal that once ran over it, to ferry trash from one end of town to the other."

"Where did the sewerage line run?" asked Abigail.

"It started at K St., the lobbyists' district, then flowed past the White House, and emptied at Congress."

They were unhappy at the prospect of wading across the filthy stream. But Abigail noticed a series of rungs that ran along the ceiling and across the divide. Franklin went first, pulling himself across, rung by rung. Abigail followed, after Jefferson lifted her up to grab the first support, and the former President brought up the rear.

A brief passage brought the tunnel to an end, where a ladder led up to a hatch. Jefferson stepped up the ladder, and with a heave upward pushed open the lid.

After climbing through, they found themselves in a small, deserted stone dwelling. Franklin called up a historical map on his smart phone, and compared it to their current Google Maps location.

"It's the old lock keeper's house," he said, scanning related links. "It's been abandoned since the city built the sewer, along the line of the old canal."

"Oh, the epochal changes that have taken place," said Franklin philosophically. "In our day, canals were the 'cutting edge', as they remark today. But we were long gone when the railroads put them out of business, and when the motor car nearly extinguished the railroads."

The place was dark, with no light switch, so they pushed open the door to the outside.

Before them was revealed a grand expanse of sky, water, and lawn.

Blinking in the light, they viewed the soaring white obelisk of the Washington Monument. On its hill, Franklin noted with pleasure, were knots of children flying into the breeze his own favorite plaything—kites. Along several roads roared those amazing motor cars that had clogged Lafayette Square. Most astonishingly, giant metal capsules reached high into the sky above them, after departing from a spit of land just down the Potomac.

They gazed at the Potomac's Tidal Basin estuary, where tourists sweated and laughed while operating leg-powered boats. On the edge of the basin was a large domed memorial with a towering statue within.

"That," said Franklin, "is the Jefferson Memorial." The Memorial's namesake blinked in disbelief.

Abigail asked, "And where, might I ask, is my husband John's memorial?"

They drank in the scene. Of the future. Their future.

"My, my," said Franklin. "Welcome to the 21st century."

"I suppose," said Jefferson, "it's time to start making a new life for ourselves…To start making the world anew."

"The Founders Visit the Founding Documents, and Have a Run-in with the Law"

Early one afternoon, not long after the escape from their captors at reConstitution Biotek, the Founders met on the National Mall.

In their first days, they'd survived with cash donations by playing music on street corners, with Jefferson on the violin, and Dr. Franklin on an "armonica" of spinning glass disks that he'd invented. The trio stayed in inexpensive motels, after Franklin forged fake IDs on the computer of a public library.

In time, to earn more money and establish themselves in their new lives, they busily took on new careers. Jefferson was working variously as a legal, architectural, and horticultural consultant, Abigail was an advisor to a new charter school, and Franklin was an analyst in information tech, meteorology, and computer graphics, among other specialties. At the same time Franklin, by emailing their pursuers phony video sightings of the Founders in distant cities, had thrown them off the track.

A Garden of Art

That day, the three gathered at the National Gallery of Art's "Sculpture Garden," which had an arresting series of large-scale outdoor figures. They wondered at pieces such as a giant rabbit and a giant pencil eraser, and wondered more how the other people in the garden could take such strange art in stride.

"The only rough analog I can think of from our time, or before, for art that is so phantasmagorical," said Jefferson, "is Hieronymus Bosch's 'Garden of Earth Delights'."

"But Bosch's subject matter," said Abigail, "is transcendent, on such matters as the Judgment Day and the depravity of Man. This material, by glorifying the mundane, may trivialize art itself."

Franklin grinned at a super-large depiction of a spider. "I think you two may be taking this too seriously. We're in a public garden, meant for relaxation, and entertainment. And outlandish art serves those purposes nicely. Think of this place as a sort of mini-Versailles."

Jefferson stopped cold on seeing another work of art, and architecture, across Constitution Avenue. "Is that a museum of classical history?" he asked in wonder. "Its front is a replica of Rome's Pantheon, the temple of all the gods!" Before them rose an enormous limestone box with a triangular façade supported by eight elegant columns.

"The reality is more mundane," said Franklin, scanning the inscription above the building's entrance with his portable telescope. "It's the National Archives: the nation's filing cabinet, if you will."

They laughed, figuring the rare documents within such a place would be far from mundane. And strode up its broad steps into the atrium.

A Tribute to Their Treatises

Jefferson, Franklin, and Adams were stunned, and touched, to find the grand lobby a kind of homage not to the gods, but to themselves. Outsized murals depicted the Founding Fathers who were involved in creating the nation's founding documents. And at the base of the back wall were the documents' originals: the Constitution, the Declaration of Independence, the Bill of Rights, as well as the medieval Magna Carta that served as those documents' distant inspiration. These lay protected in waist-high metal cases, topped by transparent glass.

Franklin gazed at the unusual mural of the Constitution's drafters, who stood outside, not Philadelphia's Constitutional Hall, but a Roman-like temple in the countryside. "It wasn't like that at all, of course," he remarked. "I should know: I somehow lived long enough to attend both the signing of the Declaration and the formulation of the Constitution."

"And longer still," added Abigail.

"Dr. Franklin, here, take this," said Jefferson with a wink, handling him a rolled-up parchment. Franklin unfurled it—to find an original copy of the Constitution! The Virginian pulled another document from his coat, and unrolled an original copy of the Declaration. "And for you, Abigail," he said decorously, "I wouldn't want you denied your own piece of history." Mrs. Adams, eyes widening, opened up an original copy of the Bill of Rights!

"When we made plans the other night to meet at the Sculpture Garden," Jefferson explained, "I did a bit of research, and learned of the Archives, and its contents, and figured we'd wind up here. So I brought along the original copies—I thought it'd be fun to compare them to the ones here!"

The three stepped up to the display cases, Franklin and Adams scratching their heads at their surprise gifts, and how their friend had obtained them.

Jefferson peered at his Declaration in its protective vault. "It's so discolored and worn," he told his friends. His comment suddenly made them all feel very old.

"They're doing their best to preserve them though," said Franklin. "It says here the containers are filled with helium gas, to slow the corruption of the paper."

"Helium, the lightest of elements," commented Jefferson, his eyes gleaming. "How fitting, for our texts helped democracy soar throughout the world!" Franklin and Abigail smiled at their companion, who was given to lofty rhetoric sometimes untethered to life's sobering practicalities.

A Criminal Suspect

In a security guard's post, meanwhile, a guard and a supervisor happened to focus their video camera on Jefferson as he fingered the Declaration.

"Wait a second," said the supervisor. "I have a funny feeling—that couldn't be, could it? Zoom the camera in!"

The guard zeroed in on Jefferson. "No!" shouted the manager. "Not him—on what he's holding!"

He focused in on the parchment. The supervisor blinked. She had undergone training on the creation and composition of the Declaration, and couldn't believe what she was seeing.

"Do a super-close-up!"

From in very close, it seemed the man was holding no cheap copy.

"Did he steal it?!" screamed the supervisor. "How did he get it out of the case? Have we had a breach?!"

The guard hurriedly checked the electronic alarm.

"Security system case is intact, ma'am," he responded. "I wonder who that guy is?"

"Well, find out!" the supervisor yelled.

Fumbling with his keyboard, the guard hurriedly copied a captured, video image of the man into the facial recognition software.

"Who *is* this guy?" the supervisor demanded.

"Here's what the system pulls up," he answered.

The display read:

Name: *Thomas J. Hemmings*
Home Town: *Charlottesville, Virginia*
Education: *University of Virginia. M.A., Ph.D. Triple Major: Architecture, Agriculture, American Studies.*
Birth Year: *1962.*
Probability of a Match: *97%.*

The supervisor grabbed her walkie-talkie, and contacted the main security desk.

Minutes later, a half dozen guards rushed toward Jefferson.

"Don't move, mister!" one shouted, and the others seized him by the arms. With a jerk of his shoulders, the lanky leader, angered to have been grabbed by common watchmen, easily freed himself. He and the flabby guards stood off in a tense confrontation. Franklin and Adams stashed their own documents in their clothes, and stood off to the side, watching anxiously.

Franklin made a downward motion with his palm, signaling Jefferson to remain calm.

"We have to think our way out of us," he whispered to Abigail, "and I have a thought."

From an open door, the supervisor strode over to the confrontation, heels clicking. The Founders watched in surprise, still getting used to the idea of women in authority.

She stated, "Mr. Hemmings, you are under arrest. You have the right to remain silent..."

Jefferson still bristled, but remained still, thinking, 'Thank goodness that my dear friend Mister Madison stuck that Fifth Amendment in his Bill of Rights there.'

"...And nothing you say will be held against you." Jefferson stayed quiet, silently thanking his old friend George Mason for pushing Madison to include the Bill of Rights in the Constitution.

A Printer's Protestations

Franklin stepped forward.

"Madame, if I might explain, and say a word in defense of my friend. That document he has is actually a reproduction from your gift shop."

"I doubt that!" she shot back. "It looks genuine; it could be an original copy!"

"But these days," answered Franklin, "it's just so hard to tell. If you might indulge me for a moment." Dr. Franklin reached into his day pack—and froze, as the guards moved hands to gun holsters.

He calmly raised his arms, palms open. "I assure you, gentlemen, I mean no harm. I seek only the truth of this matter."

The earnestness of his voice disarmed the guards, who put their arms at rest. Abigail was reminded of General Washington's way of effortlessly gaining control of a situation.

"I took the liberty, madame," Franklin continued, reaching into his pack and pulling out a dozen Declarations, "of producing, on my 3-D laser printer, a number of copies before coming here, in order to compare them against the original in the case." He handed them to the supervisor.

"I'm a printer, by trade, among other things, and I was curious about the quality...As you can see, they're virtually identical to the original, down to the smudged text and the yellowed parchment, and identical to, ahem, to Mister Hemming's copy as well.

"My friend, you see, is a historical re-enactor. He gets carried away sometimes.

"And, if you take a good look at him," said Franklin, unable to resist, "he rather looks like Thomas Jefferson!"

The supervisor snorted. She distrusted this smooth-talking printer, and the Hemmings fellow, but felt embarrassed to hold the latter any longer.

She nodded to the guards, then to Jefferson. "All right, you can go, but don't stay too long!"

A Dig from the Past

After they'd left the Archives, Franklin and Adams buttonholed their friend.

"You are a sorcerer, sir!" exclaimed Abigail.

"How in Heaven's name," asked Franklin, "did you obtain in these times real copies of the original?!"

"There's no magic involved," replied Jefferson. "Not even a parlor trick.

"Dr. Franklin, you may recall giving me a copy of the Constitution after the Constitutional Convention in 1787. My friend James Madison gave me a copy of the Bill of Rights after he passed it into law a few years later as Speaker of the House.

"Well before that, after serving with Dr. Franklin and Mr. Adams on the Declaration's committee in 1776, I had put aside a copy of it. Later, at Monticello, I made some facsimiles with my letter-copying device there, a precursor to today's 'Xerox machine'."

His scholar's mind continued spewing out dates and facts.

"Later still, in 1793, at President Washington's laying of the cornerstone to the Capitol, I undertook to hermetically seal and bury original copies of all three documents under the foundation stone. I thought it might prove of interest to some future historian excavating the site."

"Then, the other night, knowing we were to visit the Archives, and rather curious like the good Doctor about the comparative condition of our founding documents, I slipped out—while Dr. Franklin was printing out his own copies—to the Capitol. I had with me a collapsible entrenching tool, purchased from what the moderns call an Army Surplus shop. After locating the cornerstone, I rapidly unearthed the texts, whose seal I'd found to be happily intact, even after the passage of over two centuries!"

Abigail smiled at the idea of her tall friend scurrying unseen about the Capitol grounds at night. She asked, "Did no one spot you?"

"I've found," said Jefferson, "that area to be deserted at night, and that indeed, the government workers, who make up the great part of its populace, have typically vacated the area by two in the afternoon."

Abigail and Franklin chortled, and the threesome descended the steps of the Archives back into the Sculpture Garden.

Passing the giant Pencil Eraser again, Franklin remarked: "You know, Thomas, perhaps we should use this work of art to delete your documents—it might save us a batch of trouble." They doubled up with mirth, then disappeared into the crowds of the National Mall.

"The Founders Witness a Midnight Session of Congress"

Sometimes, on especially busy days, and in place of a morning constitutional, the Founders would stroll around Washington at night. They learned, as do many visitors to that town, that night-time may be the best time to walk about its monuments and public buildings, when their marble walls are evocatively aglow with artificial light.

Making the Rounds of the Capitol

Late one evening, the trio strolled around the spacious grounds of the Capitol Building. By its reflecting pool, they reflected, on the striking, equestrian statue of General Ulysses S. Grant. As usual when seeing a reminder of the war between North and South, Jefferson, a son of the South, was pensive. So was Franklin, who had doubts from the start whether the American experiment would last. But Abigail remarked admiringly, "It's a grand rendition of the man, capturing the rumpled, common-soldier aspect that I've read about."

The Founders' command of U.S. history was fuzzier regarding the nearby statue of President Garfield. They asked an out-of-town tourist who Garfield was, and received a puzzling remark about a cat. Then another passerby informed them that James Garfield was a Civil War general who later became president, and was assassinated in office, thus the effigy honoring him.

47

"I recall now reading about his sad end," said Franklin. "Before he died, the stricken president suffered terribly in the heat of a Washington summer. One of my successors in the field of electricity, Alexander Graham Bell, was brought in to alleviate his condition. To do so, he invented an early form of the air conditioner."

"That invention," noted Jefferson, "forever changed the South, and border-South cities such as Washington. It became possible to work year-round, at least indoors, and in the full heat of the summer day."

"The ability of the central government to administer, regulate, borrow, and spend year-round," replied Franklin, "is a decidedly double-edged sword."

"Single-edged perhaps," replied Jefferson. "I remember striking my deal with Mr. Hamilton to place the nation's capital here. Part of my reasoning, apart from an admittedly selfish one in being close to Monticello, was the belief that no one in their right mind would want to live here amid a tidewater swamp. We figured congress would stay in session for two months a year at most, which would greatly limit its ability to do mischief.

"In the due course of time, and the advent of air conditioning, we were proven wrong."

The mood brightened as they ascended the Capitol Building's grounds, and came upon a small, brick, hexagon-shaped building, with a Spanish tile roof and arched, stone doorways open to the air. Water bubbled through a grotto in its center, and decorative beds of flowers welcomed approaching visitors.

"What a delightful place!" cried Abigail, running her fingers over some roses.

Franklin, using the display light of his smart phone, read an inscription on the brick work. "It was built as a resting spot for summer visitors to the Capitol," he said. "It dates from 1880; the architect was Frederick Law Olmstead."

"Olmstead!" exclaimed Jefferson, ever admiring of a fellow designer. "The landscape architect of New York's Central Park. And, Abigail, of Boston's 'Emerald Necklace' of parks, including the Boston Common and the Fenway."

Jefferson felt a kindred spirit in Olmstead, who'd tried to bring the country to the city. For one thing the Virginian loved about his native state, previously and presently, was its town-and-country nature, with small, attractive cities like Leesburg and Charlottesville surrounded by tracts of open country.

Moving on, the Founders took in the vast Capitol Building, shining like the moon, with its 290-foot-high "wedding cake" dome, and 750 feet of length, including its Senate and House wings.

Abigail, normally level-headed, found herself swept up by its grandeur.

"The very summit of democracy," she enthused. "What legislative marvels must take place inside a building so grand! Surely its occupants are veritable Solons, wise men rising to the level of their majestic surroundings."

"The memories this place conjures up!" cried Jefferson, equally stirred. "Was it really two centuries ago?! President Washington asked me to form the commission that chose its architect, and I was here when the President, in masonic attire, laid the cornerstone, over there"—and he gestured toward the far side of the Capitol.

"The Senate wing on the left was completed just before I was sworn in as president, in 1801, and the House wing not until after I had left some eight years lat—"

Jefferson stopped, seeing that Abigail had become pensive herself, no doubt from mention of his election, resulting from his electoral defeat of her husband. Before reconciling, he and Adams had become enemies for years.

"Why don't we," he said abruptly, changing the subject, "take a look inside the place? To see what has changed since our day."

"Is it open at night? Will we be allowed in?" asked Abigail.

Artistic Alterations

Franklin exchanged glances with Jefferson: "That's not likely to stop us."

At the hill's summit, near the rotunda's main entrance, they paused at a French window with an electronic lock. It took Franklin and his laptop a few minutes to hack into the security system. "The main thing," he said, his face bathed in electronic light, "is to cover our foot prints."

"What foot prints?" asked Abigail. "We're standing on asphalt."

"I mean electronic footprints," said the discoverer of electricity. "It's fairly easy to break into these systems, but a bit more challenging to leave no trace that one was there."

Closing the window behind them, they entered a great lit space under the dome, and looked up at the large-scale paintings of historical events covering the walls. Scaffolding and tall ladders were along the sides of the paintings, and bits of paint speckled the floor, indicating some kind of restoration or enhancement. The vast rotunda deserted, their footsteps clattered as they approached the murals.

The first they saw was an idealized, 12-by-18-foot depiction of the presentation of the Declaration of Independence to the Continental Congress. Jefferson, Franklin, and John Adams were presenting the document to the other delegates. The formally dressed men were rendered as self-consciously posing for an epochal moment in history.

"Was John," Mrs. Adams wondered aloud, "really that short?"

"It wasn't anything like that," remarked Jefferson. "We were too busy. There was a war on."

"And we rarely dressed up formally like that," said Franklin. "Philadelphia in July, before air-conditioning? Meeting in a big brick house that absorbed every ray of the sun? We wore cut-off breeches and loose cotton shirts. And frequented the taverns at night for cool flagons of ale."

Abigail was perplexed by the other paintings on the rotunda's walls. "I was well-schooled in the arts, and the other week I read up on these paintings in a book about the Capitol Building. But they seem to have been altered."

"For instance," she said, "look at this one, the 'Discovery of the Mississippi', about the exploration of America's heartland by the Spanish explorer, Hernando de Soto." The Founders examined the huge canvas. "The painting is supposed to be about de Soto's men on horseback, carrying cannon and cross, and watched by Indians, as they reached the Mississippi for the first time." But now the canvas showed Native-Americans in primeval times discovering the river for themselves, with the Europeans absent.

"This one's been changed too," said Abigail, moving to the next picture. "I should know—it's about the ship that sailed to New England with the Mayflower—from whose passengers I'm descended." Franklin glanced upward.

"It's called 'The Embarkation of the Pilgrims', and it should show the pilgrims praying in a semicircle around a leader who has an open Bible on his lap…In this retouched painting, however, the Bible has been replaced by a captain's log."

"I recognize this one," said Jefferson, who had drifted ahead of the others. "It shows Pocahontas."

"Yes," said Abigail, "'The Baptism of Pocahontas, the Indian princess, at Jamestown: your state's first settlement, Thomas."

"Actually," replied the Virginian, "it was the *first* English settlement in America."

"Actually, replied the New Englander, "I'm almost certain it *came after* Plymouth, Massachusetts…"

"…In any event," Franklin interrupted, "this painting's been altered as well."

It was true. "The original," said Abigail, "shows Pocahontas receiving her baptism from a minister.

"This one shows her taking a shower."

A Hall of Fame

Puzzled by the alterations, the Founders moved onto a dimly lit, semi-circular chamber that, though ornate and two stories tall, seemed small compared to the rotunda.

"I remember this place," Jefferson proclaimed. "It's the old meeting hall for the House of

Representatives, back when I was president! I wrote the Rules Manual for congress at that time."

"You wrote the rule book for congress?" winked Franklin. "No wonder it's so dysfunctional!"

Jefferson laughed, but not very hard, at the dig.

"My son John Quincy served here as well," stated Abigail. "After leaving the presidency." Abigail left out the fact that Quincy had been ousted from the White House by Andrew Jackson, a follower of Jefferson's.

The Founders were startled to see, between the stately pillars girding the room, a great many statues, one or two for each state, and each depicting a noteworthy person from that place. It was a hall of ghosts from the past, visited by three ghosts in the present. The dim light of the place added to the otherworldly atmosphere.

"Look!" said Abigail. "Here's President Garfield again!" His statue represented his native Ohio.

"And here's the pride of Tennessee," said Jefferson, "President Andy Jacks—" and, seeing Abigail's face fall, he bit his tongue, and moved on to another statue, announcing: "Ah, my old colleague Robert Livingston, of New York—I sent him to Paris to negotiate the Louisiana Purchase."

"Livingston had great business acumen," commented Franklin, who'd stopped at the image of Robert Fulton, of his own state of Pennsylvania. Fulton was depicted examining his famous steamboat. "He bankrolled this fellow's steamship, with great success." Franklin wondered if his own statue was also here, as a representative of his home state, but was pleased at least that a fellow innovator in technology had been honored.

Next to Franklin, Abigail was searching in the dim light for a statue for Massachusetts, and was disappointed in what she found. "Here's my distant relation, Samuel Adams," she announced. "He was a staunch patriot for sure—but why doesn't my husband get a statue?...Or a memorial? Or a monument?..."

"I doubt," responded Franklin, moving over to Abigail, "that memories of the fiery Sam Adams have lingered outside this space. I've overheard moderns mention his name, and they seem to have confused it with a type of grog."

"Ah!" called out Jefferson, his eyes glancing at the name tag of a statue, "here is my stat—", and he abruptly stopped. "Here is Jefferson, Jefferson Davis, of Mississippi." It was another unwelcome reminder of the Civil War. He moved on, then stood frozen.

"Hah!" he cried out. "A worthy Virginian indeed!"

The others turned, and stood, almost at attention, at the soaring image, on a marble pedestal, and illuminated by a spotlight, of President Washington.

"He did rather look like that in real life," said Franklin.

"Though somewhat plumper," noted Adams.

"And with worse teeth," replied Franklin.

Jefferson thought the sculptor skillful, but something of a propagandist for his rival Alexander Hamilton, Washington's chief advisor. The artist depicted the first President leaning on a bundle of sticks, or *fasces*, the symbol of centralized power.

"I'd prefer," Jefferson stated, "the General leaning on the Tree of Liberty."

An Unwelcome Interruption

Abigail was about to defend the statue of a man who'd ejected the British from Boston, and who'd chosen her husband as vice president. But then the door to the dim chamber was thrown open, and two legislators, accompanied by security guards, strode inside.

The Founders looked around frantically, fearing arrest for trespassing, and a return to reConstitution Biotek. In moments, the interlopers were just yards away from them. The Founders didn't dare run behind the statues to hide, lest the movement give them away.

"Everyone freeze in place!" hissed Jefferson. "Don't move!" He stood motionless before the Washington statue; Franklin and Adams did the same next to the Adams one.

The lawmakers, a thin, elderly congresswoman with a pinched face, and a wrinkled senator, were deep in conversation.

"But how many billions can I get?" asked the senator, with a halting twang of a Las Vegas gambler.

"A billion here, a billion there," replied the congresswoman, in a knowing yet thin voice that hinted at a large if cloistered California city. "It's really chump change in the scheme of things." She brushed by Franklin, then stopped.

"Who is this?" she asked. The Founders hearts fell; they'd been found out!

Franklin thought frantically for some cover story. 'I'll say we're building inspectors,' he figured. 'No, we're sculptors. Or historians perhaps. Better still, historical re-enactors. No, that would bring too much attention to us. I know: we're tourists who got lost...'

The congresswoman, accustomed to walking through the darkened hall, had taken to bringing a flashlight with her. She shone it on Franklin.

"...He's wearing contemporary apparel," she continued. "So who might this be—wait—his face! My, what a perfect likeness of Benjamin Franklin! It's just as I would imagine that old geezer to look."

The senator walked over, and felt the cloth on Franklin's shirt. "The clothing on this mockup is ridiculous though. It's more 2007 than 1776. So out of date!" Dr. Franklin, ignoring the insult to his age, and his taste in apparel, held his breath.

"Oh, they probably didn't have any period dress on hand," said the congresswoman. "And what prudes, putting clothes on a statue, until the unveiling. Old Franklin was a philanderer, wasn't he? Look! There's another mockup of a new statue." She walked over. "Of Jefferson."

"He looks much taller than in real life," said the senator. "The statue must have him at least six-foot-two."

"Another terrific likeness though," replied the congresswoman. "Just like his official portraits. Had a silly view of government, though: limiting our power, and empowering the people, when it's we who know best...And look! There's another new one, next to Sam Adams!"

"I don't recognize her," said the senator.

"Oh I do, from the White House portraits of the First Ladies. It's Abigail Adams. Though the sculptor makes her look much fatter than the portraits. The painter at the time, you know, had to flatter her. Probably fat from all those babies she had: John

Quincy Adams, Henry Adams, Gomez Adams, whoever."

"I need a firm number on the subsidies for my state," said the senator, gruffly returning to business. "My vote don't come cheap."

"Why don't we talk over here?" said the congresswoman, moving away from the statues near the walls to the other, western end of the chamber. "Did you know this used to be where my House of Representatives met, back in the day, when the people those statues represent were actually alive?" And she and the senator, in subdued tones, walked away.

The Listening Spot

Franklin, relieved to breathing easier now, whispered to his friends: "I'd love to be a fly on the wall for that corrupt little chat."

Abigail, steamed at the insult to her looks, whispered back, "I believe we actually can be."

"What do you mean?" whispered Jefferson. "If we approach them, they'll discover us."

"We can listen in from afar. When my son John Quincy served here, he called it 'the whispering room.' Due to acoustics of the place, you can hear people from clear across the chamber. And the best place to listen is from where my son's desk was. He used it as a political weapon, to eavesdrop on the Jeffersonians—um, to listen in on the Democratic-Republicans, the political faction then opposing him."

"That's fascinating," said Jefferson, ignoring the slight. "But how can we find where his desk was?"

"I know where it was," said Abigail. "He told me. In his letters. Dr. Franklin, on which point of the compass are we presently located?"

Franklin whispered, "Let's see. My GPS is impeded by the walls of this great building, but I believe I can puzzle it out. We entered from the east end of the Capitol. Turned right, or north, on entering. Turned left, or west, to enter this room. Generally drifted to our right, or north, then drifted back again. We're in its eastern end."

"Excellent!" said Abigail. "My son's desk must have been near us. And my book about this building said a plaque on the floor is supposed to mark the spot!"

The three Founders got on their hands and knees, and crawled quietly about the dark ground, the muffled voices of the lawmakers in the distance. After a few moments, they felt frustrated in their search from the dim light of the room and its large extent. Franklin reorganized them to conduct the sweep three abreast, starting from the far eastern end, and slowly moving westward.

They made progress, but Franklin feared the lawless legislators would soon make their leave. He took a chance on being seen, and flipped the lid off his smart phone to employ it as a flashlight. Abigail grabbed it, stating, "Let me try!" She combed her memory for her son's description of his work place, and went off from the others. Immediately, she lit upon a worn bronze plaque. It read: "JOHN QUINCY ADAMS. Representative from Massachusetts." The others gathered around her, and intently listened.

"I won't be bought that cheaply," said the senator from the other side of the room. The Founders exchanged glances in the gloom, amazed at the clarity of the sound.

"Many of my constituents," the senator continued, "are wary of the federal government running health care. They have an image of going for a checkup, and having to get in line at the DMV."

"What about three billion?" responded the congresswoman, who evidently was a ranking member, if able to dangle such largesse.

"Five bill," the senator shot back.

"Why don't we make it a nice round number?" said the congresswoman. "Four point three billion."

"Deal!"

"Very good. I'll steer four point three billion dollars to your state, ten times what your state stands to lose under this law. Now, I have to get back to the House of Representatives—it's ready to vote."

They and their guards departed the Hall of Statues.

"Over four billion dollars," remarked Abigail, the frugal New Englander, in disbelief.

"Even accounting for 225 years of inflation," said Franklin, "that's a lot of money."

A Health Care Hush-Up

The Founders themselves left the hall, and headed to the modern House, curious to learn more about the congressional vote in the middle of the night.

They made their way to the assembly, where a crowd of legislators, lawyers, litigants, and lobbyists were milling around and inside the entrance, affording the Founders' cover. The throng was speaking in hushed tones, as if afraid of being overheard.

59

"'And ye shall know them,'" said Jefferson, quoting the Bible, "'by the company they keep.'"

"'He that lieth down with dogs," said Franklin, quoting himself, "shall rise up with fleas'."

Peeking within, the Founders strained to make out the House chamber, whose lights had dimmed, as if to cloak its activities. Its large auditorium was centered on the raised dais from which the Speaker presides, and from which the President speaks during State of the Union speeches. On the dais was a stack of papers that reached eight or nine feet into the air.

Rows of semicircular seating fanned out from the podium, and lawmakers and lobbyists, and lobbyists and lawmakers, were starting to take their seats. In the darkened space, many held penlights or had glow rings around their necks. Unusual for a session of congress, no legislator was posturing for the cameras, and no one from the media could be seen.

The Founders walked up the back stairs and sat down in the visitors' gallery, pondering the purpose and outcome of the unusual assembly.

A woman on the dais picked up a heavy gavel, and with difficulty tapped the lectern with it. Abigail said, "It's the congresswoman from the hall of statues, who proffered the four billion!" Mouths open in surprise, Franklin and Jefferson leaned forward to watch.

"It's high time we began this session," the congresswoman stated, "to pass our historic legislation," and she pointed to the tall pile of paper on the dais. "Everyone take your seats. Sergeant at Arms: shut the doors—we don't want details of what we do to leave this place."

"First order of business—an auction, for waivers to our landmark law. Anyone receiving a waiver is exempt from the healthcare law for ten years. Any money received will go into programs to promote the law, and buy votes for our re-election." With difficulty, she tapped the lectern with her gavel. "Do I hear one billion?"

"One billion!" said a congressman from Nevada.

"Do I hear two billion?" asked the congresswoman.

"Two billion," said a congressman from Nebraska. "And I raise it to three billion!"

"Three billion to waive Nebraska's unions and hospitals from the healthcare law. A 'Cornhusker kickback', if you will. Any other takers?" Gasping from its weight, she almost dropped the gavel onto the lectern. "Three billion it is! Clerk of the House: write that exemption into the law."

At her side, a gnomish-looking man keyed into a laptop, printed off something, then turned to the high stack of paper. About halfway up the pile, he carefully and laboriously lifted up the stack, and slipped the page in.

"I recognize," said the presiding congresswoman, "the gentleman from Nebraska."

The congressman rose from his seat. "Madame Speaker, may I request to read aloud the exemption from the law, to be certain of its contents?"

The Speaker almost dropped the gavel onto the lectern. "Absolutely not! No time for such trivia.

"You can read the law after we pass it."

Up in the gallery, Franklin was apoplectic. "This is abject corruption!"

"And in the dead of night, when the citizenry are sleeping, and unaware!" said Abigail.

"And what business does the central government have," inveighed Jefferson, "to interfere in such a personal matter as interaction with one's physician?!"

"I dare say," added Abigail, "that the Founding Fathers, I mean the other Founders, are rolling in their graves."

The Speaker tapped the handle of her heavy gavel. "Let's bring this business to a close." She looked at the stack of paper, some 2,700 pages worth, and with a mighty effort theatrically lifted half of it up, and plumped it back into place. "It's time to vote!" She then clutched her upper thigh in pain, and fell back into her chair.

A Legislative Sleight of Hand

Upstairs, the Founders were in a huddle.

"Is there anything," wondered Abigail, "we can do about this monstrosity?"

"Dr. Franklin," asked Jefferson, "can you, as the moderns say, 'hack' into the congress' computer system?"

"I have little doubt I could—the government's systems lag years behind those in the commercial world, and are open to attack. What do you have in mind?"

Jefferson peered at the section of the auditorium where Virginia's lawmakers sat. "Hmm, I see several are missing from their post. Dr. Franklin, could I borrow your computer tablet?"

Jefferson took it from Franklin's day pack and, drawing on his legal and legislative experience, rapidly wrote the following, which Franklin then printed out:

"SEC. 1776(a). PROHIBITION ON FAVORED TREATMENT OF GOVERNMENT PERSONNEL.—Not later than the date of enactment of this Act, all Members of this House, and all other members of the Federal Government, shall lose their coverage under the Government's private, gold-plated health care coverage, and shall be covered instead under the full provisions of this new Law."

"I see what you're up to," said Franklin, taking back his computer and getting to work. "It should only take me a minute to insert this into the online version of the law."

Jefferson took the printout of the document, and walked briskly down out of the gallery.

Meantime the Speaker, who'd apparently tore some muscle lifting up the legislative stack, called for a vote on the bill, and the health care law passed.

As Abigail was watching this, she saw Jefferson stride up to the dais, and give the printout to the gnomish-looking document keeper, who carefully and laboriously placed it into its proper section of the legislative stack. She looked at Franklin, who looked up from his laptop and gave a thumb's up. She looked back down, and Jefferson, standing tall, had rushed over to the seats of his state, and raised his hand.

The Speaker, wincing, and with pain in her voice, spoke up. "I recognize the gentleman from Virginia." Two men carrying a litter, meantime, came up on the dais, ready to take the Speaker off for medical treatment.

"Madam Speaker," stated Jefferson, "I'd like to call the attention of the House to the latest addition to the health legislation, section 1776(a), which provides all House members with the same health care coverage as the rest of the citizenry."

The Speaker, with a shocked expression, ordered the records keeper to look up that part of the bill. He did so and handed it to her, as the litter carriers placed her on the stretcher. As they carried the woman out of the chamber, she glanced over the legislative rider, and was heard to whimper: "I should have read the bill, I should have read the bill..."

Franklin and Abigail descended the stairs from the gallery, and met Jefferson at the entrance of the House chamber. There, workers were starting to set up, as required by the legislation, government-style health care for House members. No medical equipment, drugs, nor doctors were evident, but there were many desks, lengthy forms, filing cabinets, and rolls of red-tinted tape.

In front of everything were a digital readout, and a box-like container on a metal stand with a string of paper tickets hanging from it. The Speaker's litter was placed there, and she painfully looked upward.

A big arrow pointing at the tickets read, "Take a number."

The digital readout flashed:

"Your Number in the Queue: 320,000,013".

The Founders did not normally take pleasure in the suffering of others, but they did watch this with some satisfaction.

Then, suddenly, they noticed saw a mad rush of lawmakers back into the House of Representatives.

"What's everyone doing?" asked Franklin of a legislator pushing by.

"We're holding another vote," replied the congressman, "to overturn the healthcare law.

"We'll be damned if we have to get government care ourselves—and the same health care as regular people!"

"The Founders Observe Unusual War Games"

The Founders were walking early one morning from the Lincoln Memorial to Arlington National Cemetery, Virginia, across the elegant arches of Memorial Bridge. The mists from Foggy Bottom still clung to the Potomac, impeding their views. They passed the southern side of the span, feeling their way, and the purplish haze lifted, revealing a vast graveyard.

A Sad Cemetery Stroll

They stepped through a resting place containing hundreds of thousands of graves, from over 235 years of armed conflicts. After walking through the place pensively for a time, the threesome fell to thinking of the Revolutionary War.

"This reminds me," said Abigail, "of tending to the many wounded from the battles around Boston, and of my husband John away on war-time business for many lonely months."

"This reminds me," said Franklin, "of the worst episode in my life, my son William serving as royal governor of New Jersey, and turning arms against his own country, and his own father."

"I'm reminded," said Jefferson, "of my state occupied and ravaged, and my wife dying, partly from the strains of the war."

They eyed the simple headstones, dated 1942, 1863, 2013, and many other years.

"There've been many further wars," noted Franklin, "since our War for Independence."

"Including the War of 1812," said Abigail. "I must tell you, I overheard two school children talking the other day. A girl was telling her schoolmate, 'I'm studying about the War of 1812.' Her classmate responded, "Is that the one that started in 1776?' And I'm not making this up."

Jefferson and Franklin grimaced. "Indeed," said Franklin, "many of the modern Americans seem ignorant of their past." Said Jefferson: "'He who doesn't know his history is condemned to repeat it.'"

"Yes, 1812," continued Jefferson, recalling that troubled time. "The second war with Britain, and an undeclared war at sea with France, then at Britain's throat, and with us in the middle. Both powers were impressing, seizing, our sailors for their own use."

"Such actions," said Franklin, "tended to make a bad *impression* on us."

Jefferson smiled sadly. "In the years prior to that conflict, as President, I strove mightily to avoid a war. And, I might add, my predecessor Mr. Adams, as well. Both of us felt it would be foolhardy to take on the powerful British or French before America had built up its own strength."

"You weren't very supportive of John," replied Abigail with some asperity, "at the time of his presidency. In fact, you declined his request to travel to France as a peacemaker."

"John and I were then in sharp conflict on domestic matters," Jefferson answered, "so I retreated to Monticello instead." The former President hesitated. "Perhaps I should have been more supportive. Certainly the war in 1812 that my friend Madison declared, after succeeding me, brought on much destruction, particularly here, with the British burning down the capital."

They passed many more headstones. "I see numerous markers from recent broils," noted Franklin. "Several of the conflicts were near Cathay—they term it China now...Such a prosaic moniker, naming a venerable nation after dinnerware...One war in Korea, east of Cathay, and another in Indochina, to its south. Many gravestones for both of them."

"And two wars," said Jefferson, scanning the burial sites, "for Mesopotamia, or what they call Iraq today. One from 1991, and another more recent."

They reached a place of freshly dug graves, with their headstones in neat piles, waiting to be put in place.

"Just as we've been learning from the news blogs," noted Jefferson, examining the headstones' dates, and the locales where the soldiers fell. "The United States has been at war with that rugged land which Alexander the Great had difficulty taming: Afghanistan...Many wars, on many distant shores."

Filled with thoughts, the Founders walked along, to the edge of the cemetery.

Jefferson gazed south, unsure of his bearings, and of what he was seeing. He said, "Look at that immense building, and its odd, geometrical shape. It couldn't be a newer, expanded version of the Octagon House, could it? Where James and Dolley Madison resided after the British burned the White House down?"

"No," said Franklin. "It's a multi-sided building, to be sure. But extrapolating from the sides that we can see, it has five sides, not eight."

"Mr. Jefferson," Abigail gently chided, "your grasp of the capital's modern architecture fails to match your knowledge of its past. That is the Pentagon: the newer, expanded version of the old War Department building."

Franklin had called up its location on his GPS app. Even on the small map display, the shape of the place was clear. "Yes. The aptly named Pentagon. Headquarters of the U.S. armed forces." He quickly checked a related web site. "The largest office building in the world."

Jefferson's face fell. "It's gigantic. As I feared, after its founding, the nation went on to acquire a massive standing army. What a threat to our republic! History is littered with the corpses of democracies overcome by a strongman on a horse."

Abigail recalled her more hawkish husband's debates with Jefferson over the size and type of military the young nation required.

"A country needs," she stated, "a strong army to defend itself."

Franklin added, "Based on what we've seen in our time here, the military does not seem to be running the country."

"But based on what we've seen in this cemetery," answered Jefferson, "I wonder how the military has been running itself.

"Or how our leaders have been directing it."

A Ride in a Modern Carriage

Moving on, the Founders came upon a steep hill, which overlooked a wide expanse of flat terrain and streams. Several narrow roadways cut through the area, but soldiers, with the insignia "MP" emblazoned on their uniforms, were turning away traffic. The Founders approached an MP with a captain's insignia.

Jefferson, aware that federal law placed tight restrictions on use of the U.S. military within the U.S., asked him: "Don't these military maneuvers violate *Posse Comitatus*?"

"I wouldn't know about any forming any posse, sir," replied the young man.

"He means," replied Franklin, "the stricture against undue deployment of U.S. troops on American soil."

"Oh no, mister," said the captain. "This isn't an actual deployment. This is a *war game*.

"We hold simulations of recent conflicts," he went on, "and of very ancient ones, ones that Misters Lincoln and Jefferson and all those other dead presidents lived through.

"Why don't you let me show you?" said the friendly officer. And he motioned the Founders toward a squat-shaped metal contrivance, open to the air and with thick rubber wheels.

The captain took the wheel of the Jeep, and the others clambered in. The thrill of zipping along a meadow in a motorized, open-air vehicle made the 18th-century figures forget the tragedy of war for a while. Clattering along a bumpy field, Jefferson next to the captain, and Franklin and Abigail in the rear, the Founders realized how much they missed horse-drawn conveyances. The rushing air rippling their hair and clothes reminded them of sleigh rides in the back of hay-filled wagons at Christmas time.

Intrigued by the workings of the Jeep, Franklin leaned far out its right side, pressing his face almost to the rear wheel. Then the vehicle hit a rut, which nearly tossed Franklin out the side. He grabbed the back of Jefferson's seat, and some of his friend's long hair, while Abigail seized the back of Franklin's shirt, and with great effort hauled him back in.

Settled back into his seat, Franklin scarcely recognized his brush with disaster.

"I note," he exclaimed, "that each wheel turns independently, rather like the joints of the knee!" The captain laughed, amazed at the man's ability to ignore danger while analyzing something.

"Why didn't I think of that?" Franklin asked Abigail. "Each wheel has separate and independent suspension. I could have made a fortune in the carriage trade."

The captain skittered the Jeep up to the top of a steep pile of sand.

Borders and Body Armor

Stretching out from their sandy vista was a landscape reshaped to resemble a smaller version of an actual country. Acres of land, in the rough shape of a crescent, stretched from a northwesterly to a southeasterly direction. Army engineers had diverted a small tributary of the Potomac to run through the land in the same direction.

Franklin didn't need his map app to identify the facsimile country. It was obviously meant to represent the Fertile Crescent: Mesopotamia in ancient times, Iraq today.

The captain had left the Jeep, and was staring through powerful binoculars that the optician in Franklin had a burning desire to try. "Come on over," the officer said, and handed Franklin his lenses, while Franklin handed Jefferson his collapsible telescope. "The invasion," said the captain, "is about to begin."

The vague borders of "Iraq" were marked by hastily constructed fences and clumps of barbed wire.

71

Near its southern border were a modest number of troops clothed in the plain olive drab of the Iraqi Republican Guard. Facing it was a large number of troops clad in the mottled-green uniforms of U.S. troops deployed in a desert region.

Jefferson peered through Franklin's portable telescope. "What are those bulky vests on our troops?"

"Body armor," replied the captain.

"Ah," said Jefferson, "the modern soldier has gone back to wearing armor?"

"Like the medieval knights?" interjected Franklin.

"Or the chest armor of Renaissance mercenaries, to defend against the bullets of the early handguns?" added Jefferson.

Impressed, the captain told them, "I can tell you two are keen students of military history."

"Yes," said Jefferson, "I studied ancient, Renaissance, and modern—I mean, American Revolutionary—weapons and tactics. Often in the original Greek, Latin, French, or Germanic texts."

Noticing the erudite man's upcountry Virginia drawl, the officer chuckled, and asked, "What are you, a professor at the University of Virginia or something?"

"I've had some affiliation with that institution," its founder responded.

Ever the student of optics, Franklin inquired about the binocular-like instruments on the troopers' headgear. "How can a soldier see, when his binoculars are strapped to the top of his helmet?"

The officer smiled. "You're pulling my leg, right? Those of course are night-vision goggles—they tease out the infra-red part of the spectrum of light, to let a soldier see at night."

Franklin mumbled, "An absolutely brilliant idea."

An Odd Occupation

Passing Franklin's scope and the captain's binoculars back and forth, the Founders took in a broad view of "Iraq" and its borders.

Scattered about the country were roped-off camps with large signs in English and Arabic, entitled "Arms Dump." These had mounds of cartons packed with bullets, rockets, and grenades. Each was guarded by a few men garbed as Iraqi soldiers, leaning sleepily on their rifles.

"The location of the foe's arms stockpiles is clear enough," murmured Abigail.

Just over its eastern border, in "Iran", and just over its northwestern border, in "Syria", were camps of men outfitted in checkered, black-and-white headgear. At times, explosions went off near the camps, indicating the "fighters" were testing out bombs. The men brandished automatic rifles, which from time to time they pointed to the sky above them, and fired into the air.

"They should be more careful," noted Franklin. "The ballistics make it unlikely, but it is possible that some of their bullets could come back down and hit them."

"What you're seeing," explained the captain, "are mock-ups of terrorist training camps."

"The one in Iran," he continued, "was responsible for training those who blew up a U.S. Marines barracks in Lebanon, back in 1984, killing 240 Americans. The one in Syria has members of the al Qaeda group, whose leadership in Afghanistan planned the 9-11 attacks that killed three thousands of our citizens at home."

Although they were deceased at the time, the Founders had become well aware of relatively recent, momentous events such as September 11.

"What acts of terror against Americans were the Iraqis responsible for?" asked Jefferson.

"There weren't any," said the captain. "None that we could prove beyond dispute at least."

"Then why are—why did we invade Iraq?" asked Jefferson, his voice rising.

"Because it was thought Iraq was building nuclear bombs," replied the officer.

Franklin and the others had read of those devices able to destroy whole cities.

Dr. Franklin asked, "But it's my understanding that Iraq did not have nuclear weapons."

"That's true," said the captain. "But in recent times, we often go to war based on the wrong information.

"In fact, that's what makes this war game more realistic—it simulates going to war for the wrong reason, or with the wrong strategy."

Everyone's attention turned to Iraq's southern border, where the American forces—troops, trucks, and giant, roaring, armored tanks—were throwing up great clouds of dust, massing for an invasion. The Founders were stunned, and nearly deafened, when jet fighters came screaming over their heads. Involuntarily, they crouched to the ground, hands over their ears, while the captain calmly looked through his binoculars.

The Founders rose to their feet, and were astonished by Apache helicopters roaring past at tree-top level.

"What a remarkable propulsion system!" Franklin cried.

Impressed by the air and land array, Abigail told her companions, "I'm reminded of the great British fleet that appeared off Boston during our Revolution. It was a spectacular sight, meant to inspire awe."

What followed was anti-climactic. The U.S. troops moved forward, and broke through the border fences as if they didn't exist. After a brief skirmish, most of the "Iraqi" troops surrendered, with some dropping their weapons and slipping away. The soldiers at the arms dumps threw down their rifles and ran off.

The Americans then marched to the middle of the country, and set up camp, building a sturdy fence around them.

"That was almost too easy," said Jefferson.

"You got that right," said the officer.

Over the northern border in Syria, and the eastern border in Iran, the men in the terrorist camps crossed the boundaries into Iraq, and drove or marched to the ammo dumps. There they filled their packs, pockets, or vehicles with ordinance. Then they moved to different parts of the country, and began planting bombs. Some traveled near the American camp, and set up mortars to attack it.

"This is horrible!" said Abigail.

"Where is the plan of occupation for this country?" urged Jefferson.

"There is no plan for occupation," said the captain.

"In modern times," he explained, "we often go to war without any plan for what to do once the war starts.

"We're very good at starting wars," he added, "and at gaining an initial, smashing success. But we very rarely have a plan for winning, or for getting out.

"So, you see gentlemen, and ma'am: this war game is extremely realistic."

The captain saw that his guests were dismayed at the growing, if simulated, mayhem, and suggested changing the venue.

"Why don't I show you," he asked, "some of the battles we've war-gamed from the distant past?"

The Founders were too shocked and awed to offer resistance. They got back in the Jeep, and drove down the sand dune to another site.

A Revolutionary Reenactment

Abigail was deeply moved when she saw the venue of the next simulation. She instantly recognized the setting. Next to a facsimile of streets in Charlestown, Massachusetts, a long steep hill has been constructed. On its summit lay a bastion of trenches and wooden barricades.

Behind the protective barriers was a ragged but determined-looking unit of soldiers, outfitted as Revolutionary War infantrymen with muskets, and their officers with pistols and tri-cornered hats. Near the base of the hill, a larger force of well-outfitted soldiers, identified by their bright red coats, was led slowly upward by officers astride horses and holding swords up high.

"I remember that day so clearly!" exclaimed Abigail. "I watched this battle from a nearby rise, with my young son John Quincy. So many of our brave men to nurse back to health—or to bury. Those damnable British took the hill, but it was a Pyrrhic victory—they lost many more killed and wounded than we did!"

In the reenactment, the British steadily, implacably, ascended the hill. The Americans set their muskets on the barriers, drawing a bead, their officers motioning to them to hold their fire.

The captain turned to the Founders. "I think you know what comes next." They all recalled the hallowed statement, and in fact an American officer stood up at the center of the line to address his men. He declaimed the words loud enough for the onlookers to hear: "Wait 'til you see the whites of their eyes!"

The British kept marching slowly forward, to within 50 yards of the barriers. Then the American officer raised his sword, and sharply lowered it, shouting, "Now!"

The Founders held their breath for the famous volley. Instead, the colonials scrambled out of their trenches, and charged the Britishers.

"What in Heaven's name are they doing?!" shouted Jefferson.

The British officers told their men to halt. Then they ordered the troops in the front of the line to drop to their knees, giving those in the rear a clear line of fire too.

When the Americans closed to within 10 yards, the British let loose a furious volley. In the simulated battle, most of the attackers were mowed down; the remnants scurried back to the barricade, or fled down the hill to Charleston's streets.

"How can this be?!" roared Franklin.

"That's not what happened!" cried Adams.

The captain adopted a solicitous tone. "You have to put this in the context of our recent wars.

Korea—we were lured into a bloody stalemate. Vietnam—we lost our determination, and lost. The second Iraqi war—a messy occupation. The Afghan war—we withdraw without winning.

"Our soldiers simply cannot expect to win decisively anymore. So we try to drill that reality into them, even in reenactments of past victories, or near victories like here at Bunker's Hill."

"*Breed's Hill*," steamed Abigail, correcting the officer.

"Ah," said the captain, "I see that you are a student of military history too.

"By altering history," continued the officer, "we prepare our troops for the future they're most likely to face: defeat or a draw."

Dejected, the Founders climbed back into the Jeep; they felt like prisoners of war.

"Why don't we," suggested the captain, "take a look at our most recent major conflict?"

Taking a Whirl

They drove away from the simulation sites near the Pentagon and into the Arlington Hills, where the Defense Department, as the War Department was now called, had cleared out a tract of wooded hillsides as a mockup of another country.

"The land here is too rugged for a clear view!" the captain called out to his guests. "Let's try a different mode of transport."

He pulled the Jeep up to a level clearing with a big chalk circle. On the circle was a bubble-like craft with transparent walls, a large rotor on its top, and a smaller rotor jutting from its rear.

The officer jumped out of the Jeep and trotted over to the flying machine.

"I'm certified for flight!" he shouted. "Climb on aboard!"

"I believe this is one of those hell-a-copter contraptions," Franklin told the others.

"Hell—acious, yes, I'd say," commented Abigail. "It rather looks like a handiwork of the Devil."

The captain noticed some hesitation on the faces of his guests.

"Have you never flown before? In a helicopter? It's perfectly safe. We don't even keep parachutes on board," he added mischievously. "They won't be needed and, even if they were, you couldn't jump out of a copter spiraling down to the ground."

Despite the pilot's dark humor, the Founders got in and took their seats, Franklin in front this time, next to the pilot, and Jefferson and Abigail in the rear.

The trio had seen jet planes take off with great speed, and expected the same with this craft. They braced themselves, and were surprised, pleasantly so, when the craft took off slowly, and hardly moved, but hovered, not far off the ground.

"Do the rotors supply thrust?" Franklin asked the officer. "You tilt the rotor in the direction you would want to go, I assume?"

"Yes," said the captain, easing the copter higher up. "Are you an aeronautical engineer?"

"Aero Nautical," muttered the Doctor. 'Of course that's what they call it,' he thought.

"No," he replied. "I'm scientist. And a businessman. And an inventor. And a publisher. And a diplomat. And a *philosophe*—a philosopher of sorts."

The pilot looked at him curiously. The fellow was obviously smart, maybe brilliant, but odd.

Probably, judging from his pigtail and gray hair, an old hippie, maybe a college professor.

As they climbed up over the hills, Jefferson and Adams were stunned by the view. They were becoming used to looking at airplanes, which had metal frames that passengers couldn't see through, except for the little passenger windows. The fact that a helicopter had large see-through windows hadn't really hit them until they were air-borne. The view made them feel exposed and vulnerable to the elements, as if they themselves were flying. The normally resolute Abigail felt fear; the often emotional Jefferson felt a weird sense of elation.

Franklin immersed himself in examining the instrument readings on the control panel. He asked the pilot: "This global position—this G-P-S—is actually accurate to within a meter?"

"It's something, isn't it?" the captain replied. "To think that folks back in the day used an astrolabe, a quadrant, and the stars and the sun to get around. I don't know how they managed!"

"Indeed, sir."

Jefferson cupped Franklin on the shoulder, and whispered. "If only we had machines like this 'back in the day'—all the uncertainty about the unknown lands in the West, all the agony of traversing over the Appalachians, or where the British fleet lurked off our coasts, all could have been avoided!"

The craft's forward motion markedly slowed, as it began hovering high above the military's hilly preserve. The pilot put his craft on a south to north bearing, and pointed out the elements of the war game below. To the east, a border fence poked its way here and there about the hills. Beyond it was a large encampment.

"That's the eastern border," said the captain, "of this simulated, war-torn country. The other side is supposed to represent Pakistan."

Timetables and Terror

Peering through binoculars and Franklin's scope, Abigail and Jefferson saw a group of men wearing cloth head coverings, baggy cotton pants, and loose tunics, and holding automatic rifles. They vaguely reminded the former President of the Barbary Coast pirates his presidency had vanquished. The armed men milled around for a time, then gathered together and marched over to a giant, papier-mâché piece of statuary. Even from a distance, it was clear a great deal of handiwork had gone into the figure. Jefferson increased the magnification on Franklin's scope.

The ex-President recognized the statue from trinkets brought back from the vast China trade of his time. It was of the Buddha. "This simulation takes pains to be realistic," he remarked admiringly, "even recreating the religious artifacts common to the region."

He and the others watched as the men below attached explosives to the statue. They paused, and seemed to pray. Then they blew the statue to bits.

Contemporary Americans would have been disturbed enough by the wanton destruction of the religious figure. The Founders, children of the Enlightenment, and steeped in the Age of Reason, were horrified to their core.

"Can there be a purpose to this destruction?!" exclaimed Abigail.

"Are these men or beasts?!" thundered Franklin.

"It would seem," stated Jefferson, "that their creed brooks no rival."

The pilot answered, "You have a way with words, sir, and you're right.

"We have our soldiers dress as, and undertake actions similar to, our enemy, to help them better understand the foe."

The drama to the east had diverted their attention from the country to the west. Another large encampment lay there. Through their lenses, the Founders spied the familiar, in-country fatigues of the modern American soldier. More troops were pouring into the camp, evidently the start of a surge of forces.

In the middle of their camp, the American troops had constructed a tall tower. At its top was a platform, and from it engineers were operating a crane. The derrick was winching up from the ground a large, square-shaped object.

As Franklin and Jefferson tried to ascertain the platform's purpose, the perspicuous Abigail noticed that the baggy-pants bandits had moved across the border, and were moving rapidly in the direction of the American camp. She poked her friends, who turned their lenses to the east. The gunmen had stopped on a rise overlooking the encampment, and were readying grenade launchers.

Jefferson knew this just was an exercise but, as a former Commander-in-Chief, felt an urge to warn his fellow countrymen.

"Things look bad for our side," he worriedly told the captain.

The officer turned to him, and paused, a puzzled look on his face. "Did anyone ever tell you, by the way, that you look just like someone really famous?"

The Founders felt their insides tighten. This officer had armed soldiers at his command close by and, if he had them figured out, they could soon be back in captivity.

The captain scratched his chin. "What's that guy's name again? You look like, just like—Alexander Hamilton!"

"He's often mistaken for him!" interjected Franklin, realizing the officer was thinking of a modern man bearing a resemblance, not the real thing from the past.

"Yes," added Abigail, "the first Secretary of the Treasury, the supporter of a strong military, unlike his—what's the word—his *peacenik* rival, Thomas Jefferson."

"Indeed," inserted Franklin, winking, "Hamilton, that early backer of U.S. industry, unlike his farmer rival, that *unschooled* rustic, Jefferson."

"That's the one," agreed the officer, "You folks sure know your history.

"Hamilton wouldn't be an ancestor of yours, would he?" the captain asked the man from Monticello.

"Absolutely not!" huffed Jefferson, relieved, yet irked to be confused with his old rival. Eager to bring the subject back to the matter at hand, he asked if the Americans were about to suffer a surprise attack.

"Oh, I wouldn't worry about that," replied the captain easily.

The mufti militia had finished preparations for the assault, and its members were tense with expectation. At the same time, the engineers atop the platform had finished hauling the square-shaped form into position.

"Is it a new sort of weapon?" Abigail asked Franklin.

"It doesn't have the shape of any armament I can envision," Dr. Franklin replied.

Several of the engineers had laptops, and they rapidly keyed in some data. Suddenly, the square brightened with light, a crystalline display appearing on each of its four sides.

The digital display read:

"*Months*: 12. *Days*: 30. *Hours*: 24. *Minutes*: 60. *Seconds*: 60."

The display for Seconds changed: to 59, then 58, and so on with each instant.

"It can't be the countdown for a weapon," said Franklin. "12 months is too long for that."

"Look!" cried Abigail. "On the right again!"

The fighters in head cloths had visibly relaxed. They were pointing at the clock, its outsized numbers and letters clearly visible to them. Then they embraced, let out a great cheer, and fired their automatic rifles into the sky.

The captain saw the puzzled looks on the faces of his guests.

"The clock is our timetable for withdrawal," he said in a measured voice.

The Founders let that sink in.

Then Abigail asked, "But how can one know the time of retreat from a war when you're in the middle of fighting one? One can't predict the fut—"

"—Unless one is announcing one's withdrawal in advance," said Franklin.

Jefferson nodded. They thought back to their time as diplomats in France, when Britain threw in the towel during the Revolution, and stated the period of its withdrawal of ships and soldiers from the new United States.

"Exactly," said the captain. "We're announcing our withdrawal from Afghanistan well in advance."

Abigail was perturbed. "But you're sending in more troops even as you're stating your intent to leave. It seems a most confused strategy."

"It's actually pretty simple, ma'am. To win votes at home, the politicians are ordering us to bring our troops home.

"And to not lose votes, they're ordering us to make show of force before leaving. It wouldn't look good to just run away."

"But that's playing with our soldiers' lives!" Jefferson nearly shouted. "For short-term political gain!"

"I can't say I'm happy about that," replied the captain. "I have plenty of friends serving in Afghanistan.

"But for a long time, our wars have been less about fighting, and more about politics."

"This is insanity," said Jefferson. "Even for mad King George, wars had a purpose: to build or sustain Britain's empire. This war would seem to have the purpose of subduing those intolerant men in mufti. Except that we are announcing our defeat even as we fight.

"What a callous and pointless waste of treasure and lives," continued the Sage of Monticello. "What's the sense of being there at all?"

"That kind of decision is above my pay grade," replied the captain, looking at Jefferson. "It's one a president has to make."

The captain was silent for a while. Then he began steering the helicopter back to its landing zone. He said, "I guess it's time for us to leave."

To the Shoals of Tripoli

The helpful young military officer could see the Founders were disturbed by the Afghan war re-enactment, and again suggested another venue.

"Why don't we try one more simulation, one's that a little different, and observe one of our latest foreign interventions, which involves the State Department and CIA, as well as our military?"

Jefferson was intrigued by the reference to the State Department he'd founded during the Washington Administration, and they were all curious about the secretive CIA. So, after the captain placed their helicopter down at the landing pad, they clambered back into the Jeep, whose suspension Franklin so admired, and drove off to another location designed to resemble a hot, desert region.

Palm trees were scattered around three small buildings making up a whitewashed compound. Its broad iron gate blocked the entrance from a dusty road. A couple of "security guards", hired from the local population, loitered in front. Jefferson, who had studied illustrations of Libya, or the Barbary Coast as it was known in his day, when as president he'd vanquished the Barbary Pirates, recognized the landscape.

Across the road from the compound was a small building with a rooftop, on top of which two lone U.S. security guards, former Navy SEALs, stood watch. In the compound's courtyard were two other

Americans, one dressed in the formal attire of a U.S. ambassador, his visage handsome, earnest, if a bit naïve, and the second his aide de camp.

Outside the gate gathered scores of angry, shouting men in long white robes, and brandishing grenade launchers and automatic rifles.

On the roof of one of the compound's buildings were a dozen Americans, outfitted in trench coats and sunglasses, and handing grenade launchers and automatic rifles to the angry locals.

Further in the distance was a mockup of a U.S. military base in a nearby nation. The base had hundreds of special-forces troops, and squadrons of helicopter gunships and fighter-bombers, all able to reach the compound in a small amount of time. The troops were strapping on combat gear, and runway personnel were fueling the aircraft: if need be, the base was ready to launch a rescue mission.

Off to the left was an office representing a workplace in a faraway land. With its walls stripped away, it looked like a command center at the State Department in Washington, D.C. Filled with computers and display screens, it swarmed with busy officials. In fact, the place was supposed to simulate crisis management: how top officials back home might react to a sudden military or diplomatic crisis.

Built around the office was an odd construction, and both Franklin and Jefferson blinked at the sight of this. They had seen such ornate buildings, with their wrought-iron balconies, in Madrid and Paris, and had heard such buildings were frequently seen in New Orleans, in the bawdier districts of that teeming metropolis.

Its windows glowed with rose-colored light from the red bulbs in its light fixtures. A smudged sign on the front entrance read—the Founders struggled to make it out—something like, "House of Rising Sin", or "Hut of the Rising Sun".

Various U.S. diplomats—identified by their striped pants and tall, silken top hats—and various U.S. Secret Service guards—identified by the characteristic earpieces and wires coming out of their ear lobes—were strolling up the front stairs, while grasping the hands of local women in short skirts, brightly colored makeup, and long flowing hair.

Jefferson and Franklin were wide-eyed at this, while Abigail's jaw dropped.

The helpful officer explained: "We strive to be as realistic as possible in our military and diplomatic simulations, to provide the best training for our personnel. In recent years, many of our diplomats, and many of our security personnel, have regularly engaged in unapproved, uh, liaisons, with uncleared laborers. Since this is a simple fact of life in today's diplomatic and community, we decided to include it in our re-enactment."

The officer continued: "As for the war game itself, it represents certain events in Libya, whose government the United States recently helped overthrow."

"What was the reason for our intervention?" asked Franklin, trying to focus his mind back on foreign relations, and away from dangerous liaisons.

"The country was ruled by a cruel despot," the officer replied. "He was overthrown, with our help, by groups of cruel terrorists, like those gathering near our diplomatic compound there."

"Did the Libyan government pose a threat of terror to our nation?" asked Abigail.

"It had, many years before," replied the officer, "but for a long time it had in fact been damping down on terrorists, and cooperating with us on that vital matter."

"So we toppled its government anyway?!" exclaimed Jefferson. "Wasn't that exactly the mistake we made just a few years prior in Iraq?!?

"And why are these secret agents of ours handing out armaments to those angry foreigners?"

"It was thought," said the officer, "that they'd in turn give the weapons to terrorists in another country, called Syria, and help topple its cruel dictator."

"The governments of today," responded Franklin, "seem never to learn from their miscues, but to reprise the errors repeatedly, like some dull youth devoid of sense or skill."

Compounding One's Error

The three Founders, although aware of course this was just a reenactment, became agitated despite themselves at the growing throng of armed men, and the vulnerability of the unarmed ambassador. They had all served as high-ranking envoys, or as a spouse of the same, under perilous conditions in foreign lands, and devoutly wished the officials in the crisis center would take steps to protect the vulnerable envoy.

In the courtyard, the said envoy eyed the milling crowded of armed men, and spoke excitedly into a cell phone, "We're in imminent danger of being breached! Send help now!", and he and the aide scurried into the short-term protection of a small building.

The terrorists began pushing up against the gate of the compound, rattling its bars, and inducing the two local guards to flee, actually, to join the terrorists; they had been hired from the same group to provide "security".

Then one of the insurgents drove a car into the gate, making a big hole in the barrier, and the car, its driver still at the wheel, "exploded". The driver then emerged from the vehicle smiling and covered in white chalk. The simulation was cleverly and realistically put together, the Founders saw. After a pause from the stimulated explosion, the terrorists surged into the compound.

The American guards in the adjacent building, seeing this, got on a radio, apparently to the crisis management center, for the analysts there began listening and talking excitedly into their headsets. The guards also began firing into the courtyard. The terrorists paused to fire back, buying the ambassador and the aide some time.

At the same time, the Americans in trench coats paused in handing out weapons to the terrorists, and stood on the rooftop of their building scratching their heads and wringing their hands.

Crisis Mismanagement

The crisis management room, having been alerted to the attack, went into a frenzy.

"What do we do?!" shouted a programmer at a display screen, which carried live video of the attack sent by a hovering drone.

"How do we help the ambassador?!" shouted an analyst fidgeting nervously by a computer.

They were waved silent by a thin, middle-aged man, apparently in command. "We maintain the narrative," he stated, in the soothing, persuasive voice of a law professor.

"That is correct," answered a plump, exhausted-looking older woman, also in authority, whose hair style and facials tried mightily to make her seem younger than her years.

Both the man and the woman had once lived for years in the same Midwestern state, though his accent was soft and flowing, while hers was shrill and grating.

"Our narrative," she continued in a scratchy, high-pitched voice, "is that terrorism is no longer a threat. In fact, we must no longer use the term 'terrorism', as such a term is offensive, especially to terrorists."

"Not only offensive," echoed the middle-aged man, who had a handsome if quickly graying visage, "but inaccurate. For if terrorism no longer exists, due to the success of our policies, then the very term 'terrorism' is no longer operative."

He rested his chin on his hand. "What about that inflammatory video, which insulted the Prophet Muhammad, that we've heard about?" He turned to the analyst at the computer. "Do a search for that video."

The analyst tapped rapidly on his keyboard, and it was displayed on his screen.

An Internet video resembling a bad sitcom was shown, of someone doing a poor imitation of Mohammed, who was trying to clumsily ingratiate himself, inside a tent, with some of the young ladies of his distant era. The film seemed to have been cobbled together by a complete amateur. In fact, the analyst displayed the film via YouTube, and it had a total number of 17 "hits", or viewings, worldwide.

91

But the middle-aged leader watched the film with excitement.

"This will do!" he exclaimed. "We'll blame this terrorist attack on the video!"

"You're right," nodded the elderly woman stolidly. "It will give us plausible deniability."

"We can still claim we've defeated terrorism on our watch," added the man, "if the terrorist act is blamed on a film, and not on terrorists.

"Tell the military base to stand down," he ordered.

The analysts at first were astounded, and sat frozen with confusion and concern, before one finally texted out a message to that effect.

At the military base, the rotors of the copters stopped whirling, the whining jets of the bombers turned off, the soldiers stripped off their combat gear.

From the rooftop of the compound's building, the operatives in the trench coats scratched their heads, and wrung their hands, then washed their hands of it in basins of water brought out to them by servants. Perhaps fearing disclosure of their mission, they slinked back into their building, and closed tight the shutters and doors.

On the rooftop of the adjacent building, meanwhile, the two guards were overwhelmed from the terrorists' simulated mortar and grenade fire, and fell out of sight behind the roof's façade.

That distraction ended, a swarm of terrorists poured into the courtyard, then into the house where the ambassador and the aide had taken refuge. The walls of the building hid what transpired inside.

The Founders couldn't speak. Jefferson thought back to the American sailors the pirates of Libya had captured during his presidency. He had sent a mighty force of Marines and ships to get the prisoners back, and to subdue the pirates. Although the government of their time was often flawed, it would have done everything in its power to help those serving in risky overseas missions. But today…

Scapegoats and Stonewalls

…The data analyst—it was hard to make out his name tag: something like Snowing or Snowtent—looked up at the middle-aged man.

"What about the ambassador and the aide?!"

A programmer echoed: "What about the two security guards?!"

The middle-aged man shrugged slightly, and with a confident mien stated, almost to himself, "This just about settles it."

The older woman flatly stated, "Yes, the video caused this act of terr—this regrettable incident. I'll ask out our U.N. Ambassador to denounce the film before the Security Council, and on the Sunday talk shows. And as an inducement for her pretense, I'll offer her my job at Foggy Bottom."

The man replied, "And I'll have the Attorney General look into the background of the video maker. Perhaps there's something in his past we can hold him on, some low crime or misdemeanor.

"Someone that irresponsible deserves to be in jail."

"Sounds good," replied the woman. "This should take care of this matter as a campaign issue."

The man inquired: "And as to the matter of our envoys and security people, and their frequent, risqué liaisons with the local women folk?"

"Don't worry about that either," she answered, her tired voice cracking. "That's also too embarrassing to address during a re-election campaign. And it's just a sex scandal—I've handled far worse before.

"And besides, at this point: What difference does it make?!

"I'll tell my aides to stonewall any Inspector General inquiry until next year, when you're safely ensconced in your next term, and I'm safely in retirement—until I run for my first term of an even higher office."

And, with the IT wonks staring in amazement, the two actors playing the two unlikely political bedfellows sauntered out of the simulated crisis room arm-in-arm, then strode into a waiting Marine Corps helicopter, and breezily flew off.

The helpful officer saw the shocked expressions of the Founders. Clearing his throat, he explained, "This scenario shows how military affairs and political affairs, including campaigns, are intertwined today. Military strategy doesn't take place in a vacuum, but is now part and parcel of politics.

"'Spin' matters more than battlefield success. It's important for our officers and diplomats to understand this before heading to a place of danger.

"You see, this is a very, very realistic simulation."

The Founders quietly watched the end of the re-enactment. The terrorists, their business inside the diplomatic compound done, swarmed back into the dusty street.

A line of trucks pulled up with license plates marked Syria. The terrorists loaded the trucks with many of their grenade launchers, rifles, mortars,

MANPADS—the odd acronym for anti-aircraft missiles—and vast stocks of ammunition.

Then the trucks headed out of Libya eastward, toward Egypt, and Syria, trailing great clouds of smoke, obscuring their tracks.

And outside the large diplomatic building, the striped-pants diplomats, and the ear-pieced Secret Service agents, strolled out onto the wrought-iron balconies with the women in the short dresses, bright makeup, and long flowing hair. Savoring the moment, the open air, the scent of their accomplices, they paused to light cigarettes, inhaling deeply, languorously, while their escorts paused to take out their smart phones, and transmit secrets to their foreign handlers that they'd acquired in the chambers within.

"The Founders Find a Road and an Airport to Nowhere"

Of all the wonders of their new world—computers, open-heart surgery, press coffee—the Founders were most beguiled by air transport. They had taken to spending time, with many other onlookers, at Arlington's Gravely Point, a meadow which afforded an excellent spot to watch the jetliners roaring in to land or take off at Reagan National Airport.

One day, goaded by their curiosity, they walked the few miles from that spot along the Mt. Vernon bike and running trail to the airport's terminal. They had thought of hiring a taxi, for Jefferson loved the town's cab drivers, who were invariably Ethiopians, invariably from that country's capital of Addis Ababa, and invariably amateur experts on foreign affairs. The former Secretary of State always boosted his own knowledge by listening to their opinions on current events.

Fables of a Reconstruction

But it was just a short hike, so they walk they did, and they soon came upon a massive traffic jam on the adjoining George Washington Parkway. They were reminded of their initial escape into Washington during the gridlock at Lafayette Park. Hundreds of cars, their bored drivers playing with their cells, were at a virtual standstill. The cause of the delays was construction on a short, humpback-shaped overpass that went above a tiny tributary of the Potomac. A familiar sign announced the sponsor of the construction, "Economic Recovery and Reinvestment Act for New Transportation (ERRANT)".

"I recall the precursor to this route," said Abigail. "It's built over the old road leading south from Georgetown to Alexandria."

"Yes," said Jefferson, "later a canal, leading from Georgetown's Chesapeake and Ohio canal, a part of which still exists in Georgetown, supplanted it. Before it was in turn supplanted by a highway.

"President Washington, myself and, I dare say, Alexander Hamilton—with whom I rarely agreed—did agree on building more canals. In fact, my vice-president, George Clinton, was the uncle of DeWitt Clinton, the New York governor who built the Erie Canal. All those canals were how the local Chesapeake & Ohio canal got its name: it barely reached West Virginia, and hardly Ohio, but we dreamt it might, with a grand channel cutting through the Appalachians, and in so doing tie our country together!"

As they walked along in parallel with the traffic jam, the Founders observed the road construction crew. It consisted of dozens of men, and scores of earth-moving vehicles, on either side of the byway. Some of the men stood around talking, some sat on make-shift chairs; none were working. And none of their large, powerful-looking machines were in operation.

"They've been performing work on this hundred-meter stretch of road for three years," announced Franklin, reading from a wiki on his cell. "Thus far, it has cost forty million dollars."

"That's quite a price," said Abigail, "given the amount of work the laborers are putting into it."

As if in response to the former First Lady's gibe, the laborers began slowly assembling into three work gangs, one behind the other. Some in the first got into road-paving vehicles, those in the second took up axes and picks, and the men of the third readied shovels and bulldozers.

"It's good to see," said Jefferson, "these loafing fellows finally getting to work."

The first team began laying asphalt with their machines onto a roped-off section of the road, with the sickly sweet smell of the new pavement filling the air. Then, after the asphalt had solidified some, the second team struck at the asphalt with their implements, smashing it into chunks. Then the third team got into action. Using their spades and bulldozers, they gathered the broken-up pieces of pavement, and loaded them into the road pavement machines, with the solidified pieces of asphalt turned back into molten material for repaving.

The Founders stopped to watch this unusual work process.

The three squads repeated their actions. First laying down road, then breaking up the road, then preparing to lay down more road, and break it up again. Then they repeated these actions again. And again. The long line of drivers, meantime, sat fuming behind the construction gangs.

"I believe," said Franklin, "this is called a boondoggle."

"Highway robbery," said Abigail.

"It's a puzzle, isn't it?" said Jefferson. "It may be better for them to do nothing, and accomplish nothing, then to do something, and accomplish the same."

As if in response to the former President's witticism, the workers then ceased their exertions, and went back to standing and sitting around and doing nothing. With the same results.

"Modern Washington seems governed by a certain rule," said Jefferson. "The dictum is, 'Spend as much as possible, for as long as possible, to gain the smallest possible result.'"

A Terminal Twosome

The Founders passed down the slope of the small, clogged overpass, and reached the airport terminal. As they were about to enter the main building, their eyes lit on a broad expanse of soil, newly reclaimed from the Potomac, and stretching far from the airport. Obviously intended as an extension of the air facility, it had a series of newly paved runways, its own terminal building with revolving radar antennas, and scores of utility trucks running back and forth to service jetliners and their passengers with fuel, meals, and other necessities. Several things, however, seemed missing.

"Where are the aero planes?" asked Franklin.

"Where are the passengers?" asked Abigail.

"I haven't a clue," said Jefferson, who was examining a statue overlooking the new runways. It was a figure of an older man, gold-plated and larger-than-life, with a cracked foundation, making it tilt perilously close to falling. Still, the sculptor had skillfully rendered the fine details, like the thin veins on the man's nose indicating a propensity to drink, and the bulging veins on the neck showing an inability to control his temper. At the statue's base, a platinum plate inscribed in oversized letters the words, "Patrick James Moronico, Congressman for Life, Arlington &

Alexandria, Virginia," the latter indicating the towns nearest the airport.

The Founders looked out upon the pricey, deserted airport to nowhere. On the entire tarmac, which reached for hundreds of yards from the working terminal to the river, no aircraft could be seen. And only two souls, their shapes slowly becoming clearer through the heat vapor rising up from the asphalt. On the middle runway these two men, one old and one young, both bloated in body, with poor complexions, slowly approached. Though a hot day, both were dressed to impress, with three-piece vicuña suits, and Venetian crocodile shoes. The pricy footwear had been soaked in wood liquor, and cured in vats of oat flour and rye.

The older man stuck out his chest with exaggerated pride, his arms raised high, elbows sweeping, his extended chest and swollen belly almost causing him to topple over. The stocky youth followed in his footsteps, watching every gesture of the elder with vacant-eyed admiration.

As they drew near, they noticed the Founders, and the older man's visage took on a twin aspect of wariness, and what seemed a natural state of barely suppressed rage. As they met, the Founders recognized the older man as the real-life version of the legislator depicted in the statue.

"What ya doin' here?!" demanded the congressman. "You're not reporters, are ya?"

The young man strongly resembled him, and was evidently his son. As his father's expression became wary, his own previously blank expression took on the same aspect.

"I have had some past involvement with the publishing trade," replied Franklin, "but I assure you, sir, that none of us are members of the press."

"Well, some investigators was poking their big noses 'round here a while back," the congressman testily replied.

"Not that they would find much of anything here," he continued, and swept his arms in the direction of the empty runways.

"Why *aren't* there any planes here?" asked Abigail.

The congressman spat. "That's what those reporter people are always askin'! I can't help it if National Airport has excess capacity now, and no one has a need to use my airport."

"*Your* airport?" asked Jefferson.

Rep. Moronico sniffed, which drew attention to the little purple veins on his nose. His son, a chameleon, attempted a little snort of his own, and sneezed as a result, spraying phlegm onto his fancy pants.

"Well," uttered his dad, "it got my name on it, don't it? Or at least my statue does." He stuck out his chin and turkey neck, and his bulky son, although still working on just his second chin, did the same.

"I built it and I paid for it, with funds I got from my perch in congress, didn't I?"

Franklin looked thoughtfully at the vacant tarmac. "But if there's no need for an airport, why build one?"

Moronico looked at the elder with mixture of contempt, and of sympathy, for his apparent ignorance. This mix of emotions was a bit too subtle for his copycat son, who just looked confused.

"The point ain't to build somethin' 'cause it's needed," Moronico lectured, as if explaining something to a little boy. "The point is to steer cash and swag to ya district, whether the thing's needed or not. How else ya gonna get re-elected, Johnson? How else are ya gonna get ya very own statue?"

Jefferson inquired sternly: "But isn't that stealing from the citizenry?"

"What ya talking about?!" barked Moronico. "I'm their congressman—they're supposed to follow *my* instructions for how to best spend their money. That's what I'm paid for. *I'm* the expert, after all. Not some Joe Blow drivin' some truck."

"Besides," he continued, spitting violently, "it ain't their money, after we tax it and rake it in—then it's *our* money: to spend as we damn well please!"

Meeting Their Match

His son, dimly sensing his father's rising anger, clenched his fists, spat in the direction of Abigail, and took a step toward the lady.

It was the junior Moronico's misfortune to take a step toward Mrs. Adams. The lady, reared with backbreaking work on a farm, was well capable of defending herself, but in this case 18th-century chivalry and manhood came into play.

As the son started his second step, and began to raise a clenched fist, Jefferson sprang forward, whirled quickly, and grabbed the youth from behind by the neck. An instant later the stocky Franklin, his shoulders lowered, shot forward with startling speed into the solar plexus of the callow fellow, knocking him down, and knocking the wind from him.

His father stood paralyzed with rage and fear. "How dare you?!" he sputtered. "I'm, I'm a congressman! And that's his son you knocked down!"

Steaming with righteous contempt, Jefferson, Franklin, and Adams took a step towards Moronico.

The congressman, with the look of a frightened beast, jumped backward. Then, he crept, terrified, back to his son, and dragged him moaning up from the ground.

"Why, if there was a policemen here, I'd have ya all arrested for assaulting a congressman's son!"

"If you don't leave here this instant," said Jefferson icily, "I'll place you under citizen's arrest for insulting a lady."

Moronico looked with bafflement, then fear, at the former President, who seemed to loom up as tall and straight as the giant statue in his Memorial, and at Franklin, who seemed more than ready to make another fierce attack. Thoroughly cowed, he started slowly walking backwards toward the terminal, his frightened eyes locked on the formidable trio, pulling his dazed son along with him.

"Dr. Franklin and Mr. Jefferson," said Abigail, "you are both true gentlemen. My appreciation for your swift and kindly intervention.

"Mrs. Adams," bowed Jefferson, "think nothing of it."

"That villain and his corrupt seed," said Franklin, "only got what they deserved."

"The Founders Go Through Airport Security"

Shrugging off the incident with the disreputable congressman and his son, the Founders were more determined than ever to take a flight on a jetliner. The three of them entered the terminal of National Airport.

Elated over Aviation

Through the terminal's plate-glass windows, Jefferson watched the planes constantly landing and taking off. He enthused: "Remember, Abigail, when you and John and I were in Paris, and we witnessed the launch of the first manned, hot-air balloon?"

"Like it was yesterday, not 1784," she replied. "An enthralling event, but now more mundane, compared to these jet-powered vessels."

Jefferson grew more excited. "Our umbilical cord to mother Earth has been severed for good! Mankind now floats upon a limitless plane of air, with no limits to his possibilities!"

"What a means of spurring fair commerce and beneficent exchange among all people!"

"Perhaps," replied Abigail, waxing more pragmatic. "But the reach of mankind's instruments of war has been lengthened, and quickened, by such devices, and their lethal effect made far more powerful." Jefferson just smiled, lost in his reverie.

"Dr. Franklin," continued Abigail, "can these projectiles pass beyond the confines of Earth's air?"

"They cannot, due to the laws of my fellow scientist, Isaac Newton. One needs a far bigger

105

engine yielding much greater thrust. Which the technical wizards among the moderns have of course devised, for journeys outside the boundary of the atmosphere."

Franklin found himself swept up in Jefferson's enthusiasm. "Oh, to be such a voyager," he cried, "an 'astro naut' as they term it, on one of those lofty undertakings!"

"Surely, Doctor," Jefferson commented, "no one would be better qualified as a scientific specialist on such a mission."

"I must confess," said Franklin, "that I recently looked into the qualifications for such duty with the 'space agency'. But one must be under forty-six years of age."

Jefferson chuckled. "I could put on my barrister's wig and file for you, as they say today, an 'age discrimination' suit."

Again they stared through the windows, and marveled at the jet planes taxiing, landing, and taking off.

Flight Plan

Franklin, Jefferson, and Adams exchanged glances.

"Yes, why don't we?" said Franklin. "How about, say, a quick trip to my home town of Philadelphia? It shan't take but a few hours, there and back, and we can experience air travel first hand." Abigail hesitated, but felt a thrill of anticipation run up her neck, and couldn't refuse.

They headed to an airline counter to buy tickets. On route they noticed many ads and posters warning about hepatitis prevention, and HIV treatment. "Are they afraid of travelers bringing in plagues from distant lands?" asked Abigail. "I haven't heard of any in the newscasts." And every few yards of corridor seemed to have a defibrillator. "Heart attacks seem common too," said Franklin, "not surprising given how overweight so many of the moderns are."

"Nor it is surprising why they're so overweight," said Abigail, pointing to the donut shops, pretzel stands, bars, bistros, and candy stores that lined the walkways.

Portable fire extinguishers and, Franklin noticed, water sprinklers on the ceilings, were also ubiquitous. "They must have many conflagrations as well—there seems to have been little progress since I set up volunteer fire organizations in Pennsylvania several centuries ago." Bothered by the bright glare of the electrical lights, Abigail stopped at a kiosk to buy a cap, emblazoned with the insignia, "New England Patriots".

At the airline counter, they were intrigued to see one could purchase a journey from an electronic device, and Dr. Franklin, using a credit card he'd obtained, using a fake name, from Franklin Savings Bank, bought three round-trip tickets.

They saw that many travelers were handing their luggage to stewards working behind counters. "Perhaps that's customary," said Jefferson, and the three went over to the stand: Franklin with his day pack, Abigail with a handbag, and Jefferson with just his wallet.

"Do you have any carryon?" a woman asked Jefferson, who seemed surprised at the question.

"Why no, ma'am, I didn't go hunting today. Though I like to bring freshly killed quail and partridges to my relatives as gifts." The woman seemed very surprised at his response.

"I believe, Thomas," said Abigail, nudging him, "that she does not mean 'carrion'—but 'carryon' luggage."

"Ah, of course," said Jefferson, embarrassed. "I suppose it would make a mess to bring a bloody carcass on board."

"Oh I don't know," said Franklin, "I understand these planes have storage space for large items. But when in Rome…"

They walked over to their departure gate, and Franklin, the veteran printer and wordsmith, joked, "One wonders why they call it a 'terminal'. It stands to reason that just as many people depart from here as arrive at the end, or termination, of their journey."

Running the Gauntlet

Before they could reach their departure gate, they were stymied by a throng of fellow travelers, who were being shuffled by uniformed persons into roped-off lines.

"They seem like cattle being herded together for slaughter," said Abigail.

"Is it a departure ceremony of some sort?" asked Jefferson.

"Yeah, you got that right," said a passenger in line, with a heavy New York accent, "a *real* ceremony."

The Founders passed by a long table that was covered with beverages of every kind: soda bottles, beer cans, water bottles, jugs of wine.

"Is this a drinking contest of some sort?" asked Franklin. Passengers were hurriedly swilling their beverages, then plopping the containers on the table.

"Do they prohibit drinking on board?" asked Abigail.

An automated voice, resounding out of somewhere, gave the answer: "Due to new regulations, passengers are restricted to bringing three ounces of liquid on board."

Jefferson ventured: "Perhaps a monopoly controls sales of drinks on the aero plane."

In front of them, a dowdy, uniformed woman ran up with a ruler to a female passenger pulling a suitcase on a roller. She measured the item of luggage, bellowing, "This bag's too big! You have to go back and check it in!"

"But the airline already measured it," countered the passenger, "and said I could bring it with me!"

"No, it's much too big—bring it back!"

Franklin remarked to Jefferson, "*Un petit bureaucrat.*"

"*Oui.*"

Above them, a digital display blared: "Your safety is our priority. You must present government-issued ID. Report suspicious behavior. Have a nice day."

"The *government* issues the people identity papers?" asked Jefferson. "Sounds like that could lead to mischief."

The Founders finally got to the end of the line, and found to their astonishment the passengers began to strip down, with the officers directing them to take off their jackets, hats, belts.

"Are the aero planes that warm inside?" asked Franklin. "But usually objects at great altitudes, such as mountain tops, are very cold. Perhaps the heat

109

from the engines forces the passengers, for the sake of comfort, to shed some of their clothes."

"Personally, I think this has gone quite far enough!" said Abigail, fearful those around her would fully disrobe.

Officials strutted about like bantam cocks, demanding, "Take off your shoes—your shoes off now!"

Abigail, looking pale, placed a palm up to her forehead and nose, stating, "I'm beginning to feel faint."

"Fear of flying?" Jefferson asked with concern.

"No, from the smell of all these people taking their shoes off!"

The uniformed officials were flitting all around them. Most looked bored; many were ill-shaven, in ill-fitting garments.

"They seem," said Franklin, "like people who couldn't get a job anywhere else."

They ushered some passengers into a tall, transparent container. When a traveler stepped inside, a jet of air would wash over him, ruffling the clothing and hair.

"This may be a means," ventured Jefferson, "of ridding travelers of the stink from their feet."

Officials told the Founders to empty their pockets, and put the contents on a moving conveyor belt.

"Can I get a receipt?" asked Franklin, but his comment was met with stony silence.

Turning out their pockets produced an unusual hoard, including: snuff favored by Franklin, Abigail's antique nail file, Jefferson's pen knife, and the quill pens which he preferred over modern ink instruments.

"Mister," an officer told the ex-President, "you'll have to throw away those pointy-needle things. They could be used as a weapon."

"Well," replied the Declaration's author, "the pen *is* mightier than the sword."

"There must be," remarked Franklin, "a high incidence of theft on board these planes, if the fear of such simple weapons is so high."

After some badgering from an official, Franklin took his belt off. To his embarrassment, and to much snickering in the queue, his knickers fell down.

"Here," said Jefferson, bending over to take off his shoes. "Take my shoelace and use it as a temporary gird."

While they were being checked, the Founders saw two women speaking in foreign accents, and wrapped head to toe in black body cloaks, with eye slits the only apertures, breeze right on through security.

"The resemble Papist nuns," stated Abigail. "Perhaps they get a religious exemption of some kind."

Abigail noticed the passengers with babies, carrying them in strollers or in packs attached to the parents' chests or backs.

'I wonder,' she thought, 'if the infants get put on the conveyor belts too?'

She wasn't too far off, for an official demanded that one mother undress her toddler, and unsnap the diaper. Then the infant was inspected at close range.

On Closer Inspection

Several slovenly guards approached Mrs. Adams.

"You need to take off your cap!" one said.

"And hold out your arms!" said another. She did so, stating, "Am I under arrest?"

They brusquely patted her on the waist and stomach.

Franklin was shocked.

Jefferson bristled.

"Ma'am," said a male guard, "you're going to have to fully undress."

"My Lord, I can't believe this!" cried Abigail, the emotion of the moment making her native New England accent more pronounced. "This is worse than the Red Coats invading our persons by quartering themselves in our homes!"

An irate Jefferson took off his coat, and handed it to Franklin. "I've about had enough of this violation of our personal liberties," he seethed. "And I will not let stand rude behavior toward a lady!"

A guard told Abigail, "Well, if you're that upset, ma'am, you can have your choice of undressing—or a full-body X-ray."

Abigail realized he was referring to the device that could peer through layers of petticoats.

"That's a Hobson's choice if I ever heard of one!" she exclaimed.

Jefferson took a step forward, as he rolled up his sleeves.

"Hobson?" asked the guard. "Butch Hobson? You're too young, and pretty, to remember that old Red Sox player. Are you a New England fan?"

Thinking fast, Abigail replied, "I'm a New England *patriot*."

Jefferson was winding up for a punch, and Franklin was readying to tackle him.

The guard, who was from Massachusetts himself, and a big sports fans, replied, "So am I, lady!" He decided to go easy on the feisty female fan.

"Why don't you just walk on through?" he said, and waved her on, as Jefferson pulled his punch at the last second.

The guard next turned to Jefferson who, angered, had reared up again, it seemed, to the height of his Memorial statue. The guard took in this intimidating sight, and hesitated. At length he stated, "You know, sir, we do make exceptions for certain people in passing through security. For instance, are you or have you ever been a high-ranking federal official?"

Jefferson thought for a bit, and said: "I think I can prove it, if I get my wallet back." In a few moments, the guard had retrieved it. Jefferson pulled from it a piece of paper which he'd photocopied two weeks before, while going through old documents at the Jefferson Reading Room of the Library of Congress. He handed it to the guard, who perused it, looking puzzled, then alarmed.

"I'm so sorry, sir, I'm not up on my politics as much as I should be, I guess!" He led Jefferson around the security devices and through the gate, shouting at guards and passengers, "Make way! Make way!"

"I had no idea, sir," he apologized, "that I was dealing with a former Secretary of State!"

Franklin meantime had been left behind at security, clutching his knickers. Finally a guard ordered him: "Mister, come this way: We're putting the

full body scan on a suspicious character like you."
Franklin felt neither embarrassment, nor anger, but
curiosity about the electronic instrument which would
examine him. He was taken past the air-jet machines,
and made to stand at a square-sided device, which
stood about seven-feet high and four-feet across.
Next to it was a computer with a large screen display.
Abigail and Jefferson, having made it through
security, stood watching with other passengers from a
short distance away.

"Hold your arms over your head!" an officer
ordered Franklin, who did so, looking like a common
criminal enduring a search. The officer clicked on the
body scanner, and a full-scale image of the
Philadelphian, minus his clothes, appeared on the
display screen.

The women onlookers gasped, while Jefferson
and the other men looked on in admiration.

A blushing Abigail gushed:

"It isn't George Washington, but Dr. Franklin,
who should be known as the true Father of his
country!"

"The Founders' Ghastly Vision of Hell"

One afternoon, the Founders sat enjoying lunch in the second-floor restaurant of the east wing of the National Gallery of Art. A few feet above them hovered a miniature drone, no bigger than the bumble bee it resembled. Devised by Dr. Franklin, its tiny sensors kept watch for any members of reConstitution Biotek, a foreign terror group, or the National Security Agency that might be searching for their whereabouts.

A Tool for Surveillance

While Abigail liked the more conventional, classic art of the Gallery's west wing, and Franklin loved the technology in the nearby Air and Space Museum, Jefferson's favorite was the "modern art" of the east gallery, which he felt put him in touch with the creative spirits of contemporary times.

"And, for a public cafeteria, the food here isn't bad," he pronounced, savoring his baked shad and turnip greens, and a robust claret the cafeteria trucked in from the Monticello Wine Shop. While Franklin, whose gout had pushed him toward a diet of little meat, enjoyed a vegetarian soup, Abigail pushed her Maine lobster aside. As she sniffed her food, and detected an ammonia-like scent, Franklin remarked, "Yes, it is a bit spoiled, isn't it?"

"Dr. Franklin!" Abigail replied. "How in Heaven's name did—"

"—My drone did a chemical analysis of your crustacean," he replied, staring off to the side, his eyes focused on the data the device had beamed to the top of his bifocal smart glasses. "Its sensors are quite powerful, even without making physical contact with its target. The information on your New England crawl fish shows obvious decay."

Mrs. Adams smiled at the brilliant scientist, then noticed a nun and priest getting up from a table nearby. Visiting from nearby Georgetown University, they were excited about seeing the museum's modernist "The Last Supper", by Salvador Dali.

Final Testaments

Abigail turned pensive, and looked at her friends. "We've all certainly had an unusual life—lives. Which sets me to thinking: What were your last memories before reawakening in these modern times?"

"I was on my deathbed," recalled Franklin, with a stricken look. "In Philadelphia, in 1790, in great pain at age 84 from various maladies, with pus filling my lungs. For a few hours I rallied, and my daughter Sally said she hoped I'd recover. After such a long and trying illness, I replied: 'I hope not'. Soon after, with my grandsons Bill and Bennie at my side, I passed on.

"And, after what seemed but a moment, I awoke—at reConstitution Biotek. And made the re-acqaintance of you two."

"My last thoughts," remembered Jefferson, "were also from my deathbed. In 1826, on the Fourth of July itself, thinking, Abigail, of your husband John. He was himself fatally ill at the time, in Massachusetts, stating, with his last breath: 'Is it the Fourth?'"

"It is astonishing," Franklin stated, "that the two of you died fifty years to the day of our independence from Britain."

"It's even more astonishing, Thomas," noted Abigail, "that you and John reconciled, after the bitterly personal feuds of your rival presidencies. Heaven knows how stubbornly John hewed to his opinions of things. And how bitterly you attacked him, both personally, and in published broadsides."

"That was one of my life's great regrets, Abigail, that close companions in Revolution became bitter adversaries in politics. And it was one of my life's greatest pleasures that John and I, and you and I, became friends once more in our latter years."

"On that fateful day, Thomas, John was also thinking of you. As he lay dying, he muttered, 'Thomas Jefferson lives.'"

Abigail paused, in deepest thought. She added, "What happened then, Thomas, after your final moment on Earth?"

Jefferson answered, "I passed on. It was all black for an instant." The former President's eyes took on a vacant expression, as if recalling a dream.

A Founder in Limbo

"Then I awoke in a most strange place. Neither a heaven nor a hell. Though in truth, above me soared a glorious sky, with blinding light and illuminated clouds. Below was a mass of storm clouds, very dark, rumbling with thunder, and emanating heat.

"I found myself walking, in a garden. Not an unpleasant one, particularly, but lonely. I remember

117

looking at the plants and thinking, 'Ah, those are herbs that I grow at Monticello.' But it wasn't Monticello. I recall thinking of my dear departed wife Martha, and our seven children, but none of them appeared. I recall thinking of some of my indentured servants and slaves, whom I intended to free, but failed to due to financial woes or other failings of mine. I kept walking on, without destination. It all seemed a prelude to something more important."

Abigail was troubled. "Was it like a—what is it the Papists believe? A Purgatory?"

"Perhaps. I was there for an indefinite time. Dream-like, in limbo. It might have lasted just a moment, perhaps much longer. The thing is, at one point, as I was walking along, I became lost in a maze of hedges, a garden's labyrinth. I was helplessly lost, but somehow I knew I would come to an end point. And at length, I reached the exit of the garden, which opened out onto a boundary line, between the place I was in and another place. A very different place."

Franklin rubbed his grey pigtails. "As someone given to skepticism about such things, Thomas, I must say you've aroused my curiosity. Tell us about this place."

"The boundary was a wall of black rocks reaching past the horizon. The wall was about six-feet-high. As you know, I'm lanky, and by standing straight up I was able to peer down to the storm clouds. Which were not actually clouds, but a fiery land mass, with dark clouds rising up from it.

"This inhospitable place consisted of a broad plain, its grass singed with fire, in places burnt out completely. This meadow was compartmentalized, by piles of black, steaming rock, into separate locales, some of them containing buildings—and all of them containing individuals in torment.

118

"My troubled visage fell upon a series of ghastly scenes!"

Abigail straightened herself in her chair, and folded her hands with interest, as her friend went on.

General Court-Martials

"The locale nearest me was a heap of loose, wet dirt and steaming rocks, fashioned into an exceedingly steep ascent. Rivulets of salt water, formed from sweat, streamed down the hillock, turning the dirt into a viscous paste. At the base of the hill were two men. One was in a general's uniform of the Revolution. He was an American, but the uniform was British."

"Was that man the traitor Benedict Arnold," asked Franklin, "who fought for us then turned coat?"

"The same," replied Jefferson, who continued with a wry smile. "The other man was also complicit in treason, yet also of a condition more debased than any traitor—namely, a vice president."

"I beg your pardon, Mr. Jefferson," retorted Abigail, "my own beloved husband served under President Washington as vice pres—"

"—There are of course exceptions, ma'am," Jefferson cut in, "including most especially your spouse, but not to mention myself, vice president under President Adams. But this fellow I knew all too well as a scoundrel, as he was my very own vice president!"

"Aaron Burr," asked Abigail, "who plotted to separate the western half of America from the rest at our very founding!?"

"The same," said Jefferson. "And next to him was a third man, in American general's cloth: the top-ranking military officer during our nation's earliest years!"

"You couldn't mean General James Wilkerson, could you?" asked Abigail in wonder.

"I do. Since our demise, historians have shown that Wilkerson was at the time in the pay of Spain! And likely in cahoots with Burr and his conspiracy as well!"

"Well," commented Franklin, "such as scoundrel deserves a place in Hell."

"Indeed," said Jefferson. "And as you know, Burr tried to steal the 1800 presidential election from me in the Electoral College: after campaigning as my running mate. So I took a certain satisfaction in seeing him in Hades.

"But for the moment, at the base of that hellish hill, Burr stepped aside, as both turncoat generals—Wilkerson and Arnold—underwent the same torment.

"At the top of the promontory facing them were two large American flags—the original one with the 13 stars—and hanging on a tree branch, two uniforms of American generals of the period.

"Their thankless task was to trudge up the hill, in the stifling heat, slipping in the mud generated from their own sweat, and attempt the reach the place of honor represented by the flags, and change their allegiance back to where it belonged, by putting on their U.S. generals' apparel.

"Every time they attained the very top of the hill, however, they would slip in the mud, and tumble back down the hill, and start their arduous climb back up again from the bottom. This frustrating cycle repeated itself countless times."

"A truly Sisyphean punishment," commented Franklin, recalling a similar torture from Greek mythology.

"A different affliction was reserved for Burr," continued Jefferson. "As his fellow traitors ascended, and fell, he was compelled to mount another rise, a ridge or palisade that overlooked a broad river bordering a great city.

"At its summit he met a lean, handsome man with an aquiline nose, and holding two dueling pistols. The sharp-featured fellow gave him a stern look, and one of the revolvers, and then he and Burr pressed their backs to one another, pistols at the ready."

"The other man must have been Alexander Hamilton!" cried Abigail. "Who Burr shot dead, in the duel at the Palisades overlooking Manhattan."

"Just so," continued Jefferson. "As the two men waited for their 'seconds', or friends accompanying them to their deadly duel, to call out their paces before turning to shoot, Burr checked the cylinder to his revolver—and found to his horror it had no bullets!

"But his torment had only begun. As the men's seconds yelled out the ten paces prior to firing, Burr found that he couldn't move his legs, nor open his mouth in complaint. Instead he had to wait in terrible suspense as the fateful countdown was called out:

'...four, three, two...'

"...Then, at the count of 'one', Burr stood frozen in terror, defenseless, waiting for Hamilton to shoot him in the back. For what seemed an eternity he hung there in the balance, waiting for the sharp sound of his opponent's gun. But the gun's retort never came.

"Instead, he suddenly found himself back to back with Hamilton again, at the exact moment when he looked down to find his pistol lacked any bullets.

Then the agonizing countdown was repeated, and repeated again..."

..."Such a fit reckoning," remarked Franklin, "seems something out of Dante's *Inferno*."

"Yes," said Jefferson. "Though I had many disagreements with Mr. Hamilton—"

"—As did my husband John—" said Abigail.

"—He was an undoubted patriot," continued Jefferson, "and a man of great ability, so I was pleased to see him get the upper hand, in this eternal scenario at least.

Reenactments and Retributions

Jefferson paused, his brown eyes gleaming, his face taking on a stricken look.

"My vision next fell on another spot of that infernal place. It was at a lower level—so perhaps the inmates were indicted there for even greater offenses.

"I saw a seven-story brick building, its walls cut out so one could peer within its sixth floor. Books, school books, were stored in cartons about the place. In a room of that upper floor, a man was kneeling down, to dissemble a rifle, placing its component parts within a carrying case. Dr. Franklin, the gun barrel had one of those modern, telescope-like additions, for better sighting.

"Outside the window where the gunman kneeled, I could discern a group of motorized vehicles moving rapidly past a grass-covered knoll. One of the vehicles was without a top, and in its rear seat was a badly wounded man, cared for by a grieving woman, with several men hanging onto the speeding vehicle, trying to guard the stricken man, and looking about excitedly, as if expecting another attack. It was clear the man in the book repository building had fired at, and struck, the wounded man."

Abigail interjected: "From our readings of modern history, it's evident you were witnessing the famous, I should say infamous, assassination of President Kennedy, in Dallas, Texas."

"Yes," said Jefferson, "the young magistrate tragically cut down early in life, like Alexander Hamilton."

"It's remarkable," noted Franklin, "that you had this vision while you were deceased, as your own death at Monticello occurred of course well before that assassination."

"While in that strange place of limbo," replied Jefferson, "I had several visions of events that occurred *after* our own time. But I had no real sense of time in that eternal spot. Perhaps by the time I had these visions, the events had occurred on Earth!"

"And so Thomas," asked Abigail, entranced by her friend's story, "I presume this presidential assassin received his just reward?"

"After putting away his rifle," Jefferson went on, "and opening the door to the room, he found two men in uniform awaiting him."

"Were they officers of the law?" Abigail asked.

"They were in military garb," stated Jefferson, "and representatives of a unique branch of the armed forces, termed 'the Selective Service'.

"Yet despite the name, there was nothing 'selective' about their duties, which were to forcibly conscript people into a standing army."

Franklin was puzzled: "In this Hell, a presidential assassin was drafted into the U.S. Army?"

Jefferson smiled slightly. "There proved a certain justice to this.

"The officers grabbed the assassin by both arms, and began dragging him away. Then one informed him, 'The new president, in taking the place of the one you killed, has decided to launch a major war, in the southeastern reaches of Asia.

"'The conflict is waged through a novel stratagem, of 'gradual escalation', by which the few American troops there now will slowly rise over a period of years to five hundred thousand. This will give the enemy sufficient time to prepare and adjust his own strategy as the escalation takes place, even as the areas where the enemy musters his own troops is declared off limits to American might.

"'This will ensure a bloody quagmire for any Americans sent there'."

"'And sent there will you be,' the other officer said, like a judge pronouncing a death sentence. Glancing at the rifle case, he continued, 'We see you're a skilled marksman. And we know, Mr. Oswald, that you earlier served in the Marine Corps, before turning traitor and moving to the Soviet Union, so you have military experience as well. What better person to draft into the Vietnam War?!'"

Jefferson's face turned thoughtful. "I shan't burden you two with the details. Suffice to say that, in one of the repetitive tortures for which this Hell is noted, the assassin was sent to Indochina some 58,151 times, for each of our soldiers killed there. Then, for another 58,151 times, he was captured and placed in a prisoner of war camp, one notable for ignoring the rules of war governing the treatment of prisoners."

His lips dry, Jefferson took several sips of his claret. He wiped sweat from his brow, as if the Inferno's heat was still reaching him.

"There was a postscript to this particular vision. After the assassin was led away from the book repository, a man—no less than the new, replacement president!—appeared on the knoll of grass outside the building."

"You mean," asked Abigail, "the murdered president's vice-president?"

"Just so. His fate was worse even than serving as vice-president.

"For he was chained by his hands and feet to the top of the knoll, with his mid-riff exposed, revealing a surgery scar, or tattoo, at the location of the gall bladder, with the mark being the very image of Indochina!

"Biting endlessly on this sensitive spot, to the great gall of the president, was a large American Eagle.

"Rather like the eagle on the Caucasus summit!" injected Franklin. "Which, the Greek myth informs us, forever bites Prometheus, as penalty for giving the gift of fire to mankind, in defiance of the gods."

"Yes," said Jefferson. "While this president was punished for bringing the hellfire of an endless, senseless war to his Nation.

"A post-post script, if you will. At times, the president was unchained, and walked over to an adjacent building, where he stood in a long line of dejected persons who faced sleepy-eyed officials behind a dusty counter."

Abigail wondered: "Do presidents in Hell, due to their high earthy status, obtain temporary relief from torture?"

Jefferson answered: "I believe the opposite is true. For the queue was a line at a modern welfare office, a line which moved at the pace of a snail in eternity, and ended with the petitioner receiving a mere pittance, or dead-end job, or enrollment in some hopeless program of job training.

"It's my understanding the queue represented the same president's second 'war', this being a War on Poverty, and a resulting Welfare State.

"A State, and condition, which condemned has generations of less-fortunate Americans to indolence, and sloth, in contrast to the drive and hard work which previously made their country great."

"Not to mention," said Franklin, "the welfare now afforded the very fortunate, and powerful, with bailouts and low-interest loans and corporate subsidies amounting to a prince's fortune."

The former First Lady shook her head in wonder. "Thomas, that's an amazing tale. Did you come upon any other assassins or presidents in your vision?"

Jefferson nodded slightly, his eyes vacant, as he dredged up even more dreadful scenes from pained memory.

"But before I relate that tale, let me tell you briefly of someone consigned to that infernal place who was not an American, nor even a traitor, but someone who had done incalculable harm to America.

"The person in question was Osama bin Laden."

"The villain chiefly responsible," said Ben Franklin, "so we've learned, for the September 11 attacks that slaughtered so many of our citizens?"

"The very same," said Jefferson. "His punishment was—to go through airport security.

There he is patted down and jostled and probed, for all eternity, by the same intrusive security apparatus his own actions brought about."

"A very appropriate punishment," commented Abigail.

Another Assassin's Agony

"But onto the next American inmate of the place. Near the book repository was another structure, a three-story, red-brick building, whose second floor was peeled away. This revealed a balcony that, along with the ground floor, contained the seating for a theater. Starred-and-striped banners marked a presidential box on the upper floor, which overlooked the stage below.

"The theater was full, with the audience cloaked in apparel from the War Between the States, or the Civil War as they say in the North," continued the Virginian.

"The theatergoers were in a state of fear and suspense, as if a terrible event had occurred. The banners cloaked the presidential box, making it impossible to discern what had happened there. But a mustachioed, and oddly dapper-dressed man, stood posed on the box's balustrade, a smoking pistol in one hand, and a bloodied dagger in the other. He leapt in the air and—"

Abigail interrupted: "—You must have seen John Wilkes Booth, the actor who—as we've learned—murdered President Lincoln, at Ford's Theater I believe it's called."

"What special punishment," asked Franklin with interest, "was meted out to such a scoundrel?"

Jefferson's face took on a look of mild surprise.

"As I far as I could discern, the vicious assassin's fate then proceeded along the lines of his mortal life. He jumped from the balcony onto the stage, smashing his leg. In great pain, he limped outside the theater to a waiting horse. Then for thirteen long unlucky days he was pursued through the swamps of Virginia and Maryland, like a hunted animal. At dawn on the thirteenth day, soldiers surrounded the barn where he'd taken refuge, and set it afire.

"He began choking and burning like, well, like a denizen of Hell. He was then shot in the neck, and dragged outside the conflagration, where he lay paralyzed for three agonizing hours from bullet wounds to the spine and neck, before expiring, with his last breaths muttering, 'Useless, useless.'

"This scenario was then repeated over and over, until in revulsion and contempt I turned away."

"No traitor or assassin," noted Franklin, "ever met a more fitting end."

Mrs. Adams was starting to feel downbeat from Jefferson's gruesome stories, but curiosity pushed her onward.

"Thomas, you mentioned that more than one president dwells in that infernal place."

Eating Jim Crow

"Yes, Abigail, so let me close my narrative with an account of that condemned personage.

"In one of the lowest levels of the Inferno was a town square with the new—well, I suppose the not-so-new, technology—of a railroad, which ran along the border of the square. One corner contained a federal building, a headquarters for the Infernal, that is, the Internal, Revenue Service. Another corner of the square contained a bank, actually a very large federal bank.

"In front of the revenue building—to be accurate I should say the tax or Impost Building, for 'revenue' is one of those terms, beloved in Washington, which obscure its true meaning—before that building gathered a crowd. The crowd was led by a thin man with a sallow complexion, a rather pinched, mean face, and wearing pince-nez glasses, a silken top hat, a top coat, and striped, silken pants. He presided over a ceremony, whereby he cut a ribbon on the building's entrance way. He and the throng then strolled confidently to the federal Bank, and he cut a ribbon there, marking its opening as well."

"Was this bank," asked Franklin, "the Federal Preserve, or Reserve, or some such, that we've heard so much of?"

"The one," asked Abigail, "that now hands out cheap loans to bankrupt, yet politically connected institutions, while offering nothing to profitable institutions without Washington ties, and nor any special favors to the great mass of the citizenry?"

"The same," said Jefferson.

"This elegantly dressed leader then strolled to a twin set of newly constructed buildings, between the Bank and the Impost House. These were utilitarian structures; they served as eateries and commodes, respectively, for the workers in the two government buildings.

"One set of these was sturdily constructed of stone and metal; the other set was shoddily made of wood and paper.

"He cut inaugural ribbons to both sets of these buildings as well. As he did, the workers from the government structures streamed outside, and walked over to lunch, and to use the privies.

"At his command, the workers were divided into two groups, by race.

"The white workers were directed into the more substantial structures, while the Negro, or African-American, to use the contemporary term, workers were directed into the separate, and much-less-than-equal, structures, with the hearty approval of the man in the top hat and pince-nez."

"I must say," interjected Jefferson, with some asperity, "having been myself a resident of the Old South, I was peeved to see federal sanction given to this apparatus of 'Jim Crow', and racial discord.

"The fellow then strolled confidently, if a bit abstractly, to a lectern set up between the new buildings. He addressed the assemblage, though he seemed to be speaking more to himself than to the citizenry.

"He told the crowd that he 'had kept us out of war', and pledged to continue to do so.

"Strangely, he then stood on his right leg, tip-toe, and spun himself 360 degrees to his right, before pronouncing: 'The world war we enter will be 'the war to end all wars'.'

"He then stood on his left leg, tip-toe, and spun himself 360 degrees to the left, before pronouncing, 'With the war over, we now need a League of united Nations, a league guaranteed to end all wars'.

Ben Franklin scratched his pate, and thought back to his diplomacy in France during the bloody American Revolution, to the savage French and Indian wars which had preceded it, and to the brutal wars between France and Britain that had followed it.

"This man," he remarked, "seems to have an unfortunately naïve view of foreign relations."

"Or a duplicitous one," said Abigail. "Yet I must say that, for a time in Hell, he seems to be enjoying a reprise, if not an outright celebration, of his major actions in office, however destructive, such as the imposition of an onerous levy on the earnings of enterprising citizens, and giving official sanction to an unfair system of race separation."

"His comeuppance," answered Jefferson, his lips pursed, "swiftly came.

"After he finished with his speechifying, and pirouetting, and ribbon cutting, a train rolled in along the railway, coming to a stop in front of the lectern. When the man sauntered over to enter the first-class compartment, a banker and a tax agent, from the buildings he had opened, ran over to him.

"The banker demanded: 'Sir, our policies, by setting interest rates to near-zero, have debased the savings of all the people, including you. So I must request half your personal assets.'

"Looking even more sour than normal, the man in the top hat took out his fat wallet and handed the banker half of his cash.

"Then the tax agent demanded: 'Sir, to pay for your wars, and your expensive new institutions, I must request half your personal assets.

"Looking more pinched than usual, the man took out his wallet again and handed the agent the rest of his cash.

"As he approached the train compartment, and was greeted by a Negro porter, he took a few remaining coins from his pocket—three Woodrow Wilson dimes.

"The porter informed him, "Mister, that amount is far from enough to pay for first-class. You'll just have to ride in the caboose—in the Negro section of the train!"

As he trudged to the back of the railcars, the man turned deadly pale, and pressed his hand to his chest, as if stricken by a deficiency of the heart."

Abigail, smiling wanly, remarked: "My dear Thomas, such a conclusion, although an ironic denouement, hardly seems a fit punishment for such a villain. At my husband's farm in Quincy, Massachusetts, after all, we employed African-American servants—as indentured laborers or wage workers, and not as slaves—and their acquaintance was compatible, if not amicable. So sitting with Negroes in a train surely does not qualify as torture."

"Abigail my dear," replied Jefferson, "it wholly depends on the character of the person in question. Believe me, as someone intimately acquainted with the Virginia of yore, nothing would have been more torturous to a bigot of that type than to have to made such a journey, cheek by jowl with a people he despised, and unjustly maligned."

"The Founders Find Out Fannie and Freddie"

During their first weeks in Washington, the cash-strapped Founders had lodged at inexpensive motels. As they took on occupations and earned more income, they began staying in ritzy hotels. Although the accommodations were comfortable, and provided a base of operations to learn about their new era, their itinerant lifestyle added to their sense of being out of time and out of place.

Homesick Blues

One day, as they were strolling along the sumptuous homes of Embassy Row, Abigail remarked to the others: "Living out of my luggage is unbecoming to a lady, and vexsome to the spirit. I, and perhaps all of us, could use a home."

"A more permanent place," replied Franklin, "could provide a safer means to avoid our pursuers, conduct our business affairs, and plan our future moves."

Jefferson rubbed his chin in thought. "Perhaps a simple town house would do. Like the one General Washington had across the Potomac in Alexandria, to manage his affairs when he wasn't at Mt. Vernon.

"We could make it into a 'duplex,' with Mrs. Adams residing on one side, and Dr. Franklin and I taking up rooms in the other."

"So, how do we find such an abode?" asked Abigail.

"Why not put someone else to work for us?" said Franklin, ever the savvy businessman. "There are signs for realtors all over Washington."

"In fact," noted Abigail, "I noticed a very large mortgage enterprise the other day. We could go there to try to find a home, or at least collect information about doing so."

Not ones to laze about, the Founders determined to head out immediately.

"Should we take a cab?" asked Abigail, amused that the modern word for an automobile for hire was their outdated term for a horse and carriage.

But her question was met with a scowl from her friends.

"What's the matter?"

"Why," said Jefferson, "that would violate 'Rule Number Three'." He winked at Dr. Franklin.

"What's Rule Number Three?" asked Abigail.

Franklin replied: "Rule Number Three is: 'Never take motorized transport, when walking, running, bicycling, swimming, or canoeing will suffice.'"

Abigail laughed. They had all often remarked on how sedentary and overweight many modern Americans were. A fact which had affirmed their determination to stay as fit and physically vigorous as in their prior lives. So they walked to the nearest Capital Bikeshare, which had racks of sturdy city bikes for cheap rental, and cycled over.

The venue Abigail had mentioned was two miles up Georgetown's Wisconsin Avenue. On reaching it, they were deeply impressed.

"It looks," exclaimed Jefferson, "just like the old Governor's Palace, in Williamsburg, Virginia!"

Spreading out over acres of lawn was a broad, three-story building, in classic colonial style, the lower two floors of red brick, the top one a slanted tile roof.

At the center of the construction was a second, fenced roof with a church-like spire, surrounded by four brick chimneys.

"As Virginia governor," enthused Jefferson, "my family, as did Patrick Henry's before us, lived in a dwelling like this. A house fit for a prince! That is, for a democratically elected official."

Despite its allure, the lawn leading to the entrance was deserted, except for two squat figures, standing in thick weeds that had incongruously sprung up there, as if the manse had been abandoned. Next to the persons, who had a forlorn, or even foreclosed, demeanor, was a sign, which read: "Federal National Home Loan Mortgage Enticements Association."

The Terrible Twins

As the Founders walked over, they looked at the name tags on the twin personages. Large enough to discern from a distance, the tags read, "Fannie May", and "Freddie Not."

The two were a woman and man, to judge from their names, but their look and behavior were almost identical. Their tight shorts bulged from their ample stomachs, their tight shirts seemed stuck to their skin. They both had double chins, which made four chins in all. Crowning their faces were beanie copter caps.

They said little at first, and moved less. It was hard to tell the man from the woman. Perhaps they were identical twins.

Standing under a chestnut, or money, tree, which indicated that money does grow on trees, each had an arm placed slackly around each other's shoulders. Making them seem two parts of the same being.

Most realtors affect a positive manner, but both were dour when not outright sour.

Fannie May twirled her, or his, beanie copter, and glumly stated: "Wish the copter lifted us off the ground."

Freddie Not twirled his, or her, beanie copter, and said, "That's not likely, given our girth."

Fannie May shook her head. "Trying lifting up one of your legs—that should lighten you enough."

Freddie Not shook his head. "I doubt that will work. But there's one way to find out."

Simultaneously, they lifted up a leg, Fannie May her right, and Freddie Not his left. They took on the appearance of a crumbling Roman arch with a top-heavy center, ready to collapse, as they stood together unsteadily.

Then each slipped his, or her, right hand, somewhat awkwardly, into a pocket. Each took out a short plastic handle with a hollow circle at its end and, blowing into the circle, began to blow bubbles. The bubbles got very big, then burst.

The Founders watched all this in amazement, then approached the duo.

Franklin looked at their name tags again, and said, "In truth, I'm having trouble telling the difference between you two."

"That's Freddie, and I'm Fannie," said Fannie May.

"I'm Freddie, and that's Fannie," said Freddie Not.

And they curtsied, on one leg each, which made them even more unsteady, and on the verge of collapse.

Jefferson hesitated, then asked: "Fannie—", or was it Freddie?, "—Can one get a loan for a mortgage around here?"

Freddie answered, "Have you owned property before?"

"Over two thousand acres, in various parcels throughout Virginia."

"You must have had to hire a lot of help."

"Well," said Jefferson, "I have had up to 200 servants."

Freddie, and Fannie, speaking together, stated: "We bet you could pay a mortgage off in cash!"

Jefferson replied, "I do have a horror of debt, personal or public."

Freddie, and Fannie, or was it Fannie, and Freddie, replied, "We bet you could put up a lot of collateral!"

"Actually, I own many rare documents and books; many of them are now in the Library of Congress."

In treating with the odd twosome, Jefferson and the other Founders felt as if this wasn't like a real conversation, but a kind of dream.

Freddie and Fannie stamped their two feet that were on the ground, and almost fell over.

"Stuff that's in a Library," said Freddie, "doesn't sound like it's available as collateral."

"Unless he steals it from the Library," said Fannie.

"But then it would become overdue," retorted Freddie.

"I am a bit short of collateral and cash right now," Jefferson offered. "And, actually, my servants are—unavailable. But I'm filing for patents—on the swivel chair and the copying machine, both of which I invented. In fact I invented the patent office.

"And I assure you I can guarantee a steady stream of income: I'm a professional farmer, and an amateur scientist, and a top-notch diplomat and linguist, a fair violinist—a polymath in fact: I've even founded a university and run a large government."

"That's very impressive," said Fannie.

"Therefore," they cried in unison, "you should take out a loan!"

"What?" asked Jefferson.

"And understate your income and property," said Fannie.

"In fact," said Freddie, "the lower your means, the greater a loan we'll give you."

"I don't understand your reasoning," said Jefferson.

"There isn't any," said Fannie.

Ben Franklin interjected, "Is this the normal way of granting mortgages in recent times?"

"Yes," said Freddie. "The more risky the borrower, the more we give him."

"Yes," said Fannie, "The more a borrower can't afford a loan, the more likely we are to grant it.

"And grant it we did," said Freddie, "to tens of millions of borrowers, many of whom couldn't afford it."

Jefferson quietly told Abigail, "As a former politician, I suspect all of that is a way to buy votes."

Fannie and Freddie fell silent. They placed their legs in the air on the ground. Each slipped the left hand, somewhat awkwardly, into their right pocket. Each took out wrapped chewing gum and, even more awkwardly, unwrapped the chewing gum paper with one hand. They began chewing the gum, then blowing bubbles. The bubbles got very big, then burst.

"These bubbles," Franklin told Jefferson and Adams, "and all those loans, remind me of the tulip bubble the Dutch engaged in a century, um, three centuries ago.

"The Dutch bid up and up the price of tulips which, though nice to look at, aren't really all that valuable, and the price collapsed, wrecking the whole Dutch economy."

Franklin turned to the odd twins. "Aren't you building up a house of cards?"

"But we like parlor games," said Fannie.

"And parlor tricks," said Freddie.

"No worries!" they exclaimed together. "It's all good. Whatever. And if the House of Cards collapses, the Fed will pick up the pieces, and make everything well again."

"What is this 'Fed'?" asked Abigail. "I've heard many people in Washington talk of it, but it's very hard to find."

"You really should visit it sometime," said Fannie.

"It would be to your credit," said Freddie.

Parrying a Poison Pill

The Founders briefly huddled. "As a businessman," noted Franklin, "they seem the shadiest of business folk."

"As someone who took out some very bad debts in my previous life," said Jefferson, "I think taking a loan from them would be like taking a poison."

"These two," said Abigail, "are simply charlatans."

Jefferson turned to Fannie May and Freddie Not.

"Gentlemen, uh, or gentle lady—gentle people: Frankly, this all sounds like a swindle to us. We must be going."

Fannie and Freddie then moved from their position for the first time, and took several steps forward.

"But you can borrow against your mortgage to buy a car!" shouted Freddie.

"You could borrow against your car to improve your home!" shouted Fannie.

"You could borrow against your mortgage to get another mortgage!" Freddie and Fannie shouted together.

Abigail grimaced. "What ever happened to thrift?"

"To cash on the barrel head?" said Jefferson.

"'To a penny saved, is a penny earned?'" said a disgusted Franklin. They strode away, back to their bikes.

"Wait, wait!" cried Fannie and Freddie in unison.

"If you really don't want a mortgage: how about a student loan?!?"

"The Founders Visit a Climate Alteration Lab"

The Founders were taking their daily, brisk constitutional, in a spot not far from Constitution Avenue, and Foggy Bottom. In fact, a thick fog roiled the ground as they came up to a complex of glass-and-steel buildings, linked together by gravelly paths and elevated walkways. The mists covered the lower floors of the buildings, such that the higher floors seemed to be floating in air, free of the earth's weighty and practical concerns.

"Where are we?" asked Abigail, normally sure of her surroundings.

"We're near the National Academy of Technology, and the Department of Environmental Energies, I think," said Jefferson, "but I'm really not sure."

Franklin looked at the GPS on his smart phone, then at his Garmin GPS watch, then the GPS on his ultrathin laptop, then his Apple mini tablet, but found in that locale that all technical instruments were malfunctioning.

A sign outside the main building read, "La Puta Isle—Where Our Science Meets Your Dreams." Its doorway was open, so the Founders, curious, went in.

Before them, stretching down a long corridor, were a number of laboratories. Many were large rooms of transparent plastic or glass, inside of which experiments were underway.

"A dream come true!" exclaimed Franklin. "Modern science labs—I wonder if they're anything like the Royal Academy of Science I joined, or the Silicon Valley centers I've heard so much about. What wonders of logic and discovery must lie within!"

A Hothouse Haven

They walked over to an oven-shaped room with see-through walls. Inside were a dozen or so people, sweating profusely, and on the verge of fainting. Around them were researchers with clip boards, observing them and jotting down what they saw.

"This could be a medical research lab," said Jefferson. "Perhaps they're treating the sufferers of some disease."

"I hope it's not smallpox," said Abigail, recalling the awful sickness that afflicted her family in the Revolutionary War.

At the lab entrance, a portly, bearded man in a doctor's smock greeted them.

"You must be the outside observers," he said. "Why don't you come in?"

Franklin and Jefferson eyed each other, and winked. The honest Abigail, though hesitant, saw her friends' tacit agreement to play along, and tagged along herself.

They followed the man into a small, sealed antechamber.

"Here, put these smocks on," he told them. "They're a cool cotton fabric...Who do have I had the pleasure of meeting?

"Dr. Frank Benjamin," ad-libbed Dr. Franklin.

"Dr. Jeffrey Thomason," said ex-President Jefferson.

"Abigail, eh, Dr. Abigail, Adamson," said the former First Lady, blushing from the deceit.

Their guide nodded, pushed a button on an electronic lock, and the door to the lab slid open. The Founders gasped, almost overwhelmed by a blast of hot air.

"Quickly, get inside!" urged their guide, shooing them along. "Faster! The lab will lose its heat!!"

The Founders entered, and the door behind them closed. They were immediately immersed in sweat. In front of them were the subjects of the experiment: red-faced, dripping sweat themselves, almost falling over, or sprawled out exhausted on chairs and divans.

"Over here, please," the guide motioned. He was pointing to a temperature gauge on the back wall, next to a light stand.

The Founders walked over, past the distressed test subjects, becoming more distressed themselves. Franklin's heart pounded, Abigail almost swooned. Jefferson, a Southerner more accustomed to high heat, was less affected.

The guide stated, "When we started the temperature experiment three weeks ago, the gauge read, '20 degrees, Celsius'. That's about 70 degrees Fahrenheit, or about room temperature."

The man pointed to the temperature reader. Franklin, his bifocals misted with humidity, took them off and squinted. The gauge read, "36.67 degrees, Celsius."

"About 100 degrees, Fahrenheit!" the guide noted.

Franklin looked up from the display: "The temperature has sharply risen."

"Thank you for your confirmation!" exulted the guide.

"You see," he continued, "to test the 'greenhouse gas' theory, that the temperature of the

Earth is dangerously rising, from greenhouse gases like carbon dioxide, we've kept these brave volunteers in this closed room for 21 days. No air in, no air out. No air conditioning. The only thing added to the air is the carbon dioxide they exhale. So it's clear that carbon dioxide causes the warming."

Jefferson whispered to Dr. Franklin, "I had greenhouses at Monticello, and they only thing toxic about them was the fertilizing manure from our draught horses."

The former President asked the guide: "Don't the temperatures rise from the heat released from the subjects' bodies?"

"And there's no open doors or vents," noted Abigail. "It's a closed space. Like a barn in summer. Or a hothouse. So it would get hotter, wouldn't it?"

The guide smiled. "You're such good sports, being devil's advocates. Yes, heat is released from their bodies, mostly from the carbon dioxide they exhale, just like that released by industries world-wide. And other heat is a byproduct of their sweat. And their sweat is composed of not just water, I might add, but salt, which, as the Mayor of New York has proven, with his restrictions on that substance, is also dangerously toxic."

Giving his handkerchief to one of the suffering subjects, Franklin told the guide, "I find this climate experiment fascinating."

In fact, in the 1760s, while sailing to and from America and Britain, Franklin had taken regular measurements of the ocean's temperature, and discovered there was a warm-water current, a "Gulf Stream," pushing up from the Gulf of Mexico to the British Isles, helping keep the islands temperate.

Franklin mentioned this, stating, "Actually, I've worked in climate-related research myself, in regards to my Gulf Stream, and—"

"—Oh I know," said the guide, and for a startled instant Franklin thought his identity been found out. The guide continued, "Yes, those evil Gulf Stream planes: contributing to global warming by polluting the upper atmosphere with their exhaust fumes. I trust you three didn't fly in one to get here!" The guide lowered his voice. "I fly in them myself, in all honesty, but only to get to global conferences on climate change, to fight the problem they help cause."

Wiping sweat from his forehead, Franklin assured the man that they had walked, not flown, to the lab, and the guide, believing they were from out of town, found that most admirable. Then Franklin added, "I actually knew Daniel Fahrenheit, the inventor three centuries ago of the thermometer, the precursor to your temperature gauge." Franklin almost kicked himself, after seeing the confused look on the guide's face. "I mean," he added quickly, "I know of Fahrenheit's groundbreaking work in this field, having studied it closely.

"And, if you look at the hard data," added Franklin, "you'll find the outside temperatures that Fahrenheit recorded, some 300 years ago, are almost unchanged, and statistically insignificant, from the temperatures recorded today."

The guide hesitated. "But of course," he finally stated. "Mr. Fahrenheit's temperatures were in, Fahrenheit. But today's are in Celsius. Let's see: a hundred degrees Fahrenheit is only 27 degrees Celsius. So each degree of Celsius, the modern measurement, is much hotter. That's more proof of warming."

"Well," the guide stated, as he sauntered back over to the temperature gauge, "thank you all for stopping by at our lab, and for verifying our results." He flipped a switch on the light stand next to the gauge, and four bright heat lamps turned on. Though already broiling hot, the Founders could feel the added heat of the lamps, two of which shone on the temperature gauge.

Abigail asked the guide, "Don't those lamps, when activated, affect the measurements?"

"Oh, they are merely a health precaution," the guide assured. "Our subjects, being cooped up indoors like this, don't get enough natural sun light. We wouldn't want them to be deprived of vitamin D, which the body gets from exposure from light, so we encourage them to keep use these lamps as much as possible."

"Feel free," the guide concluded, "to look in at our other experiments. You may find them interesting."

A Breathless Experience

In departing, the Founders felt guilty about abandoning the test subjects to their earthly hell, but relief on reaching the refreshingly cool corridor. Sweeping sweat from their brows, they went down the hallway, and chanced upon another lab. Its door was open, and they walked in.

In the middle of it were six persons in white smocks. At a signal from a woman in a white coat, they all stood still, and clasped their hands over their mouths and noses. After about 60 seconds, their faces turned white. Soon, their chests were heaving, their cheeks were puffing, and then they all passed out, or fell to the floor gasping for breath.

"What is this chamber of horrors!?" demanded Abigail.

"Are they being poisoned with some sort of toxic gas?!" asked Franklin.

A climate scientist observing the proceedings answered Franklin. "You're kind of right, sir. Carbon dioxide is a main contributor to greenhouse gases, and thus a very real poison. Unfortunately, whenever we exhale, we breathe it out, thus ruining the atmosphere and, over time, ourselves. So we're trying to train our test subjects to not exhale."

"But don't these unfortunate people," asked Jefferson, "have to exhale eventually?"

"True," replied the scientist. "But we still hope to slow their rate of exhaling."

He gestured toward the subjects, who had gotten back on their feet, and were starting to hold their breaths again. "Let's say we train citizens to hold their breaths for one minute, for six times every hour. That's six minutes, a cut in carbon dioxide of 10 percent, every hour. If we can get everyone on the planet to do that, it will mean a huge reduction in emissions.

"Not to mention," he added, "the natural decrease in the rate of breathing that comes from sleeping. So another idea we have is to give every citizen sleeping pills, to have them exhale less, by dozing more."

"I think," said Abigail, "that you've already solved that problem: It's called cable television."

A Cock and Bull Story

After watching the group of testers collapse again, the Founders moved down the hall to a large, bowl-shaped lab. The activity there was strikingly different. At first glance, the Founders thought they were witnessing a bull fight or a rodeo.

Through the glass they saw three bucking bulls: legs kicking, necks swiveling, horns slashing the air. Lab assistants attempted to tame the beasts by climbing onto their backs, but were thrown off, and landed hard into what appeared to be thick brown soil strewn onto the floor. Meantime a steady stream of doctors and stretcher bearers entered the lab and carried out the injured personnel, their places taken by another stream of healthy researchers.

The researchers in the lab seemed oddly outfitted. Many wore the dungarees and ankle-high boots of farmers, and all had bandanas or surgical masks over their mouth and nose. The clothing of everyone was stained with brown.

But this wasn't the oddest thing. While some attempted calming the bulls, others warily tried to strap large pieces of cotton cloth to the creatures' behinds. As they did so, the animals—either from spite or necessity—would defecate, spewing fecal matter all over the researchers. Being large bulls, the feces produced were considerable, often erupting in a cannon-like blast that could knock a large man off his feet.

Stranger still, another group of researchers was carrying spades, which they used to try to shovel the expelled feces back into the animals' orifices. These persons carried the greatest risk of harm, for many were kicked or trampled by the bulls, which seemed to take the greatest offense at having their anal passages violated by their own dung.

The watching Founders realized with shock that what they had presumed to be soil was in fact an accumulation of feces. The researchers were constantly slipping on the muck, and so their masks, boots, and dungarees were covered with it.

Jefferson and Franklin watched, appalled yet fascinated, while Abigail watched in abject horror. Normally steely-nerved, she began to feel faint, and fainter still. Jefferson caught her as she fell, and he and Franklin gently laid her down on the hallway floor. The Virginian aristocrat chivalrously took off his coat, and propped up Abigail's head with it.

A passing scientist saw this, and kneeled down next to the trio. "Here, have her take this," he said, giving Franklin a glass vial. "People often faint around here, though usually inside the lab—from the fumes."

Dr. Franklin administered the smelling salts, and Abigail woke up, coughing but alert.

"What in Heaven's name is the purpose," she asked the man, "of these dreadful experiments?"

"Yes, they must seem weird," the fellow replied, laughing softly, "to those unaccustomed to it. Let me introduce myself: I'm Dr. Hans Jamison, chief of this lab, and its Excretion Execution Experiment."

"Your people place an awfully high value on dung," said Franklin. "Are you some kind of medieval alchemist, trying to turn shit into gold?"

Abigail blinked at her friend's vulgarism, but was curious to hear the answer.

"Oh no, I'm simply trying to stop the planet from warming, and stop the tides from rising. Our ambitions are quite modest."

"But we've yet to reach midsummer," remarked Jefferson, "so of course it's getting warmer."

"I mean over the long term," answered Jamison. "And mid-term. And short-term. It's getting measurably hotter on Planet Earth all the time!"

This surprised his listeners, who had found the weather in the region, during their stay this time, much as it had been 225 years before.

"But the bulls," said Abigail. "What do they have to do—"

"—Why, I'd have thought that obvious. The bulls emit, and rather spectacularly so, large amounts of greenhouse gases and—"

The conversation was interrupted by a popping noise that penetrated the laboratory walls. In the lab, researchers with moisture-proof gloves extending well up their sleeves were endeavoring to attach large rubbery sacs to the bulls' rear ends. However, the fecal matter around the opening of the anus was slippery, and the sacs kept slipping out.

One lab assistant, they realized, had succeeded in attaching a sac. It had rapidly filled with gaseous emissions from a bull, then—POW!—the sac had exploded with a great bang heard from the corridor. Bits of plastic were flung all over, with some clinging to the lab window. The bull now had a large, ragged rubber bag hanging from its anus.

"We need bigger balloons," lamented Jamison. "But we keep plugging away. Bulls, cows, and other cattle are key contributors to methane, carbon dioxide, and other dangerous stuff. So we must devise a foolproof mechanism of capturing their gases. And of returning the fecal matter that retains the dangerous gaseous residues back to their intestinal tracts."

"Your efforts here are, um, impressive," said Franklin. "But a bull is only one species of animal, out of many thousands on the planet."

"Quite right, sir. But we're working on that. Why don't you all come with me, and I'll show you."

A Whale of a Tale

Intrigued, Franklin and Jefferson helped Abigail to her feet, and they all followed Jamison to a computer room. The lab chief made some printouts, and handed the images to his guests. The Founders looked over photos of wolves, elephants, eagles, whales, bears, and other wild animals. They were outfitted, along with tags for studying their migration, with diapers to block their emission of digestive gases.

Seeing their keen interest, a scientist in a diving suit walked over to them.

"Are you a marine biologist?" asked Franklin, pointing to her suit.

"No, as a zoologist, I specialize strictly in land animals. I wear this suit to try to keep clean when working in the Excretion Execution Experiment.

"Though the marine biologists deal with some thorny problems," the zoologist added, noticing the photo of the whale, with a leviathan-sized diaper, that they were examining.

"For whales, they have to use diapers, which are normally water-absorbent, that are water-*proof*. That was a tough knot to crack for our materials scientists.

"But the biggest worry is the plugs they put into the whales' blow holes, to cut down on their greenhouse emissions. When these creatures, with their giant lungs, exhale, they can blow the plugs out with great force. The plugs have blown holes in the hulls of our research vessels. They've even sunk a few ships, and drowned some sailors."

Abigail commented, "These noble animals supply much of the lamp oil—um, they *used to* supply, the oil for lamps back"—she searched for the contemporary expression—"*back in the day*." She added, "I'm so glad the hunting of them has mostly ended, with the substitution of other fuel sources like natural, uh, gas." She immediately realized her error.

The zoologist exploded. "Natural gas and oil are far, far worse than whale oil! At least whale oil was a natural substance, obtained in sustainable, hunter-gatherer expeditions on pollution-free ships powered by the wind—wind that was free of toxic gases like carbon dioxide or oxygen, or the methane produced by bull shit!

"Where'd all of you get your degrees, anyway?!"

Dr. Franklin defended them. "I received a doctorate in science from Oxford University, two other diplomas from Harvard and Yale, and a master's degree from William and Mary." He whispered to his friends, "Honorary degrees, but they count."

The zoologist sniffed like a snorting rhino. "Well," she harrumphed, "all that learning should have taught you something."

Changing the subject slightly, Jefferson turned to Jamison and asked, "I'm wondering about the safety of the whales. Won't the plugs in the blow holes choke them?"

"Well, they can always exhale through their mouths," replied the climate scientist.

"The real problem," he continued, "is they keep blowing out the plugs. We contracted with SeaWorld to try to train blue whales to exhale less explosively.

But the trainers there got so frustrated that they asked to work with orcas instead.

"So we've started paying the Japanese fishing fleets to increase their quota of whale takings, to reduce the source of these dangerous emissions."

The zoologist offered another ray of hope. "Large land creatures like elephants are another big problem, due to the great amount of flatulence they produce." She held up a supersized bottle of pink liquid. "But we've developed PPA: Pachyderm Pepto-Abysmal. It puts a lid on the amount of pachyderm farting which, frankly, is positively elephantine in its stench and sound.

"And, as with the Japanese whaling fleets, we're putting out a no-bid contract with Chinese ivory poachers to hunt down more elephants in Africa's nature preserves. That should lessen the problem."

Franklin found it hard to believe what he was hearing but, winking at Jefferson, decided to prod the zoologist a bit.

"But madam," he said, "pachyderms, like bulls and whales, are large creatures, and few in number. What about animals that are small and numerous? Like the vast numbers of pigeons in big cities. They're everywhere, as are their droppings. What can one do about them?"

Jamison stepped in it, the conversation: "Glad you brought that up. In fact, the Mayor of New York, who's been so innovative on food-related issues, has issued a city-wide ordinance against feeding bread to pigeons, especially if the bread contains salt. Hungrier pigeons should flatulate and defecate less as a result. And eating no-salt bread should lower the birds' blood pressure."

Opining on Odiferous Emissions

Franklin had pulled his laptop from his day pack and, using its built-in printer, made some printouts. "I just have to share this with you folks," he said, handing copies to Jamison, the zoologist, and his fellow Founders. "I once wrote, in fact, a treatise on flatulence."

The document read in part:

> *"It is universally well known, that in digesting our common food, there is created or produced in the bowels of human creatures, a great quantity of wind. That permitting this air to escape and mix with the atmosphere, is usually offensive, from the fetid smell that accompanies it. That all well-bred people therefore, to avoid giving such offence, forcibly restrain the efforts of nature to discharge that wind.*

> *"My Quest therefore should be,* To discover some Drug wholesome & not disagreeable, to be mix'd with our common Food, or Sauces, that shall render the natural Discharges of Wind from our Bodies, not only inoffensive, but agreable as Perfumes. S*urely such a Liberty of* Expressing *one's* Scent-iments is *of infinitely more Importance to human Happiness than that of, say, Liberty of the Press."*

The document concluded:

"Fart for freedom, fart for liberty—and fart proudly."

As Jefferson, and even the prim Abigail, strove to stop from laughing, Franklin told the climate expert, "Forgive my old-fashioned language, sir, for as you can see, I am old."

"Not at all," said Jamison, smiling broadly, and scanning the document with interest. "I can see that your heart and, ha ha, your stomach, are in the right place. Although the scent of the gases emitted is not really our prime concern, altering their odor could produce desirable changes to their chemistry, and toxicity.

"In point of fact," he added, "we're conducting research on this very matter. He turned to the zoologist. "Could you demonstrate for us?"

The animal scientist, still clad in her diving gear, reached into a drawer and pulled out a package wrapped in plastic. She tore it open and placed, with difficulty, a diaper around her weight belt and underwater suit.

"Here we have our newly developed disposable fart deodorizer," explained Jamison. "They're the sort of product that climate scientists, and people with digestive disorders, have been dreaming of. The user simply places the pad around her bottom, and any gases emitted activate the deodorizing pad, which absorbs the farting odor."

"That's exactly the sort of thing I was thinking about," remarked Franklin, with a wink.

Jamison smiled genially. "Perhaps I can steer a federal grant your way to further your own research into this important matter."

157

"I appreciate your kind 'scenti-ments', sir," said Franklin.

Gaseous Disposals

"Let me show you all," said Jamison, "one more of our labs that bears on this very subject."

Down from the computer room was a large, spherical-shaped space, with a number of wooden posts stuck in the floor. The top of each post had a pulley and rope, and burly research assistants with gas masks were hoisting large animals, mostly bears and sheep, up into the air. As they did so, other workers would dart out with bellows and, while the animals dangled in air, would insert the instruments into their orifices, and draw out their intestinal gases. Then they injected the noxious vapors into balloons made, this time, of sturdy, unbreakable material.

However their work, though innovative, the Founders saw, was complicated by several things. One was the loud discomfort of the creatures being violated in this way. Another was that the bears would sometimes take swipes or bites at the sheep. Yet another was that the bears, being intelligent animals, would begin to sway back and forth on the hoists, moving them closer to their hoped-for prey. Yet another group of aides attempted to remedy this, by using grappling hooks to poke and push the bears back toward the posts.

"The sheep are making such a woeful bleating," lamented Abigail.

"Though whether more from the bears or the bellows it's hard to say," replied Jefferson.

Franklin asked Jamison, "As a practical matter, how do you dispose of the gases?"

"There's a vast underground cavern in Nevada," he replied, "that was built to store the waste from nuclear energy. Fortunately, lawsuits shut down the use of that facility, as nuclear energy, which produces no greenhouse gases, is very dangerous. So we're hoping to store the gases there. But some Nevadans think the gas will seep and leak out of the cavern and into their drinking water. It's an example of the 'Not In My Backside' syndrome. People really need to learn how to sacrifice for the common good."

Franklin wanted to ask Jamison about something that was bothering him. A few weeks earlier, while his friends were otherwise occupied, he'd taken a train to the mid-Atlantic shore, and spent the day exploring and studying some seaside spots he'd visited in his earlier life.

"I was wondering about something, Dr. Jamison," Franklin stated. "I'm something of an amateur historian, and I've, uh, I've studied accounts and drawings of coastlines and harbors from centuries ago. According to your theories of warming, the sea level in such locales should have risen by many feet." He thought back to the coasts he'd recently visited. "But in many cases, those shore lines of old are practically identical to today's. How do you account for that?"

Jamison eyed Franklin with some suspicion. Then he smoothly replied: "The answer is simple. Warming has been melting the ice caps, which should make the sea levels rise.

"But the ice caps, being icy, are cold, and when icebergs from them fall into the ocean, some of the warming is mitigated. Think of the icebergs as giant ice cubes, cooling off the seas, and the ice caps.

"Further, the planet has warmed so much, that it's evaporated the water that has melted, resulting in sea levels, and coast lines, that are nearly equal to before."

The Founders had seen, and heard, enough, and, after thanking the smooth-talking Jamison and the emotional zoologist, made their way out of the building, their minds filled with the odd science they'd seen.

Passing by the research center's warehouse, they glanced through an open doorway into a vast dark space. They dimly perceived hundreds of metal racks stacked with cartons stretching far into the gloom. Suddenly, a gleeful scientist came bursting out of the entrance, and grabbed Dr. Franklin by his long, gray hair, exclaiming, "Eureka! Eureka!" He then grabbed Mrs. Adams, and to her horror planted on her lips a moist kiss.

Abigail pushed the man away toward Jefferson, who kept him away at arm's length and demanded, "What is the matter, sir?!"

"We found it!" the man replied. "We found a cheap, easy way to store carbon dioxide!"

"Well, what is it?" Jefferson asked.

The scientist skipped back inside the storehouse, and flipped a light switch. The entire place was illuminated, and the labels on the cartons became clearly visible.

They read: "Coca Cola".

"The Founders Observe a Redistributive Sporting Event"

Early one Saturday morning, the Founders were ambling along the Potomac from Memorial Bridge toward Georgetown. They went along the paved running trail along the river, passing the squat Kennedy Center and a crowded, adjoining highway.

"Although it's a weekend morning," noted Abigail, "the road is clogged with mechanical carriages. I wonder if some significant event is in town."

"You may be jumping to conclusions, Abigail," replied Jefferson. "This region is always clogged with traffic."

But Mrs. Adams proved correct. Uniformed officers, holstered revolvers on their hips, started to place barriers in the roads, and turn away automobiles.

At the end of the running trail, the land broached into the river, and the Founders came upon a pier and boathouse for college rowing crews. They saw dozens of sculls racked in a storage shed whose garage-like doors were open to the riverside.

"Along with rowing in Philadelphia's Schuylkill River," Franklin remembered fondly, "I loved swimming in Boston Harbor."

Post-Modern Pastimes

Their attention turned to a milling crowd of oddly-outfitted people. The mostly youthful throng was wearing pricey running shoes, and tight-fitting shorts and shirts of new-fangled Spandex, or body-length suits of a rubbery material. Strangest of all to the Founders, some wore stiff shoes with metallic soles that made a loud clicking sound.

"Have Dutch wooden shoes made a comeback?" wondered Abigail.

They walked up to a wide, fenced-off lawn filled with thousands of two-wheeled, metal contrivances, placed in endless rows of racks. Jefferson and Abigail watched with interest, not surprise—accustomed to their friend's non-conformist behavior—when Dr. Franklin slipped through a fence opening to inspect some of the contraptions.

The Philadelphian lifted one of them up with the finger of one hand. "They're amazingly light," he enthused, "probably some composite! How anything so light could withstand the pounding of the roads?"

The trio slipped through the crowds to the shore, where they watched clumps of people in their tight, rubber-like suits wading into the Potomac.

"It's a swim race!" enthused Franklin. "Perhaps combined with a competition involving those two-wheeled contrivances.

"I must say I was one of the better swimmers in my day. Perhaps I'll join in."

In his previous life, Franklin had believed nudity to be a healthful practice. During business and scientific trips to London, he'd sometimes scandalized neighbors by appearing in his front yard in the buff. So it seemed natural to him, as he stepped into the river, to start stripping off his knickers and ruffled shirt.

As often with the free-thinking Franklin's actions, Abigail was openly mortified, while Jefferson, inwardly amused, looked on with a poker face. Seeing that some astonished spectators had noticed her friend undressing, Abigail cried: "Dr. Franklin! I believe you have to register first for this event, and pay a fee!"

Franklin stopped in mid-undress, his shoulder straps drooping below his waist and modest paunch.

"Oh that's a pity," he replied. "The water, though somewhat dirty, is bracing; I daresay I would acquit myself well."

Grinning, Jefferson asked a swimmer the cost of the race.

"Two Ben Franklins, sir," came the response. "A two-hundred fee, for some racers."

"Two hundred dollars for a swim?" wondered Franklin, shaking his head, at the cost, and that his frugal image was imprinted on such inflated currency. "I think I'll pass.

"After all, a penny saved is a penny earned—and two hundred unspent is a fortune on the way."

Star-Spangled Memories

Just before the start of the race, a hush fell over the assembly, as a young woman, of African descent, began singing, "The Star Spangled Banner."

The Founders were impressed at the crowd's patriotism. The athletes had been stretching their muscles, inspecting their bicycles, chatting with cohorts, or splashing in the water. Suddenly, almost all fell silent, and stood at attention.

With the athletes, the Founders placed their hands over their hearts. Jefferson whispered to his friends, "I recall when that poem was printed in newspapers during my friend Mr. Madison's war.

"It was written by a local Tidewater solicitor, Francis Scott Key. His son, tragically, was shot to

163

death not far from here, in the Marquis de Lafayette's Square, by a Congressman Sickles, after Key had an affair with the legislator's wife."

Abigail commented: "A fitting end for such misbehavior."

Franklin noted: "Sickles, eh?—A fitting name for such a bringer of doom."

They listened in admiration to the singer, who interpreted the anthem in a soulful and emotive way.

"The affecting mournfulness of African spirituals," noted Jefferson, "resounds into the present day."

They were thrilled to hear the crowd cheer at the anthem's crescendo, "And the Land of the Free, and the Home of the Brave!", and applaud loudly at its conclusion.

The Founders felt dizzy. Events they'd been deeply involved in, several centuries before, still had, through a long chain of events, an impact on the citizens of the present day.

But abruptly, the mood of the emotional former President changed, as he reflected again on the War of 1812.

"I left office three years before the war," he told the others, "trying everything to keep the nation out of it."

"And nearly crippled the country," retorted Abigail, "especially my region of New England, and its merchants, with your embargoes on British and French goods."

"It was damned if you do, or not," sympathized Franklin. "Economic collapse with an embargo, or military debacle if we took on the mighty British or the overweening Frenchman Bonaparte."

"I must admit, Abigail," conceded Jefferson, "after long reflection, and after some two hundred years, that your husband John, my friend—

"—Your *former* friend at that time!" snapped Abigail. She couldn't forget, or completely forgive, the bitter personal and policy disputes between Jefferson and her husband, and herself, from that era.

"—That President Adams," continued Jefferson, somewhat shaken, "did have the best approach to dealing with those foreign potentates."

"You mean," smiled Franklin, hoping to break the tension, "his 'Porcupine' policy?"

"Yes," said Jefferson. "Keep your head down, and try to stay out of those foreign brawls. But build up your defenses, and let the powers abroad know you're ready to fight if fighting comes—bristle a porcupine's quills, if you will. And if a bully reaches down to grab you, stick and sting him hard."

"It's true the war in 1812 was a near disaster for us," reflected Dr. Franklin, with a professorial air. "Our invasion of Canada at that time, as during the Revolution, was a bust. Canada, in fact, is the only country to ever defeat or tie the United States twice."

"Actually more than that," interjected an athlete who had overheard Franklin, "if you include all those Stanley Cups."

One Hand Greasing the Other

With the Anthem over, a slim, nattily dressed man, with an accent that seemed to mix Cook County with Kauai, appeared at the head of the proceedings. Very lean, his limbs seemed as long as an octopus' arms, his airy physique tipping somewhat in the wind.

165

And he spoke in rolling, ringing phrases, full of air and wind. As the leader held court at the start of the race, a number of dignitaries came up, and handed him cloth bags, the contents of which he carefully counted. He generously awarded each one a token of respect, such as an ambassadorship, or a contract to procure some good or service for his government, in particular energy devices such as solar panels.

The only condition, in the case of the latter, was that the company in question expend at least a million dollars in the hiring of each employee. As his government greatly valued the working man, and insisted that no expense be spared in the employment of workers, including the "administrative costs" of hiring, which after all make up the bulk of such expenses.

He also afforded such firms interest-free loans, of a minimum of a billion dollars, with the sole proviso they must fail in their business, and file for bankruptcy, in order to receive a bailout, to demonstrate to all the seriousness of his government in sparing no effort or cost in the fight against joblessness.

Lines, Fees, and Litigations

The Founders turned their attention back to the sporting event. Near the swim start was a wooden table, behind which sat race officials accepting cash and credit cards from a line of people in athletic attire.

"Look, Dr. Franklin," said Abigail, "it seems people can still register for the race."

At the front of the line was an obese man, who was struggling to put on his wetsuit. An official asked him for his name, date of birth, email address, Social Security number, and other information.

"I know what an email address is," said Franklin, "but what's a social security number?"

"I've read up on that," said Abigail. "It's an identifying numeral for taxes the government collects from, and pensions the government accords to, every person. And, as a unique number, it can be used to track every person."

"The Government now provides everyone a pension?" asked the frugal Franklin. "Doesn't that undermine everyone's incentive to save?"

"The Government can now track every person?" asked the liberty-loving Jefferson. "Isn't that what the likes of King George or Robespierre dreamed of doing?"

The official handed the heavyset racer a very long form with very tiny text.

As a printer, among other things, Franklin was curious as to its purpose. "Pardon me, sir," he asked the official, "but I'm new to this pastime. What is the document for?"

"Just the standard legal release form," he replied. He deemed it odd Franklin was puzzled over the form, for the geezer seemed well-spoken and had clearly been around the block a time or two.

"You know what I mean," the official continued, "it protects the event from lawsuits in the event a racer gets injured."

Though a skilled and experienced attorney, who'd studied under law legend George Wythe, Jefferson had never heard of such a thing.

"The thought of having to sign a legal waiver before a sporting event," he told his friends, "instead of just doing it, on an honor system, as a free individual, beggars belief.

"Today's Americans," Jefferson told the official, "seem an awfully litigious lot."

"You got that right," the official shot back. "If we didn't make everyone sign a liability form, we'd be out of business in a flash."

The official scrutinized the papers the racer had given him. "Just to double-check, your best time for this Olympic-distance event is four hours, correct?"

"That's right," said the racer, struggling to get his thick thighs into the suit's narrow legs.

"OK, then that will be ten dollars."

The Founders chuckled inwardly at the now-ubiquitous use of the term "OK", first popularized by the expression, "OK Kinderhook," a nickname for President Martin Van Buren, a native of Kinderhook, New York, and a follower of President Jefferson's political party.

"Ten dollars seems quite reasonable," Franklin told the others, "for a competition of this magnitude, accounting for the great inflation that's occurred since our time."

They watched a trim young woman in a close-fitting wetsuit step up to the table and fill out the required documents. The Founders shook their heads, still astounded that women now took part in athletic competitions, and in great numbers.

"How could one manage," asked Abigail, "to have six, eight, or ten children, and find the time to train for and compete in these events?" They were also surprised at the sheer number of sporting events in modern America, shown everywhere on electronic screens.

They were of a mixed mind on this. On the one hand they were all keenly competitive, and Franklin,

Jefferson, and Abigail, as a swimmer, horseman, and hiker, respectively, had been excellent athletes in their own right. On the other hand, sometimes they felt that the modern, all-pervasive sports and entertainment culture distracted citizens from more pressing matters.

The week earlier, Abigail had had a conversation with a young mother of three, who complained that she was a "football widow," that her husband spent most of his time with something called "fantasy football," in which he concocted entire seasons of computerized play for various sports teams. Mrs. Adams couldn't fathom such a thing.

The official told the woman racer: "So, ma'am, your best time for this distance-race is two hours, right?" The woman nodded, and the official replied, "That will be two hundred dollars, please."

A surprised Abigail remarked, "That's twenty times as much as the gentleman paid." She asked her friends: "Does the large discrepancy in cost reflect the evident need for the lady to change clothes after departing the water, no doubt in a private facility, far from prying eyes? Such a structure could cost a lot of money, I suppose."

The penny-wise Franklin decided to find out. "Why," he asked the official, "did the lady racer pay twenty times as much as the prior gentleman?"

The official was amused at the pigtailed elder's formal style, and his ignorance. "Well, her race times are twice as fast," he responded. "So we charge her twenty times as much. It's one way to help level the playing field, and to burden the more talented people, who due to no fault of their own are highly qualified."

Equalizing Inequalities

Not quite comprehending the official's point, the Founders headed back to the shore, where many racers were readying to enter the water.

Most of the swimmers were wearing wetsuits, for greater buoyancy and speed. And some of the men, generally the older, or heavier fellows, strapped on life vests, which some jokingly referred to as "Mae Wests", over the suits.

"I recognize that term 'Mae West'," said Abigail, blushing, "from the history records at our biotech firm. Miss West was a, um, a buxom actress, from the early part of the last century." The former First Lady coughed with embarrassment. "The rather, full, vests that these men are strapping on were nicknamed after her."

At his friend's discomfort, Jefferson suppressed a smile. Franklin, an accomplished swimmer, and student of the physics of motion, wondered if the vests would help or hinder a racer. He asked a male competitor, "Why are only men putting on these 'Mae Wests'? Are they afraid of drowning?"

"It's to make up for the natural advantage of female swimmers," the man replied, as he put on the flotation device. "Women have more body fat, especially in certain places, than men, and these vests counter that advantage.

"The race seeks to make sure all genders compete on an udderly, that is, an utterly, equitable basis."

"But don't men," asked a puzzled Franklin, "have their own advantages, like size, and muscular strength?"

"Sure," said the racer, who swiveled his hips and stuck out his vest, to the delight of some male friends. "But believe me, the race takes pains to even out every unfair edge any group might have."

As if to prove this contention, the Founders watched as a group of young, fit men and women stood in the river's shallows, and strapped diver's weights to their ankles and wrists. Franklin asked a nearby official about this.

"Yes, sir, these swimmers are all among the fastest. To allow the slower folks to better compete, they tie themselves down with weights. The faster the swimmer, the more the weight. That way, everyone and everything should come out even in the end. And society on top."

Alongside this group were a bunch of old, out-of-shape, and slower men and women. As they stripped off their own wetsuits, volunteers handed them new, sleeker-looking wetsuits. Franklin, who'd invented swim goggles to aid in his own youthful swim contests, inquired about this.

"They're the so-called 'laser suits', the most aerodynamic ever created," an official said.

"I think you mean *aqua*dynamic," corrected the scientist-inventor.

"'Aqua-dynamic', to be precise, yes!" laughed the official. "They have a special material and design that make swimmers markedly faster. In fact, many races have banned them. We give them to the less gifted swimmers, to make up for their disadvantages."

The official, with other race officers, then hoisted a series of banners that read, "30-34", "45-49", "Over 70", and so on. The swimmers began assembling under the signs, which were apparently meant to signify different age groups. But the Founders saw that some elderly swimmers were placed under younger age-group banners, like "20-24", while some obviously younger swimmers stood under older age-group banners, like "55-59".

"Aren't they confusing the age categories?" Jefferson asked Franklin, who asked the official about it.

"Actually," the officer replied, "we're evening things out. There shouldn't be any discrimination on the basis of age. Surely you, sir, can appreciate that." Franklin took the slight in stride. "However," the official added, "it's an unfortunate fact that younger swimmers, and cyclists and runners, tend to be faster than their elder brethren and sisterhoods. So we mix up people of all ages in every age category, to afford everyone the same opportunity."

Keeping Current with the Rules

After much putting on and taking off of wetsuits of various kinds, and vests, and weights, the athletes were finally ready to head to the starting point. Two ferries pulled up along shore, with the older, heavier athletes tending to go aboard one, and the younger, leaner athletes tending to the other tender.

The ferry with the less-skilled racers chugged upstream, toward the Francis Scott Key Bridge. The ferry with the more-skilled racers slipped downstream, toward Arlington Cemetery's memorial bridge.

A wide-eyed Abigail told the official, "Well, this certainly seems, uh, fair. To hold separate races for the slower and the faster."

"In fact, ma'am, they're all in the same event. But we make the faster ones start downstream, and swim upstream against the current, while the slower ones get the downstream edge."

The Founders took all this in. Jefferson thought back to when he was U.S. ambassador to Revolutionary France, and the more extreme actions Paris took during the height of the Revolution, for the sake of *égalité*.

They watched as the swimmers in both tenders began to strap bicycle helmets over their swim caps.

Franklin asked, "Is this a stratagem for saving time, during the transition from swim to cycle? But surely the helmets will slow them greatly, and nearly equally so, for both groups in the water."

"No," said the official, "the helmets are required for their protection. When we mix swims like this, with one group struggling upstream and the other flying down river, and all nearly blinded by the muddy Potomac and the mists of Foggy Bottom, terrible head-on collisions ensue. The National Water Sports Safety and Health Protection Board requires the protective headgear."

At length, the ferries took the racers to their respective starts and, on shore, the crowds of athletes, spectators, and Founders quieted down with expectation. Near the swim exit was the finish line for the bike and the run and for the triathlon race as a whole: it featured a large plastic arch with a digital clock on top, to mark the official time. The clock was set not to zeroes, but to "-10:00:00"—minus ten minutes—to show empathy for the competitors, by giving them extra time. As guns were largely banned in the District, an official blew a whistle for the start, with ear plugs given those who might be bothered by the whistle blast.

The triathletes took off, those in the slow group struggling, from lack of ability, those in the fast group also struggling, from the weights and the contrary current. Soon many swimmers were calling out for help, from the volunteers in kayaks watching over the race. By the rules, those in the faster group were allowed to hang onto a vessel for a few moments to catch their breath; those in the slower group were allowed to hitch a ride.

Many of the faster were, despite the obstacles placed on them, swimming faster. One reason was that the slow swimmers, because they were swimming down current, were moving toward the rising sun in the east, which blinded many, causing them to slow or veer off or even reverse course, an unintended consequence unforeseen by the planners.

Indeed, the Founders saw that, despite the best-laid plans of the organizers, most athletes were not moving at the same speed, but were scattered all over the river.

"There are too many factors and variables," said Franklin, "to try to predetermine an event of this magnitude!"

"Yes," agreed Jefferson. "It reminds me of the *dirigistes*, the rigid directors, of Europe's *ancien régimes*, the projectors, postulators, and planners, trying and failing to direct their complex societies from the top.

"Make that Europe's current regimes too.

"And America's."

Spinning Their Wheels

After what seemed an eternity, especially to the swimmers, athletes began stumbling to shore, and to the path marking the transition to their bikes. The faster ones took keys they'd strapped to their ankles, unlocked the weights, and tossed aside the shackles. The very fastest ones were made to continue with the weights still on, and trudge through a long meadow to their bicycles. Their ordeal didn't end there.

While the slower mounted lightweight titanium or carbon bikes provided them, the speedier had to take their pick from a rack of Capital Bikeshare bikes. These were clunkers designed for taking the pounding of city streets, and heavy enough to dissuade thieves from carrying them off. Not only did the fast athletes have to ride these but, they had to stop and pay for their rental before riding off.

With horrid fascination, the Founders watched the slow and the fast, on titanium and carbon bikes and on iron clunkers, roll onto the bike course, which wound its way through the city's byways. Most of the routes were HOV lanes, and police stopped and ticketed many for riding just one person to a seat, as two-person tandem bikes were rarely, if ever, seen.

Along the route, police on motor scooters, normally assigned the task of accompanying the leaders of a race, were flagging down the fastest—by trying to enforce a speed limit of 14 miles per hour. Franklin and Jefferson watched those caught speeding, as Abigail turned away mortified, being subjected to urine tests to check if they were doping. The cops also made the rule breakers "walk the line," and breathe into the open end of a cylinder.

"What's that device for?" Franklin asked a fan.

"It's a breathalyzer, to determine the content of a person's blood."

"But certainly," Jefferson pointed out, "no serious competitor would imbibe before a race."

"Certainly not!" said the fan. "But he'd blood-dope like crazy to make up for the burdens placed on him!"

The bike portion of the race, the Founders learned, was made up of three loops, starting from the swim to the bike transition, and wending through downtown past the Jefferson Memorial, and then back to the start. There, volunteers set up tables where the thirsty racers could grab drinks. The energy drinks for the slow were of the normal composition, while the drinks for the fast were watered down to ensure they did not get enough sugar.

As in the swim leg, however, the organizers' hopes to even out the race were dashed. Near the end of the 25-mile ride, some cyclists were seen approaching the transition. And all of these, despite the clunker bikes and the speeding tickets, were fast, even elite, athletes.

High-Spirited Harriers

They rolled their heavy bicycles into the rental racks, and officials directed them to the footgear changing tents. The Founders peeked through the flap of one tent, and saw the athletes pulling on footwear—hiking boots, sneakers, loose sandals, clod hoppers, weighted diver's boots—aimed at slowing their pace.

The Founders followed these racers as they hobbled out of transition to the run course. Some of the slower athletes started to come in from the ride, and put on spring-soled "bouncing shoes," aimed at letting them bound along briskly like a rubber ball.

On a curbside, Abigail and Dr. Franklin were looking on with rapt interest when they noticed Jefferson drop to his knees in evident pain.

"I can't believe it," he groaned. "They, they brought it back!"

"Thomas, what's the matter?!" pleaded Abigail, dropping to his side to help.

"I thought it was dead, dead and buried for good," he gasped, staring up at the race. "But it's back! Oh, the horror, the nightmare! Will we never rid the country of this wretched institution?"

Mrs. Adams and Franklin followed his stricken gaze, which alighted on a half dozen racers running near the leaders. All wore heavy boots, and all were evidently African. Not African-American, for their skins had a darker hue more typical of many native Africans. Abigail and Franklin looked closer, and saw what had sent the former president and ex-slaveholder into his faint. The racers were extremely thin, even emaciated-looked, and had on their ankles and wrists the unmistakable signs of chattel slavery: bloody marks on their flesh from cold irons bound.

The New England-bred Adams recalled her horrifying exposure to Southern slave labor and slave auctions during her time as First Lady. Feeling faint herself, she grabbed a water bottle from out of Franklin's day pack, put the bottle to her lips—and then impulsively ran onto the course, and went along with the Africans.

"Are you all right?" she asked a tall, slat-thin man who seemed the leader of the pack, and offered him water.

"Doing pretty well," he said in a clipped, somewhat-British-sounding accent. "Those bikes were stinkers, but now we're on our strength—the run." He took a long grateful swallow from the bottle, and handed it back.

"But won't those clodhoppers," she pointed at his weighty boots, "greatly slow you down?"

"Hey, ma'am, they'll speed us up! Most of us, didn't have shoes at all, running to school and church, as kids in hill country."

Abigail presumed from the remark that he was from the upcountry of Kentucky or Arkansas, and the plantations there, though his accent didn't sound American South—she figured that inflections could have changed a lot over two centuries.

Running alongside, Abigail continued, "I feel terrible when I see those marks on your skin. My Lord—you're bleeding a bit there too! You must have taken an awful beating."

"That is so true! Those weights were very heavy in the waters, drained our strength, and left cuts, and indentations, on all of us."

Abigail realized with surprise that she, and Jefferson, had been wrong in the assumption about the shackles.

'Could our general assumption also have been wrong?' she wondered. 'This fellow has a resolute spirit which one does not usually associate with prolonged servitude.'

She attempted, "What, what is your—position—what is your work, back home?"

"I'm a marketing representative," he replied in between breaths, "for a running store, in my hometown, of Nairobi." He saw the blank look on Abigail's face, and figured she, like so many Americans, was ignorant of foreign geography. He added, "That's in Kenya, in East Africa. We sell, sell running shoes, and, and other athletic stuff."

Abigail, making a mental note to learn more about current world geography, was embarrassed she'd assumed this "free man of color," as they termed it back in her day, was a slave.

The Kenyan continued, "What neighborhood of Boston are you from?"

Abigail was again surprised. "How do you know I'm from New England?!"

"Hah! Your funny accent is a giveaway," he said, breathing hard. "A bunch of us ran, ran the Boston Marathon, and you sound, sound like the locals. Actually, ma'am, you sound like, someone, from Maine, with that real, that real strong, 'old-time' Yankee accent!"

The racer was elated to be running, and to have met this kindly, high-spirited American. Catching his second wind, he added, "Our real occupation, our passion, I must confess, is sports. We're elite runners, and we skip from town to town, running, or doing triathlons like this, for cash purses. It's not much money—but it's great fun."

Abigail took this in, and the man asked, "What races are *you* doing?"

"Why, sir," she said, surprised yet again, "I'm not *doing* any races." The thought of women engaged in sporting contests, so common in the present time, seemed so alien to her.

"Well, that's surprising," the Kenyan replied, "for we've been, been running a six-minutes-a-mile pace, for the past five minutes, and you've hardly, hardly broken a sweat. And in shoes like that!" He pointed at her "sensible" business shoes with the moderately high pumps.

"I'd have taken you for a top runner, for your age group," he added. "Which is likely a very young age group, of course," he added flatteringly.

179

With this, Abigail blushed deeply. She realized she should get back to help her friends. She bid the fast, friendly foreigner *adieu*, and jogged back to the transition, her mind swimming with thoughts.

When she returned, Jefferson had fully recovered. The observant Franklin had deduced that the indentations on the runners were from the race weights, and conversations with spectators had confirmed this.

"Abigail, please," said the chivalrous Virginian, smiling, and taking off his tapered, cape-like jacket, "you're all sweaty from the exertion." He handed her his silken overcoat to towel off.

His mood had grown giddy after learning that slavery was indeed buried for good, while Adams felt invigorated by her run. But all their spirits fell, when they again began watching the many obstacles officials placed before intrepid racers like the Kenyans.

An Unceremonious End

At length, the three-part race neared its end. Again, contrary to the organizers' designs, the athletes performed the run portion of the event at varying, and unequal, times. Despite the many impediments, the speediest, including the Kenyan group, finished near the top.

In admiration of the racers' determination, the Founders stayed for the awards ceremony. On a lawn near the bike racks, they saw tables stacked with trophies, next to which were sets of three wooden stands of differing heights, each wide enough for one person.

"This is so exciting," a spectator told them. "They're going to present all the awards at once! Gold, silver, and bronze medals for the three top finishers—in every category!" The race was busy getting ready for the presentation, with workers making adjustments to the many series of platforms.

Dr. Franklin watched the laborers with interest. "How you noticed something odd?" he asked his companions. "For each set, they're only working on the second and third stands. They're leaving the first one, for first place, untouched."

"Perhaps," said Abigail evenly, "the work on the first-place platforms was already completed."

"But I was observing the workmanship earlier, before the changes were made," replied the perceptive Doctor. "It was exactly the same for all three types of stands. I can't fathom why they would change just two of the three." Jefferson shook his head, and scratched his locks. "It is a puzzle."

Then a white-haired gentleman rushed up to them, crying joyfully: "This is my daughter's first triathlon, and she finished second overall! She'll be getting a silver medal!!"

Proud parents themselves in their previous lives, they were genuinely happy for, and a bit envious of, the elated father, who urged them, "Why don't we all check out the race results?" Congratulating him, they walked together over to a wide metal post, to which were attached video screens and sheets of text.

"Look," Franklin told his friends, "it has digital displays, and computer printouts, of the results."

The beaming dad took off his eyeglasses and squinted at the top of the first sheet.

"You know," Franklin advised him, "you really should wear bifocals."

"I know," the elderly man replied, "I need to keep up more with recent innovations."

"There she is! My Jennifer!!" he shouted, pointing at the printout. The Founders bunched up behind him, looking over his shoulders. The listing read:

Women. Final Results.
1. Melissa Evert, 4:03:17
2. Jennifer Kyoto, 4:05:42
3. Helen Cairnes, 4:06:27…

A loudspeaker announcement broke their attention. It blared:

"Gentlemen, ladies, laborers, citizens—we're pleased to announce the medalists for today's activities…"

The Founders and the proud parent looked up from the printout to the platforms, where the top athletes had taken up positions. Two sets of platforms away was Jennifer Kyoto, blushing, smiling, waiting for her medal.

"…And now, our recognition for your efforts!"

With that, a whirring noise was heard. Most of the athletes on the stands visibly swayed, and some of them almost fell over. In fact, most seemed to be growing in height!

For a moment, Jefferson wondered if the race, as a kind of strange reward or training aid, had given the winners a growth hormone. He had read that many of the most competitive athletes now gave themselves such substances. However, as races typically banned those things, it seemed odd this event would provide them.

"They're raising them!" Franklin shouted, interrupting his train of thought. Franklin was pointing excitedly to the base of the platforms. "It's a device for elevation!" he continued. "Don't you see!?"

Jefferson and Abigail stared at the bottom of the constructions. The wood for some of them, for the second and third in each set, was literally pushing out of the ground, like a shoot emerging fast from the soil, making the stands taller.

For every set, the second and third stands continued to grow, until they reached the exact height of the first. Then they stopped growing. The athletes who'd been swaying from the rising platforms then regained their balance, and stood still, and very surprised.

Next, a swarm of officials rushed over to the stands, and reached up to hand everyone exactly the same medal.

A medallion of tin.

Franklin and Jefferson looked at each other in astonishment. Out of the corner of her eye, Abigail saw the pained look on the face of the father; he'd looked away from the platform, and at the electronic display. Which now read:

Women. Final Results.
1. Melissa Evert. 4:03:17
2. Tied for 1st. Jennifer Kyoto, 4:03:17
3. Tied for 1st. Helen Cairnes, 4:03:17...
......3,427. Tied for 1st. Rosie Ruiz, 4:03:17

Everyone in the race now had the exact time, and finishing position!

Jennifer stood on the platform crying. Her father came over, and they trudged away wiping off tears. Then the other competitors dispersed, a hollow feeling hanging over the race. The Founders stayed were they were, in a reflective mood.

Finally, Franklin stated, "Thomas, to quote a good friend and namesake of yours, Thomas Paine: 'These are the times that try men's souls.'"

"A 'Paine' indeed," muttered Abigail. "An event like this."

Jefferson suggested, "Perhaps all of us could use a strong drink." And even Abigail, normally not an imbiber, and certainly not one who would drink with men, agreed.

"The Founders Compete in a Retro Sporting Event"

In the wake of the disappointing athletic contest, the Founders were ready for a stiff drink. As they were about to depart the Potomac for the nearest tavern, they noticed coming on scene another large group of athletes, with the now-familiar gear of wetsuits, bicycles, and running shoes.

Playing by the Rules

One fellow who had cycled over, his equipment in a backpack, dismounted next to them. Abigail noticed the man's jersey, which was lettered, "LIVESTRONG," which certainly sounded sporting, and asked him, "Is another contest taking place?"

"Yes, ma'am," he replied. "Another triathlon."

Franklin asked him: "Why would people compete in another race, when their times are going to be redistributed? What's the point of it?"

"Well, this will be a retro event."

"What do you mean—retro?"

"It follows the old rules, namely: the rules. Whoever wins, wins. There's no redistribution of awards.

"Some of the old-fashioned types," and the man looked at Franklin, who seemed to fit those category, "prefer it that way. So a retro race is held for them."

The Founders were intrigued, and heartened, that such a sportsmanlike contest still took place.

"I wonder," winked Franklin to the others, "if we should compete in it?"

Before Jefferson and Adams could answer, the cyclist fellow told them, "Registration is over here, and it's allowed up to race time. Follow me."

As they walked over, Abigail told Franklin, "I must say this notion of women competing in races—and together with men!—is very odd. I do have a sporting spirit, though." She turned to Jefferson and held out her hands to him and Franklin. "However, I'd hate to compete against you two gentlemen, my friends."

The cyclist overheard them, somewhat puzzled, as sometimes half the competitors in endurance events were women, and this woman looked trim and fit. Perhaps she was from Europe, where female racers were rarer, though her accent sounded New England. He told her, "You could all be on a relay team, and compete together."

"That settles it," said Franklin.

"But who will be in what event?" asked Abigail.

"Dr. Franklin," stated Jefferson, "was a noted swimmer in his day."

"Yes," said Franklin, "I won many races on the Charles River growing up, and later on the Thames in London. In fact, I invented swim fins."

"Is there *anything*," said Abigail, "that you *didn't* invent?"

"Yes," said Franklin. "The ones Mr. Jefferson invented."

They laughed heartily. By then, they'd reached the head of the registration table, and a volunteer gave Franklin an entry form for a relay team.

He filled out the swimmer's info, absently writing down "306" in the Age category, before crossing it out and penning in "65".

"So the swim is settled," said Jefferson. "But we've a problem. We need a—"

"—I could build a bike," said Franklin.

"Even with your talents, sir," Jefferson replied, "we may not have enough time for that."

Counsel from a Swift Cyclist

The cyclist, overhearing them again, said, "You could borrow mine."

"Aren't you competing?" asked Jefferson.

"I had hoped to," he glumly replied, "but the registrars say that I'm banned from this race."

The Founders could see his disappointment. He surely looked like an athlete, without a trace of fat, and thickly muscled, with massive calves and thighs for his size. He was holding a futuristic "space helmet" that had tapered ends to slice through the air while riding.

"Whatever are you banned for?" asked Abigail.

The cyclist smiled. The threesome, though likeable, knew nothing about endurance sports and its well-known competitors. "Most of the races won't let me compete," he answered. "They say I cheated, by taking illegal substances to make me faster. Too bad, because I mostly race now to raise money for charities."

The Founders were disturbed at the charges, especially when preparing to race in a by-the-rules, retro event, but were impressed by the fellow's competitiveness and seemingly charitable nature.

Jefferson asked, "Who banned you?"

"The United States Anti-Doping Agency—it's a quasi-federal government organization."

"The *federal government* polices sports organizations!?" asked Jefferson incredulously. "What

188

business does it have doing so? Why don't the organizations police themselves?"

"Good question," replied the cyclist.

"If the Leviathan hand of the State," said Jefferson, "can regulate even mere sporting events, what sphere of society can remain outside its domain!?

"You know," he told the cyclist, "I've practiced quite a bit of law. You should let me look into your case. Why don't you send me a letter about the banning?"

"Snail mail?" asked the cyclist, puzzled.

"I believe it would be more customary," interrupted Franklin, "for the two of you to exchange business cards."

"That's so '20th century'," said the cyclist. "Here, take my e-business card." And he handed Jefferson a small computer chip. "It has all my personal data, and pertinent information about my case. Just plug it into your computer."

The cyclist eyed Jefferson up and down. "You're lanky and lean—the perfect build for a biker. I bet you'd spin the wheels around like a roulette wheel. You're a bit tall for my bike, but we could raise the seat and handlebars some." The cyclist hesitated. "Usually my team takes care of all the maintenance. I don't think I have a bike wrench with me."

Franklin pulled a metal gizmo out of a pocket. "I have this multi-purpose tool," he said. "Will it do?"

The cyclist eyed it. "Is that a Swiss Army knife?"

"In part," said Franklin. "I added to it some useful tools of my own: a barometer, digital clock, electrician's blade, toothpick, magnifying glass." Dr. Franklin quickly adjusted the bike, while Jefferson filled out the cyclist section of the entry form.

"You're quite a mechanic," the biker told Dr. Franklin. "Here, let me give the three of you my radio sets." And he handed them three ear plugs, each with a tiny microphone. "They let you communicate during a race, to exchange useful information about course conditions and competitors."

Jefferson hesitated in taking his.

"Don't worry," said the banned but generous cyclist, "they're perfectly legal."

"It's not that. It's that we seem to have made Abigail the runner by default. That's not very chivalrous."

"Quite right, Thomas," said Franklin. "Abigail, please make your choice: swimming, biking, or running."

"I fear it's a bit late for that," replied the practical lady. "I would never fit on that bike. And swimming is Dr. Franklin's strong suit.

"Besides," she added, "although I've rarely run since childhood, Mr. Adams and I were accustomed to taking long strolls on our farm, and steep walks up Beacon Hill, and bracing hikes through the Blue Hills between Boston and Quincy, Massachusetts." Her demeanor became fiercely confident. "I will do my utmost to hold my own, and to not disappoint my friends!"

Franklin and Jefferson had no doubt about that. "But," said Franklin, looking at the feet of the other competitors, "the runners here all have impressive footgear. What will you wear?"

"I do not intend," said Abigail, "to put on 'running shoes', as they call it. I'll wear what I wore when playing as a child, or when playing with my children: I'll go barefoot."

"That's very trendy of you," commented the cyclist, again listening in. "Barefoot running has become more popular. Some think it makes you faster. And it certainly is the natural, and 'retro', way to go."

A Swimmer's Strategy

Abigail filled out the runner's form, as Franklin hurried over to get ready for the swim. When she and Jefferson arrived at the shoreline, they thought for a moment that the Sage of Philadelphia had learned, like the geneticist Dr. Meddlesohm, to rapidly manufacture life. Franklin had set up his portable printer, and from it were emerging two legs, then a torso, and two arms, though these were very flat, and—it was a wetsuit!

"A couple of my fellow competitors are wearing the superfast, aquadynamic 'laser' suits," Franklin explained. "But they're all sold out here, so I had to make my own.

"With a computer-aided design tool, I made a few enhancements—I'm confident I'll have the fastest suit in the race, if not the 'strongest engine'."

The Doctor pulled on his suit, which proved quite snug, given the mature-man's paunch sticking from his midsection.

"And tell me what you think of this!" Franklin turned his back, pulled something from one of the hidden pockets in the suit, and turned to face his teammates again. The top of his head was now covered by a swim cap looking much like a Napoleonic soldier's cap, or a cyclist's space helmet, tapered long on both ends.

"The 'prow' of the cap, like the beak of a swordfish, will slash through the waves!" he enthused.

191

"Its 'stern', meanwhile, will cover, like the rear of a lady's swim cap, my pigtails.

"It's odd that most men's hair is so short in this era," he noted, "when everyone should know that long hair is a sign of virility."

Abigail blushed, while Jefferson nodded, shaking his lengthy, reddish-brown locks with emphasis.

"The wetsuit," Dr. Franklin added, "by covering my limbs, will allow me to forego what both the men and women swimmers of this era do to maximize their speed: shave their arms and legs."

The good Doctor grinned. "I'd rather go nasty and unshaven into any contest."

An event official was strolling by, and Franklin asked her for a copy of the race rules. Flicking through the pages, he remarked, "It's as I thought. There are no regulations prohibiting its use."

"Use of what?" asked Abigail.

"Oh, you'll see." Franklin licked an index finger, and held it above his head. "I'd say about 20 knots, in a generally westerly direction."

"That's very smart, Dr. Franklin," commented Jefferson. "The wind will affect the water current, and thus your swim tactics."

"It will, and much more than that," Franklin replied mysteriously.

His friends accompanied him to the start, where Franklin waded into the Potomac with the other swimmers, and made sure his bifocal goggles were snug. Then a singer sang, "The Star Spangled Banner," which officials had considered banning from the previous, heavily regulated event, as jingoistic. To start the race, an official fired off a gun, which had been prohibited in the previous race, as handguns were normally banned in Washington, except among criminals. And they were off!

Franklin was unfazed by the violence of the start, with some swimmers trying to elbow him out of the way or even swim over him. In his day, he'd witnessed bare-knuckle boxing matches where fighters fought to exhaustion or death; he was not gulled. He swung hard with his own elbows, powered by his sloping, muscular shoulders, and knocked off the goggles and stunned the noggins of those challenging him, clearing out a personal do-not-enter zone.

He found the aquadynamic suit fast and buoyant. Another big aid was his enhanced bifocal goggles, which he'd taken to carrying around and using in local pools. The distance lens was his own improvement over night-vision goggles he'd recently purchased. It allowed him to see through the murky Potomac like it was the crystalline Caribbean, letting him know the exact position of his rivals. The computer chip he'd implanted in the lens displayed the latest current and wind conditions, allowing him, like a sailboat, to tack in the direction of least resistance, while his rivals stayed on a slower, straight-line approach.

He built up a lead on his younger rivals and, at the turnaround point under the Francis Scott Key Bridge, saw on his lens display that the wind direction was aligned for the ploy he had planned. He flipped onto his back, and while backstroking with one arm, pulled the device out of a hidden pocket with the other, then unfurled it in the churn behind him. Soon the current and the wind pushed the item out of the water and into the breeze. Franklin felt a tremendous surge pull himself up and onto the top of the water. The kite fully unfurled in the wind, hauling Franklin, his feet skimming the waves, along like a water skier, at a good 25 knots.

"How wonderful!" he exclaimed, exhilarated by the onrushing air and the spray kicking up into his face. "Just like I did as a young man, on Philadelphia's Schuylkill!"

The officials observing his swim from their river-borne kayaks couldn't quite believe what they were seeing, and before they could pull out their smart phones to take a photo, Franklin—now with a big lead—cut the wire to the kite, and with a head-first dive from his standing position sliced back into the Potomac, and resumed swimming.

A Revolutionary's Revolutions

As Franklin approached the exit point of the swim, Jefferson was changing into the bicycling attire he'd purchased from a vendor at the race. He sported a bright-red, tight-fitting Spandex jersey, its zipper pulled down to his stomach, white Spandex shorts, and baby-blue bicycle shoes. And he fielded tips from his new cyclist friend.

"Stay in a pretty easy gear," he was told, "so that you can do as many revolutions as possible."

Jefferson nodded, "I rather like revolutions.

"In fact," he told Abigail, *sotto voce*, "a Revolution now and again, to replenish the Tree of Liberty with the blood of patriots, is a Good Thing."

"Remember," continued the cyclist, "this is a triathlon, not the Tour de France, so drafting is not allowed."

"I would think," Jefferson responded, "there'll be plenty of draughts and toasts after our victory."

The cyclist shook his head, while Abigail laughed at her friend's confident, cavalier attitude in the face of a difficult challenge.

"And take this," said the cyclist, handing Jefferson his space helmet. With the helmet, the red, white, and blue attire, and a black cape draped down his shoulders, the former President cut a striking figure.

Then Franklin came running up from the water, with surprising speed for his age and portly physique. He expected Jefferson to take the timing chip off his ankle, but the ex-President was already on his bike, poised to go. Abigail kneeled down to tear the chip off Dr. Franklin's leg, and attached its Velcro strap to Jefferson's leg.

The latter took off, eager to protect the lead. He tried to maintain, as the cyclist had told him, an even, circular motion with his pedaling, and found his old habit of horseback riding had built up his core strength and stamina. Meantime, Franklin and Abigail trotted over to the nearby Washington Monument, and took the lift to its windowed top floor, which afforded a superb view of the bike course.

Abigail borrowed Franklin's powerful, portable telescope, and told Jefferson through his radio headset the location and relative speed of the nearest cyclists. She also spotted four of his pursuers whom, she was angered to see, were cheating, by drafting behind one another. Manipulating his radio set, Franklin broke in on the race officials' chatter, informing them of the transgression, which led officials patrolling the course on motorcycles to find and penalize the cheaters.

Dr. Franklin, examining the weather radar on his tablet, warned Jefferson of an incoming storm front, with heavy winds, near the course's hairpin turnaround at Hains Point, a spit of land close to the Tidal Basin. The lanky Virginian got into an almost horizontal position, on the "aero bars" protruding from the bike's frame, and reached 30 mph, holding on determinedly at the banked swerve of the turnaround.

As the storm front hit, a 40-mph tailwind benefited him, while a 40-mph headwind buffeted his pursuers still approaching the bend, practically stopping them in their tracks. Seizing advantage of the gust, Jefferson stood up on his pedals and, cycling without hands, grabbed ahold of his cape, held it up like a sail behind his helmet, and picked up even more speed, sailing past the Jefferson Memorial on the route back to the finish.

Atop the Washington Monument, meanwhile, a watching Abigail murmured, "A bravo performance, Thomas.

"But how come my husband John doesn't have a memorial too?.."

Franklin had brought his swim kite with him, and thought about making a parasail of it to glide down from the Washington Monument, but a wary Abigail vetoed the notion. After taking the lift back down, they obtained Capital Bikeshare rent-a-bikes, and quickly rolled back to the transition area.

At the bike finish Jefferson, as he'd often done with his horses, dismounted in one seamless action, and dramatically held out a leg. Franklin ripped off the timing chip and strapped it to Abigail's ankle.

Fashionably Fit

The former First Lady was fashionably if demurely attired for the run. Although she appreciated their function, she was astounded at the current fashion for sports bras, horrified that women would run in public in what was in effect an undergarment. So she pulled a loose-fitting red blouse over her white-colored bust support. She was equally disturbed by the very short shorts of some female harriers, and gratified that running skirts had not only become popular, but had been on sale in a bright white color at the race, along with the other items. Abigail was pleased that something called "compression socks" had become the rage, allowing some mystery to remain about a lady's legs, and sported a blue-colored pair pulled up to her knees.

Finally, in a concession to concern about the broken glass and metal shards in the District's unswept streets, she wore a pair of thin-soled Vibram "barefoot" running shoes, ultra-light yet affording some protection to her feet. A concession to the rather lower-class style of the times was to wear a sports cap, emblazoned "New England Patriots," as a sun shield. Bonnets, she sensed, though far more lady-like, would induce mockery.

Jefferson and Franklin, to scout the course for Adams, rode back to the Washington Monument. Abigail, determined as her friends not to let the team down, made a common beginner's error, starting off at a blazing, not measured, clip, then growing exhausted, before catching her second, and third, wind.

Luckily she found, as the others had, that the hard, pre-industrial life of colonial times had steeled her for the challenge. Franklin had made a life-long fetish of personal discipline and improvement. Jefferson had spent years supervising plantation work from atop a horse in often sweltering weather. Abigail had spent her marriage doing difficult physical labor

197

on a farm while raising five children. They all had had to walk or ride or climb everywhere, make many of their possessions themselves, and make do without any modern appliances or conveniences like elevators, convection ovens, or air-conditioned cars. It made them tougher physically, and mentally.

Benefitting from the lead her friends had given her, Abigail was challenged only once during the run by a relay team member—the Kenyan she met during the regulated race! He pulled up to her, politely greeted Mrs. Adams, then fell back exhausted from his back-to-back racing efforts. The only other person close to her, and finishing second, was the young woman whose prized medal had been stripped away during the previous event's awards ceremony, and who also had courageously taken on a second straight race.

The former First Lady broke the tape for the fastest relay team, as the crowd and her fellow team members whooped and cheered. Later, at the awards, the Founders proudly stood atop the highest platform, and shook the hands of the Kenyan and the daughter's teams who had taken the silver and bronze.

There was just one sour note. As they and the other winners filed out of the event, officials seized the gold, silver, or bronze medals from them.

"Are you redistributing them?" an upset Jefferson asked an official.

"No," she replied. "The government has been printing so much money that it fears the dollar will become worthless. The people may resort to alternative currencies, based on precious metals that are still worth something.

"So we've been ordered to confiscate any metal from the medals."

"The Founders Watch a Film about a Founding Father"

One time, while visiting the downtown theater district, Franklin, Jefferson, and Abigail Adams happened by a movie house. They stopped cold after seeing the marquee, which read:

"BENJAMIN FRANKLIN—WEREWOLF SLAYER!"

"You know," suggested Jefferson, "We've never actually seen one of these motion pictures in a public theater."

"I doubt," said Franklin, "that many have actually ever seen a movie with such a theme."

Transfixed by a Flickering Screen

Curious, the three entered the lobby, suffused with a dim electrical light. Snacks and beverages were on sale, but as each cost an average person's monthly wage the frugal Franklin insisted they head straight for the show. After they had purchased their tickets, they walked to the theater's entrance, but an usher held them up, and handed them paper spectacles.

"Oh cool," said a young couple nearby, "this film uses 3-D: three dimensions!"

Intrigued, the Founders placed the flimsy spectacles over their eyes, and were disappointed in the effect.

"I can see less well than before," said Abigail.

Franklin looked the spectacles over. "They seem to be a way of improving depth of field. But the paper material is inferior—I'd never purchase them for my old optometrical shop."

The Founders forgot about 3-D lenses after entering the theater. Dropping into their seats, they popped on their spectacles, and for the first time took in a cinematic spectacle. The vivid images seemed to explode form the screen. Loud mechanical music assaulted their ears. They were instantly seized up in what seemed a vivid dream.

They took in the image of a dark forest, spot-lit by moonlight creeping down through thick storm clouds. In the foreground, on his hind legs, stood a terrible creature, half wolf, half man, baying at the rising moon, its jaws dripping saliva and blood.

A shocked Abigail whispered, "It almost seems the moderns have learned how to call up heavenly, or hellish, visions."

"Despite the supernatural theme," said Franklin, "I suspect a rational, scientific explanation is behind this spectacle."

Jefferson nodded. "Remember the moving series of pictures we all saw in London and Paris back when, with images similar to one another placed side by side, and moved around a small carousel?"

"Where each picture was slightly changed from the next," said Abigail, "giving the impression of change and movement when flashed rapidly past the eye?"

"Yes," whispered Franklin excitedly, "It must be the same principle. But greatly speeded up by electrical transmission of the images, and their quick manipulation by machine!"

The scene shifted to a young woman, a fair part of her upper abdomen exposed to view, stepping anxiously and alone through the stormy forest. Then the man-wolf spotting her. And the man-wolf joined by a pack of wolves. Next the man-wolf leading the pack across a meadow to attack the defenseless maiden, as dark clouds unleashed pouring rain and lightning all about.

"It's terrifying, but wondrous," breathed Abigail. "Though the Puritan in me thinks the maid should wear something more demure."

She added, "Wouldn't people who frequently watch these entertainments lose themselves in the powerful illusions like some narcotic, and never return to reality?"

Although seized by the images, Franklin had managed to steal glances at the members of the mostly young audience. They chatted loudly over the sound track, tossed popcorn at each other, and checked their smart phones incessantly.

"I'd say that's unlikely, given the short attention span of modern youth."

The Founders ignored the constant interruption of cell alarms and text alerts to watch the movie's conclusion.

A Bolt from the Blue

As the wolf creatures were closing in on the maiden, the scene shifted to an elderly man rushing through the forest in her direction. The elder wore a frock coat with ruffled shirt, breeches and boots, had narrow-lensed spectacles pushed down his nose, and sported a raccoon hat trailed by a gray ponytail. Jefferson and Adams had seen the stock image in countless periodicals of their time, and had recently and often seen it in the flesh. It was the spitting image of Dr. Franklin!

"Do I really look that old?" asked their friend.

"The actor imitating you is quite handsome," assured Abigail.

"If that *is* an actor," said Jefferson, "and not purely the creation of a machine."

The Franklin image rushed toward the wolves and man-wolf that were circling the woman. He carried a kite, made of metal and a red, white, and blue cloth, with a set of keys attached to it, and he sailed the kite up into the thundering clouds. The lightning intensified, and he adroitly steered the kite over the man-wolf just as it jumped at the throat of the lass. In a dazzling explosion, a lightning bolt crashed down upon the evil creature, vaporizing it in a flash. The circle of wolves, startled, ran away.

The grateful young lass threw herself on Franklin, and kissed him passionately. The Franklin image turned his face to the audience, his cheeks covered with lipstick, and smiled smugly.

The real-life Franklin smiled broadly. The real-life Adams frowned. Jefferson arched his brows.

Then a long string of text identifying the makers of the vision rolled down the screen. The vision itself disappeared as bright blinding lights came on in the theater, destroying the illusion. The abrupt transition was startling to the Founders, who awoke as if from a reverie. But the other audience members were already leaving, and they realized it was time for them to also go.

Back on the street, the sun light was dazzling, adding to their general sense of disorientation, as motorized wagons sped by, buildings of steel and glass towered above, and winged, jet-powered cylinders from National Airport arched into the sky.

"Do moderns spent much of their lives in dreams?" asked Abigail, rubbing her eyes. "Watching movies, in theaters or on the electronical computer, gazing continually at televised imagery, and playing with their electrical speaking and texting devices? Also, flying and driving in practically an instant to faraway realms?"

Mrs. Adams thought back to the daily grind, and welcome little pleasures, of farm life in the 1700s. Sowing and harvesting, helping the neighbors, raising her children. Sun rise, sun set.

"This seems a charmed and easy life, but one that is rather unreal."

"The Founders See an Exhibit on Immigration"

One hot afternoon, Dr. Franklin, Abigail Adams, and former president Jefferson were walking along the National Mall. They passed the Air and Space Museum, whose vintage aircraft fascinated them; Franklin recalled Leonardo DaVinci's prescient sketches on manned flight.

Outside its entrance were protestors—calling themselves something like "the Falling Gong"— handing out leaflets against China's central government. Reading one flyer, Jefferson noted proudly the democratic revolution they'd ignited was still having effects world-wide.

Near Air and Space's vast, plate-glassed building, they wandered over to a squat, one-story structure marked by yellow plastic arches. Noting the arches, Jefferson asked, "Is this another federal building, like the Capitol, that copies the style of ancient Roman architecture?"

A Nattering Nanny of Negativism

A clerk from the Smithsonian overheard Jefferson, and the fellow, mistaking the Virginian's drawl for the accent of a foreigner, amicably interjected, "I guess you folks are from out of town! No, nothing Roman about that joint—it's just a convenient place to grab a bite. Some folks object to it, as it doesn't blend with the elegant look of the other buildings around here. And, though it's been adding salads, juices, and fruit of late, others object to—"

Suddenly, they were all accosted by a squat man, with curly, thinning gray hair, like that of a satyr, who'd rushed abruptly out of the Smithsonian metro exit. Cloaked in an expensive business suit, with a lapel button of a big apple, he was about 70 years old, though with the willful energy of a 17-year-old.

"Don't you dare!" the fellow commanded, in a grating New York accent, grabbing Franklin by his rumpled shirt top, and pushing a pamphlet on nutrition into his hands. "Don't enter this place of Evil! And if you do, at all costs don't take any packets of sugar! You will lose your immortal soul!"

The startled group watched the excitable busybody run off, his beady eyes fixed on a hot-dog stand on the Mall. He pushed a pamphlet into the hand of its surprised vendor, and demanded to know the salt and fat content of his "half smokes," as the local delicacies were called.

"Judging from his pomegranate icon," said Jefferson, "the man appears be a vegetarian advocate of healthful produce. Nothing wrong with that, though he is a bit high-strung."

Next to the arched, eat-a-bite bistro was a large, venerable building, of red sandstone, that resembled a castle of yore. A wire-mesh fence of sorts surrounded it.

"This is the original Smithsonian building," the clerk informed them.

"A striking edifice," said Jefferson.

"This learned institution," said Franklin, recovering from his accosting, "was endowed by that beneficent Brit, John Smithson, thus its name."

"Smithson was following up the work of your life, Dr. Franklin," noted Abigail, "and your establishment of scientific bodies and philosophical clubs."

Waiting Is the Hardest Part

Gathered outside the castle was a lengthy line of folks, dressed in the varied apparel of countless foreign lands. Waiting patiently in the heat of the sun, they spoke all the languages of the Earth, and many could be heard trying to practice and master English.

Each pushed along, in a creaky wheel barrel, stacks of paper taller than themselves; some pulled out the forms as they slowly moved in line, and painstakingly filled out the paperwork. At times, officials would come up to some of them, and accept a check as some sort of fee, then pile more stacks of paper onto the wheel barrels.

"What admirable patience and persistence these persons have," lauded Abigail.

The clerk noted: "The Smithsonian has many history exhibits, and this is a reenactment of immigration in America, from the early days to the present time. The people in line represent today's immig—today's, legal immigrants.

The clerk pointed out a small group of high-ranking officials who, standing off to the side, were keenly observing the queues and busily jotting down notes.

"Immigration, both legal and otherwise, is a big issue in Washington. So those officials—from the immigration and naturalization agencies—are attending this exhibit, hopeful of gaining new ideas on how to best run our immigration system."

"A simulation of sorts?" asked Dr. Franklin, reminded of the war games they'd witnessed. "To help spur creative thinking on the matter?"

"Exactly, sir," replied the clerk.

"And inside the Castle," he continued, "you'll find more of the exhibit on, for instance, the mass immigration, over a hundred years ago, through Ellis Island and Castle Clinton Island."

"And where are those isles located?" asked Abigail.

Franklin tugged on his gray pigtails, and queried the clerk: "Castle Island—you mean the old Dutch battery on lower Manhattan, where they built a fort, and battery of cannons, to safeguard New York's harbor? Thus 'The Castle.'"

"That's right," replied the clerk. "Today's New Yorkers still call the place 'The Battery', or 'Battery Park'."

Jefferson remarked: "From before our day, and since, of course, a tide of immigration has broken upon the nation's shores. The immigration surge grew so great that, by 1820, a service to both welcome, and vet, all immigrants was set up on Castle Clinton Island, and then later on nearby Ellis Island, in New York's harbor."

The clerk blinked. "I'm surprised at your knowledge, sir. Did you know that most people, when they hear the term 'Castle *Clinton* Island', think the place is named after President William Jefferson Clinton—"

"—It's actually named," Jefferson quickly stated, "after the son of *President Jefferson's* vice president, George Clinton."

"As opposed to," answered the clerk, "George Clinton, the musical master of funk."

"I wouldn't know who that is," replied Jefferson.

As the "immigrants" in the simulation shuffled slowly to the building's exhibit marking their entry into America, the Founders gazed proudly on the scene.

A preening Jefferson exclaimed: "So we *did* become a bright light to the rest of the world! A true Empire of Democracy, as I foresaw."

Dr. Franklin adjusted his bifocals. "Yes, John Winthrop's 'shining city on a hill.'"

"The tens of millions who came here," added the clerk, "made up the greatest migration in human history."

Cutting the Line

The clerk shifted uncomfortably from one foot to another, and turned his gaze toward the south of the Mall. "But things have, uh, changed a bit," he said, "from the time of Ellis and Castle Islands..."

Abigail, and then her two companions, turned their gaze that way.

They watched as a second line of people steadily approached from South of the Mall, and drew near the Castle's fence. Many in this large group wore work belts, studded with screwdrivers, pliers, hammers, though none pushed along stacks of papers, and no officials approached them for a fee. Some carried babies, others carried plastic bags filled with white powder or dark-green seeds. They spoke not in a multiplicity of voices, but in one language, although that tongue wasn't English. It wasn't clear whether this group consisted of re-enactors, or actual migrants.

As this exodus approached the fence, the Founders noticed for the first time that the barrier was an unusual one. Although ten-feet-high in spots, in other places it was hardly a bump in the ground. And there were many gaps. So many, in fact, that the barrier seemed a series of clumps of wire and metal, instead of a continuous and impenetrable barrier.

Around and about the clumps were re-enactors in the guise of contractors, sitting on dump trucks, cranes, bulldozers, and other construction equipment, but not operating any of them. Government officials walked up to some and handed over large bags of cash. The contractors accepted these, then went back to doing nothing.

"Seems like good work—if you can get it," noted Jefferson, recalling the slow construction work they'd seen near National Airport.

The clerk replied: "The government keeps spending billions of dollars to build a border fence, and paying contractors to do the work: as a fee for services."

"Seems more like a fee for non-services," noted Franklin.

"Well," said the clerk, wiping sweat from his face, "congress keeps spending the money for the barrier simulated here, then some of its committees drag their feet, or the Administration declines to execute the project. The money gets spent, though, the contractors get paid, and their lobbyists pushing for the expenditures get a raise. So the system works, after a fashion."

The onrushing crowd reached the fence clumps, barely hesitated, and streamed forward. The contractors buttonholed a few of the newcomers, made them a proposition, then put them to task building small sections of the fence.

"The newcomers work," the clerk explained, "for low wages—allowing the contractors to pocket more of the money they're paid to build a fence—to keep out the newcomers."

Jefferson wore a troubled expression. "This reminds me a little of ancient Rome," he remarked.

"Do you mean," asked Franklin, waving a hand to fan himself, "when the degenerate Romans, near the end of their Empire, began hiring the hostile German tribes on their frontiers to defend their frontiers?"

"Perhaps that too," Jefferson replied. "Though most of these folk don't seem hostile per se. I was thinking more how the very need to construct such barriers reflects the decline of a nation: the end of its expansion, the decline of its native-born population, the need to build artificial barriers to defend itself.

"An America whose population was expanding rapidly from the Atlantic to the Pacific shores, and its economy and culture flourishing, as in its past, would have never dreamed of putting down barriers to mark the terminus of its glorious growth."

A few seemed the least reputable of the newcomers: they were mean-faced, sporting ugly tattoos, and clutched bags of crystalline powder. Then a group of persons, in well-attired business suits, of a type a lawyer would wear to impress, approached them. Although clearly white-collar professionals, they were pushing wheel barrows as if common laborers. The Founders saw work badges on these persons identifying them as high-ranking officers of the Justice Department.

Peering from the far-sighted lens of his bifocals, misted with sweat, Franklin saw these re-enactors strip the tarps off the wheel barrows, and transfer hundreds of firearms, new-fangled automatic weapons, to the unsavory arrivals. These then turned around and—fast and furiously—walked the weapons back toward the Southern horizon, presumably for use there.

The bulk of their fellow countrymen continued marching toward the castle. Some of these veered off, entered the arched restaurant, and took up work behind the counter there. The bulk, however, cut to the front of the line of those patiently waiting and filling out their stacks of paper.

The people previously in the front of the line, and now pushed to the rear, reacted in various ways. Most shrugged, saying nothing, with many going back to playing with their smart phones. Some sharply demanded the officials taking fees do something about the apparent lack of courtesy and fair play. The officials uniformly said and did nothing, and went on collecting fees and handing out new stacks of paperwork to those now in the back of the line.

The Founders were surprised at this abrupt change in the immigration queues.

"Who are these people getting special access?" queried Jefferson. "Are they inventors, entrepreneurs, yeomen laboring by the sweat of their brows, skilled craftsmen, physicians—those a nation would want to attract to its shores?"

"These are 'illegal immigrants'," responded the clerk. "Actually, that term might get me into trouble: let's call them freewheeling travelers. The Smithsonian wanted to make this exhibit as realistic as possible, so both types of migrants are included."

Abigail dabbed sweat from her face and shook her head. "I don't understand."

The clerk was surprised at her lack of knowledge. "With today's immigration system," he explained, "a legal applicant has to wait years, fill out innumerable forms, and pay expensive fees to get into the country. But an undocumented migrant can simply enter the country instantly and for free. And get free medical care at a hospital's emergency ward, and get free college tuition."

Franklin took off his bifocals, and blinked hard in disbelief.

"In this way," added the clerk, "there's little red tape, and fewer forms to fill out. It's a lot simpler."

"But surely," said Abigail, "the gendarmes will arrest the illeg—these freewheeling visitors—and deport them."

"Not a chance," replied the clerk. "By law the authorities cannot ask them their immigration status, and so cannot take them into custody."

A Neighborhood Detour

Dr. Franklin then turned white, and began visibly shaking.

"Forgive me," he stammered. "I'm accustomed to the cooler climes of Pennsylvania, not this swampy Tidewater place. I'm feeling, I'm feeling quite faint." Abigail and Jefferson rushed over to their friend, and propped him up.

Eyeing Franklin closely, the clerk figured he was probably even older than he looked. He proposed: "You know, sir, my home is right down the street. Could I offer you an air-conditioned break from the weather there?"

Concerned about the good Doctor, Jefferson and Adams accepted the man's generous offer, and the foursome slowly walked the few blocks to the clerk's town house.

They soon passed giant, concrete structures, containing the bureaucracies for housing, energy, human services, and other functions. Glancing at the agency names on the buildings, a sweating Franklin muttered to himself, "Such hubris that the government thinks it could administer, from a single, central location, such complex, diffuse matters as the housing of a continental-wide nation." Jefferson was struck by the impersonal ugliness of the buildings, whose style resembled those he'd read about, built by Russian and German tyrants of the previous century.

They soon entered the Southwest quadrant of the city, and passed under a wide elevated highway, Route 395.

Immediately a desolate urban landscape loomed before them. Ruins of old apartment buildings, abandoned stores, shuttered churches with lonely spires, and vacant lots defaced by rubble filled their view. Jefferson the architect scanned the cityscape and the elevated byway. It was clear the road had been built after the neighborhood.

"The viaduct destroyed this venerable district," he pronounced.

The clerk looked at him with surprise and replied, "So you're familiar, are you, with Jane Jacobs' mighty work, *The Life and Death of Great American Cities*?"

Jefferson gave him a quizzical glance, and the clerk continued, "The urban renewal projects of the 1950s and 1960s, funded by the federal government, were intended to revitalize the nation's cities, with works like this highway. But they resulted in the opposite effect. As Miss Jacobs detailed in her book."

"They surely produced, in this case, unintended consequences," answered Jefferson. "The highway must have acted like a giant moat, cutting the residents off from the rest of their fair city, and suffocating their neighborhoods.

"I'm rather shocked," he continued, "the Central Authority presumed to plop this monstrosity atop the citizens' very living quarters."

"Well," noted the clerk, "the residents of this area were mostly poor and black, as they remain, and didn't have much say in the matter."

"It seems," noted Abigail, "that some things in Washington haven't changed since its founding over two hundred years ago."

They arrived at the clerk's townhome. Jefferson admired its sturdy architecture, which dated from the city's early years.

However, the home had an unusual entrance— no entrance at all. The front door had been pulled off its hinges. And a stream of foreigners, resembling those who had streamed up from the South to cut the line at the Smithsonian, freely entered in and out.

The clerk ushered the Founders into his domicile. Although the air-conditioning was on full, it provided little relief, due to the lack of a door. And to the lack of windows, which had apparently been carried off from the house as well. Fortunately, Dr. Franklin was by then recovering his customary strength. With his friends, he looked around the first floor with eager curiosity as the clerk brought them cold refreshments.

Newcomers sat at spots about the house, engaged in assorted activities. One was refinishing the clerk's kitchen. Another was on the clerk's computer, filing for welfare benefits. Yet another was vacuuming the floors. And two men, with handkerchiefs over their faces, were carrying a television set and an antique chair out the open doorway to a waiting car.

"Some of my visitors are terrific," said the clerk, handing out the beverages. "They tend to be great with their hands. One even redid my basement for next to nothing."

Looking out the doorway, he watched the two men place his valuables into the car. "Others are not as good.

"It's an experiment," he continued, seeing the puzzled looks of his guests. "I got really taken up with the exhibit at my place of work, the Smithsonian. So I decided to try the modern approach to immigration in my own house. An open border approach, if you will."

"I must conclude," Dr. Franklin told him, watching the two men return to take away the refrigerator, "that an 'open door' policy, for your house, and perhaps the nation, is something of a crap shoot."

"You might be right," the clerk replied. "Sometimes nice things happen: like getting my laundry finished and folded for me. Or someone growing and picking vegetables in my garden. But sometimes, not so great things: like getting robbed.

"But I can tell you one thing: I'm never bored. I never know what to expect; each day at home is an adventure!"

The Founders rested for a few minutes—on the floor, as the thieves had reentered again and taken the sofa. Then Dr. Franklin pronounced himself fully fit again, and they all walked back to the Smithsonian.

The Declaration of Immigration

There they found the group of high-ranking officials still observing the exhibit, taking notes, and scratching their heads. The Founders listened in.

"Our agents in the field are giving us hell for not enforcing the border," said a man with the name tag reading, "Head of Immigration and Customs Enforcement (ICE)".

"But the higher-ups are pushing to grant amnesty to the newcomers," replied a woman whose tag identified her as the deputy chief of ICE.

"I'm beside myself trying to figure out a reasonable compromise," her boss responded. "Most of these arrivals are hard-working, family-loving types. But some are dangerous criminals."

"And moving to the front of the line," said the deputy, "isn't fair to those who've played by the rules. But the country's businesses need more workers. It's a true dilemma, isn't it?!"

Former president Jefferson cleared his throat, and stepped forward. "Might I propose a possible remedy," he quietly remarked.

The two immigration officials turned to face the tall man, rather elegantly if quaintly dressed, and speaking in a quaint Southern accent.

Jefferson held up his hands dramatically. "Why don't you look to your own past for a solution? To Ellis Island?"

The officials looked at him with vacant expressions. Jefferson sighed, and turning back to Abigail and Franklin, whispering, "I'm ever amazed how ignorant modern Americans are of their own history."

"Well, America's always been a place of rapid change," suggested Franklin. "There're a lot of things to remember here, and to forget." He looked at Abigail. "Especially for those of us who've lived here twice."

Jefferson turned back to the officials, and stated: "Ellis Island, and Castle Island, may provide a way out of your dilemma. The exhibit inside explains what their role was. Your agency, or its predecessor, took in tens of millions of newcomers at those places over a century ago.

"Why not do likewise?" he continued. "Enforce the current law, while taking in millions of legal newcomers. Check them, as at Ellis Island, to accept those eager to work, who want to establish families, and offer valuable skills. In short, those seeking liberty, life, happiness.

"At the same time, shun those with criminal pasts, or who seek an easy life on the dole."

The officials looked at each other, surprised. The man's idea seemed outlandish, but logical, and he presented it with an aura of authority.

"Perhaps adjust the numbers of people permitted in," Jefferson went on, "perhaps for the most needed skills. In that way, you make the nation stronger, by attracting the brightest and best from throughout the world to these fair shores."

Franklin chimed in. "America already has the greatest model for immigration, in Ellis Island, in the history of the world. It could be scarcely improved upon."

"Why not go with what works?" added Abigail. "With what's practical, and legal.

"Case closed."

The officials were amazed. 'Why hadn't they thought of this?!' they figured.

They reached over to shake Jefferson's hand, and scribbled down some notes on the conversation.

Then they raced off to congress to make a proposal for real immigration reform.

The Founders headed back over to the hot dog vendor, and purchased some "half smokes" and sugary lemonade.

"It is satisfying," concluded Jefferson, "to help out our fellow Americans from time to time."

"The Founders Take a White House Tour"

In their excursions about town, the Founders had often passed by the White House. Naturally Abigail, as the first First Lady to inhabit it, and Jefferson, who had helped design it, and Franklin, keenly curious about it, all had a desire to see the place.

They learned the best tours of the Executive Mansion were through a congressman from a person's state. And, as natives of Massachusetts, Virginia, and Pennsylvania, they were able, by supplying IDs that Franklin made up, to wangle a VIP pass.

A Trip to the Executive Mansion

One morning, they went to take their exclusive tour. While waiting outside the White House, Abigail was struck by the contrast between the manicured lawns of today, and the swamps and tree stumps that had girded the place when she and Mr. Adams had lived there in the 1790s. As she and the others entered the gleaming mansion, which for 70 years had been the largest house in the country, Abigail was impressed by the opulent furnishings and, in jarring contrast to her dim and dingy time there, by the electric lights blazing in every room.

Mrs. Adams was also heartened that there were no slaves. They had supplied construction gangs for building the White House, and had been servants there in the early years.

"No more living," she told Franklin, "off the sweat of others."

"Yes," he answered, "except now the nation's living off the loans of others."

Jefferson, who had managed for President Washington a competition to select the architect of the White House, was interested in the changes made over time to its basic structure. He was pleased his idea of adding stylish and useful additions—low colonnades in his day for horse stables, and later on, south and north porticos, an East Wing, and a "Truman" balcony facing Pennsylvania Avenue—had been consistently followed.

"Were those old rumours true, Thomas," Franklin asked him mischievously, "that you anonymously contributed your own designs to the competition for building this place?"

As he often did when asked an uncomfortable question, Jefferson took on a Sphinx-like visage, and didn't directly answer. "I was pleased to help execute the ideas of the original architect selected. And later as president, with the assistance of the esteemed designer, Benjamin Latrobe, to make certain improvements to the original design."

Dashed Expectations

The tour began with a knowledgeable guide showing the Founders the Cabinet Room. This was a rectangular space with large windows and an oval mahogany table, around which the President's closest advisors would sit and offer intimate counsel. Looking through its open doorway, Abigail proudly recalled the small but inestimable group making up the first federal

Cabinet under George Washington. There was Alexander Hamilton, the financial genius who put a bankrupt nation on a sound financial footing. John Jay, the first Supreme Court Chief Justice and, as New York governor, the executive who abolished slavery in his large state. Jefferson himself, the first Secretary of State. And John Adams, the first Vice-President.

'What a collection of talent!' Abigail thought. 'Like the ancient Athens of Pericles and Plato, or the ancient Rome of Cicero and Seneca. To think that our sages all sat in the same small room together!' She looked over at Franklin, and was reminded of the quality of the first American envoys sent abroad.

"Dr. Franklin," she said, "I look back with pride on our ambassadorial mission to France, during the Revolution. Our representatives were yourself, Thomas here, and my husband John: that had to be the most skilled diplomatic mission in history!"

Jefferson was too embarrassed to speak, but Franklin answered: "Abigail, when one considers it, in the early years of the Republic, for the post of Secretary of State alone, we had the most impressive group of foreign secretaries of any nation in history. Along with Mr. Jefferson, holding that critical position were James Madison, James Monroe, and your son John Quincy, all four of them future presidents, and other luminaries such as John Jay, Daniel Webster, and Henry Clay.

"Few nations have been so fortunate at their creation to have their interests so well-represented abroad."

"Such personages," replied Abigail, "set a grand precedent for our nation. Let us hope that those who serve in these times are discharging their duties as ably and as responsibly."

221

The tour guide, seeing the visitors were enjoying themselves, announced a special treat.

"Since you are VIP guests, and obviously appreciate what you are seeing, we're going to let you stay to watch the start of a meeting in the Cabinet Room—of current, and recent, high-ranking officials."

The Founders moved with high expectations to the doorway of the honored space. Since their reconstitution, given their backgrounds, the Founders had become avid consumers of the news. So they recognized many of the figures who began filtering in.

They saw a Treasury Secretary, a tax cheat who urged sharply higher taxes on an overburdened citizenry.

They saw a Secretary of Defense, who launched a major invasion of a foreign land without making a plan of occupation for that country after its rapid defeat.

They saw an Attorney General, who shipped to a neighboring land high-powered guns that thugs employed to murder hundreds of foreign citizens.

They saw several visiting, former Treasury Secretaries, who were also former heads of Wall Street's biggest investment firms, and whose policies of rising mortgage debt had padded the profits of such firms while setting the stage for a nation-wide economic disaster.

They saw a Secretary of Energy, who steered billions in taxpayer loans to now-bankrupt firms that made major campaign donations.

They saw a Secretary of Health and Human Services, who promised to reduce the health care expenses of the people, but in fact was pushing premiums sky-high, and who had violated First Amendment guarantees of religious liberty by ordering religious institutions to follow health-care laws that trampled on their most deeply held beliefs.

They saw a National Security Advisor and a former Secretary of State, who had both covered up the killing of a U.S. ambassador to a North African nation.

They saw a Secretary of Agriculture, who padded his department's budgets by enticing millions more Americans into the indulgence of food stamps and a life on the dole.

And they saw many others of that ilk.

Abigail was angered, and Franklin outraged at these rank visitors. But less so than Jefferson, who was on the verge of exploding. He took off his caped jacket and handed it to Franklin, and rolled up his sleeves, and his fists.

He asked Abigail, "You know the story of the Galilean preacher, on seeing the corruption in the Temple?"

"Of course I do, Thomas. When Jesus flew into a rage, and overturned the tables of the corrup—". She stopped, terrified of the scene her friend was about to make. He could land them all in the custody of the Secret Service, their identities exposed, and back at reConstitution Biotek. Seeing his friend's rancor, Franklin prepared to tackle Jefferson, and stop a mad bull rush into the Cabinet Room.

Congressional Connivers

With great good fortune, at that very moment their tour guide returned.

"I see you've all been happily absorbed watching our little gathering," he told them. "So we'd like to offer you another treat. Recent and current members of congress have been invited here to a special meeting, to offer their sage advice to the Chief Executive on pressing matters of state. How would you like to see the start of this session as well?"

Before his friend could respond, Franklin half-dragged Jefferson from the Cabinet Room to the other conference space.

"Just think, Thomas," he urged, "of what we may have to look forward to at this session.

"Think of the sterling lights in congress you observed during the legislature's first sessions. Your dear friend James Madison, the first Speaker of the House, who guided through passage of the Bill of Rights. There was Abigail's son, John Quincy, serving after his presidency as a congressman; like ourselves a friend of science, and a founder of the Smithsonian. Also in the early congress was the future president and hero of the Battle of New Orleans, the young Andrew Jackson, senator from Tennessee.

"Not to mention congress' very own creator, Connecticut's Roger Sherman, who devised the rules granting each state two senators, and granting the states congressmen proportional to their population. Sherman the patriot, of whom you stated, Thomas, that 'he has never said a foolish thing in his life.'"

Franklin concluded: "We can expect, and pray, that the current constellation of congress approaches the stellar accomplishments of its predecessors."

Buoyed by Dr. Franklin's admiring, if selective, recollections, the threesome stood excitedly in the entrance of an adjoining meeting space, to watch the legislators saunter in from a side door.

As with the Cabinet Room, the Founders recognized many of the figures who entered.

There was a congressman from New York, a combative fellow prone to wrangles, and the head of the House tax committee, who'd neglected for years to pay his taxes.

There was a handsome ex-Senator and former vice-presidential candidate from the Carolinas, a man who'd been indicted for hushing up with campaign cash the birth of a love child, which took place while his wife was ill from cancer.

There was an ex-congressman from a bayou state, of the name Jefferson, who kept thousands of dollars of bribes literally on ice, by storing it in his freezer.

"I assure you," Thomas Jefferson told his friends, "that *this* Mr. Jefferson and I are *not* related."

There was a senator from Idaho who retired prematurely, after undercover police noted his attempted solicitations and "wide stance" in an airport toilet.

There was a former congressman from New York City, who had quit congress after posting online videos of himself preening to the camera in his underpants, and who then had the temerity to run for that city's mayoralty.

And more of that ilk strutted in.

On observing these notorious persons, and reflecting on their manifold breaches of the public trust, the Founders reacted sharply.

Their guide, after checking on the next tour group waiting to enter the White House, returned to see how the trio was doing. But before he could get a word out, Jefferson, Franklin, and Adams sprinted past.

"Is the exit this way?!" called out Franklin.

"Need a breath of fresh air!" exclaimed Abigail.

"We really must be going!" shouted Jefferson.

Safely outside, in Lafayette Square, Dr. Franklin recited a quotation from the founder of his state, William Penn:

"As governments are made and moved by men, so by them they are ruined too. Let men be good and the government cannot be bad.

"But if men be bad, then the government be never so good, as they will endeavor to warp and spoil it to their turn."

"The Founders Visit a Central Bank and its 'Wizard of Odd'"

Franklin, Adams, and Jefferson were on
Constitution Avenue, for their morning constitutional—
a brisk, two- or three-hour hike they liked to take each
dawn, to stay in trim and to explore their new city.
Jefferson joked that the term for their exercise, "a
constitutional," was a tribute to his friend James
Madison, who'd largely devised the Constitution.

A Washington Walkabout

They found the District, though the repository
of odd governmental practices, filled with pleasant
neighborhoods, strung in a necklace of pearls that
encouraged ambling from one locale to another.
They'd often start their walk from Capitol Hill,
then head to the 7th St. complex of art galleries, to
the National Mall's museums, across downtown to
Dupont Circle's shops, to Adam Morgan's restaurants,
past the ever-expanding George Washington
University, then to the ugly, functionally-designed
State Department, at the aptly named Foggy Bottom,
go along the Potomac to Georgetown, move across
the Francis Scott Key Bridge to non-descript Rosslyn,
and finally up steep hills to the vibrant new Virginian
neighborhoods of Court House, Clarendon, and
Ballston.
"It reminds me of New York City," said Dr.
Franklin, "with its multiplicity of neighborhoods,
though without the wide mix of ethnic communities,

except for the diplomatic corps and the recent immigrant arrivals."

"I'm ever uneasy about big cities," said Jefferson, "with their propensity to control and corrupt the common folk of the unspoiled hinterlands. Though I must admit that, for culture and cuisine at least, this place compares not unfavorably with 18th-century Paris."

Earlier, they'd passed by several cinemas, which brought up the subject of motion pictures. Since viewing "Ben Franklin: Werewolf Slayer", the Founders had become ardent fans of the movies, in particular classic American films. A favorite of Jefferson's was "The Wizard of Oz" which, he was told, was loosely based on a popular protest against central bankers, a cause he had been the first to champion. This naturally brought up the subject of the Federal Reserve, an organization the Founders had read about, but whose operations they had trouble grasping.

Now the Founders found themselves on Constitution Ave., the Korean and Vietnam War Memorials to their right. They stopped to admire the slightly-larger-than-life, yet grimly realistic, figures of the Korean War Memorial. The bronzed soldiers on patrol, gazing warily into the distance, captured the ambivalent memories of that conflict among the present-day citizenry.

A Presidential Swoon

Nearby, the design of the Vietnam War Memorial deeply affected them. They stepped down a subtly declining ramp, and passed by the inscribed

229

names of all the war's fallen. It was as if the downward slope of the memorial recreated the quagmire which that conflict represented. At the midway, and lowest point, of the slope, where the casualties were greatest, Jefferson stopped. His bent his head, tears welling up, his handkerchief dabbing at swollen eyes.

As often happened when he reflected on war, the former president thought of the two British invasions of his Virginia, when he was its Revolutionary War governor. Of the devastations wrought, of his own family put to flight, from Richmond and Williamsburg and again from Monticello, his servants scattered, some dying of disease, of his wife Martha dying, after giving birth to their seventh child, worn down from the disruptions of the war. The thought of Martha in turn brought back his black depression after her death, when friends like Madison feared he might take his own life.

Tourists at the Wall who saw the grieving figure assumed he was a Vietnam veteran or relative of one of the war's fallen. His two friends led him back across the boulevard.

"Thomas," said Abigail, reading his mind, "having lost one daughter at birth, and another at the tender age of two, I fully share your anguish."

"Friends in need, indeed," replied Jefferson. For a while, he regained his normal composure, and the three walked further up Constitution Ave. Then suddenly, the former President, still affected by the Memorial, turned quite white, and swooned, and fell onto the sidewalk…

…When Jefferson awoke, he was again striding up Constitution with his friends. On their left was a long white construction, with tall vertical windows, rather like the slits of an ancient fortress. The place was plain in appearance, at least compared to the magnificent marble edifices of the town's other public buildings. Its window shades were drawn, as if to hide the interior from sunlight and prying eyes. It was set far apart from the avenue, as if to blend into the background unseen.

Normally the building wouldn't have drawn their attention, but the Founders couldn't help notice a yellow-brick path of gold, leading from the sidewalk toward the entrance. Astonished, they stepped along the golden road, following its path, which must have cost more than one of the region's gold-plated road construction projects.

As they moved along, the walkway's gleaming gilt gradually turned into less lustrous metals, of progressively decreasing worth: from pure gold, to a mix of gold and alloy, then silver, and bronze, to a dull lead, then cheap tin. The metals then petered and pewtered out entirely, changing over to paper, first of fine and durable paper stock, rather like that in dollar bills, then of a progressively cheaper kind, until they and the path ended in toilet paper.

The Federal Preserve

Despite the unprepossessing look of the building, security guards manned a checkpoint at the entrance. The monitors' eyes were glassy, and their stomachs bulged over their belts like most of the other security personnel in the city.

Franklin moved out of their view. From his day pack, the venerable publisher took out his redesigned laptop and 3-D printer.

"What is this place, Doctor?" asked Abigail. Franklin took a quick photo of the exterior with his smart phone, and his image app identified the place as, "The Federal Reserve". He rapidly hacked into its database, and called up the specs of the security cards used to gain entry.

Jefferson approached his friend, "What have you got for us, Doctor?"

"This place piques your interest, doesn't it?"

"Certainly."

The portable printing device, able to create perfect replicas of items in three dimensions, quietly hummed. Soon, Franklin handed laminated cards to Jefferson and Adams, while taking another for himself.

"We are now members of the Federal Reserve Board—of Philadelphia, of Richmond, Virginia, and—oh, Abigail, sorry, I entered Braintree, not Boston, Massachusetts. But I doubt these sleepy monitors will notice."

Abigail felt uncomfortable about engaging in a deceit, but compelled to join her friends on what promised to be an interesting adventure.

Once inside, the trio picked up the pathway again, which again had turned a golden hue. The yellow-brick road gleamed, even indoors. But Jefferson, who'd once poured over rocks and ore sent him by Captains Lewis and Clark, soon realized the metal was mere Fool's Gold, to gull the impressionable.

The faux yellow-brick way led through a series of empty corridors, ending at the closed, twin doors of a walled amphitheater. Franklin and Jefferson each took a handle, and pulled the doors open. Abigail, shielding her eyes, peered into the vast chamber that appeared, with its steps and rows of seats leading down to a brightly lit stage. The three entered and descended the stairs.

The platform, ceiling, and walls of the stage were covered in mirrors, and shrouded in mists of dry ice. Klieg lights shone on the mirrors, lending the place the intensity of the sun. A group of shadowy figures could be glimpsed standing around what appeared to be a man at a raised podium.

In the rows of seats flanking the stage were hundreds of disheveled persons, in cheap business suits, listening attentively, respectfully, devoutly, unquestioningly, scribbling down notes, not with quills, but with modern ink pens, or through electronic tablets, and making recordings. In front of the journalists, and in the seats nearest the center of the stage, were about a dozen people in expensive business suits. In passing them, the Founders noticed they wore badges from other cities that were regional headquarters for the Federal Reserve. The rest of the audience was made up of independent bankers from various parts of the country.

A Wizard of Wealth

The Founders had discovered the wonderful invention of sunglasses, and they put on their lenses to shield themselves from the glare. Up close, the mists cleared somewhat, and they saw at the podium a ChairMan, and next to him four others with large, identifying badges—a TinMan, a StrawMan, and a

Lyin'Man. As well as a Wicked Witch of the Western states.

The ChairMan was bald, with a white beard. But he wasn't so much a man, they noticed, but an image projected onto the rostrum: a giant, shifting oval face of green, the color of money. On either side of his constantly chattering visage were the images of flames, and the continual burning of cash, bonds, IOUs, and other financial paper. Below his podium was a digitized horizontal display, on which flickered a stream of lettered codes, each associated with a positive or negative number.

The Founders noticed that the ChairMan's voice, like his image, was altered. It was amplified through speakers, like those they'd heard at modern concerts. His voice boomed.

"I am the Wizard, your wonderful Wizard, listen!

"We are on the verge of an economic abyss! So we must print more money! If we print enough, money will become so cheap that anyone will be able to afford it. And then everyone will be able to afford homes, cars, and college loans!!"

The scribes and officials in the front seats watched the Chairman with rapt and unquestioning attention.

"I'm ordering our Federal Reserve Bank here in Washington," intoned this wizardly ChairMan, "and our branch banks all over the country, to make more and more of the stuff! Money's a good thing!"

The imagery blurred, and was transformed, and the appearance of fire was replaced with those of chestnut trees, and of dollar denominations sprouting from their branches and leaves.

Abigail noticed that the faces of Franklin and Jefferson, and Washington and Hamilton, along with other notables from the past, were on the denominations. 'Why is it?' she wondered, 'that my husband John is not on any currency?'

With her friends, Mrs. Adams also noticed that the values on the digital display changed with the ChairMan's words. For instance:

IBM, +1.5; XOM, +2.25; KO, +.65...

"I don't recognize the abbreviations," said Jefferson.

"I do," said Franklin, "from my financial research." Dr. Franklin had been trying to find sound investments for their earnings.

"They're stock-market symbols, representing large technology, energy, and food-products firms, among many others."

"Almost every single one on the screen," noted the keen-eyed Abigail, "has risen since this fiery wizard began speaking."

"You're right," responded Jefferson. "The potential for manipulation of the financial markets, from this central banking authority, is immense."

"Now you know why I'm having so much trouble finding a place to invest our earnings," complained Franklin. "How can I trust the value of any stock or bond, when their values are so changeable, and based on the actions of one man?"

"Nowhere does our Constitution," Jefferson stated, "authorize a financial despot. Without any say from the people, he arbitrarily controls the value of the people's money!"

The ChairMan spoke again: "At the same time, we must guard against inflation, against the value of money falling too much, and prices rising too much as a result."

The image of the money trees were consumed with flames, the trees and the money and the wizard himself disappearing in a fiery holocaust.

"Look at the screens!" declared Abigail.

APPL, - 2.75; GE, - 1.3; GOOG, -.75…

"Now almost every item is falling," remarked Jefferson.

Straining to recall a famous man's quotation, the former President recited:

"'If the American people ever allow banks to control the issue of their currency, first by inflation, then by deflation, then the banks and the corporations that grow up around them, will deprive the people of all property, until their children wake up homeless.'"

"What a prescient remark!" commented Abigail. "Who said it?"

"I did," replied Jefferson.

On the ticker, the stock prices kept falling.

"I daresay the Rothschilds themselves," said Franklin gloomily, "could not make money in this environment."

"What about safe investments, cash deposits?" asked Jefferson. "What do they call them today— commercial deposits, 'C Ds', right?"

"Please don't jest, Thomas. All this easy money from this wizard has pushed the rates of return from such instruments to under one percent, well below a rising cost of living."

"Doesn't that punish people who are thrifty and responsible?" asked Abigail. "Those who carefully save for a rainy day, or for their children's schooling?"

"It's worse than that," replied Franklin. "It punishes the elderly who've put away money their whole lives, and are now living on savings with fixed rates of return—and getting nothing in return."

"It goes against the wisdom of the ages," said Abigail sharply. "I'm reminded of the folk tale of the ants and the grasshopper: The frugal ants saved up for the winter, while the reckless grasshopper spent the summer singing, then starved. This awful place turns common sense on its head!"

"It's legalized theft on a massive scale," railed Jefferson. "The piling up of debt and the transfer of a ruined currency to unborn generations!"

The ChairMan's image reappeared on the screen, and the flames flickered around him, seeming to singe his beard. His voice roared: "But we mustn't worry too much about higher prices. The great fear is another Great Depression.

"Every general must fight the last war, even though the next war is never like the one before it. So let us fight the last war, the Depression, and have a big party, and print more money!!"

His visage was consumed with flames, and the money trees appeared again, with big-dollar denominations like that of Dr. Franklin, making that apostle of thrift aghast at the misuse of his image.

And the screens' values were again stood on their head:

GOOG, +3; APPL, +2.5; MCD, +5...

"I must confess that I do own a few tech stocks," admitted Franklin. "And they're doing rather well right now."

"Is even Dr. Franklin corrupted?!" declaimed Jefferson, smacking his forehead in despair. "Is Ben Franklin now a mere stock jobber?!"

"Don't worry, Thomas," he replied soothingly. "It's only play money, really, of a very small amount."

The ChairMan's Right-Hand Men

After the ChairMan had set, for a while at least, the nation's money policy, his acolytes took to the rostrum in support.

The Lyin'Man averred, "We can through careful and precise intervention in the market prevent recessions from ever occurring again."

The TinMan declared, "A gold standard would set the nation's money to an arbitrary value like that of gold. Better to set it to a cheap metal like tin, that all can afford."

The StrawMan offered, "The Federal Reserve has abolished for all time the boom and bust cycles of the market, be they in real estate, the Internet, gasoline prices, college education, or the economy generally."

The final speaker, in fact at one time an actual Speaker, was the Wicked Witch of the Western states. She was a withered, sunken-cheeked woman, from the Federal Reserve Board of San Francisco.

In another role, as legislator, she had once passed, at midnight, when all good souls are asleep, yet evil spirits roam the earth, a law nationalizing the nation's health care, saying at dawn's early light that the people could read the law now that she had now passed it. She looked vaguely familiar to the Founders, who thought they might have seen her around Capitol Hill, but they couldn't quite place her.

The Witch from the West had made an apparently Dorian Gray-like pact for, although of evidently ancient vintage, her face, perhaps through chemical and cosmetic means, appeared to retain the visage of a somewhat younger woman. One time in fact, she had nearly died of mortification when a heckler threw a pail of water in her face, which melted away her makeup, revealing an image that seemed older than, well, Ben Franklin.

Screeching approval for the wizardly ChairMan, she tried to raise her broom with glee— and stopped on hearing a blood-chilling cry: she'd mistaken the StrawMan's arm for the broom, and nearly ripped its weak material asunder.

With each statement from the rostrum, the scribes and officials rose to their feet in applause.

But the utterances, and the uncritical responses, irked the Founders.

"Obviously I'm no expert," said Franklin, "in modern American history. I wasn't here. But even the average man knows the nation, far from banishing busts, has been in recession for years."

"And even someone with a passing knowledge of this Federal Bank," said Jefferson, "knows that, since its founding, early in the last century, the nation has suffered through a Great Depression, and a severe downturn combined with inflation in the 1970s, as well as the current hard economic times.

"Back in our day, yes, there were busts, and sometimes severe ones, but they were transient and, over the long term, left to its own devices, without such meddling and propping up from the Central

239

Authority, the Nation prospered mightily, more than any other nation in history."

"This stuff about abolishing any economic variations," added Abigail, her Puritan background showing, "is mere twaddle.

"It is in the nature of life that life is sometimes hard. And when hard times arrive, one should face it like, well, like a man. And not delay facing up to such difficulties with an avalanche of other people's money, which after all is mere theft from such persons."

Peeling Back the Curtain

The Founders felt they were in the right, but felt helpless about doing anything about it. Then Jefferson noted, "Behind all this dazzle and roar, there must be a real organization here, and perhaps a real chairman."

"Should we look around?" suggested Franklin.

Fed up with the patter and the pyrotechnics, they left their seats, and strode over to the side of the stage, and began poking about. They came upon several doors.

One had a sign, "Electrical Closet," which intrigued Dr. Franklin, but he put away his boundless curiosity about electricity for the moment. For another door had a sign, "Federal Reserve—Finance Dept." This portal had multiple locks, but that proved little bother to Franklin who, using the skeleton key and wire in his handy toolset, quickly unlocked them.

Jefferson threw open the door, which revealed a large chamber that bordered the side and rear of the stage. The room had hundreds of filing cabinets: the drawers of most of them were wide open, and many had been pushed onto the floor, scattering the file folders all around. In fact, the carpet was littered with documents, of cheap loans in the trillions to banks and firms, foreign and domestic; in spots, the piles of paper were many feet deep.

"This rather reminds me," said Jefferson, "of the way the Continental Congress ran the financing of the Revolutionary War."

"Yes," said Abigail, "when Washington's troops were forever short of weapons, food, and ammunition."

The Founders looked past the debris to the wall adjoining the stage. It had a small platform with a small raised dais, the top half of which was shielded by a curtain. Below the curtain they discerned two skinny, hairy legs descending from an old man's boxer shorts.

From the hall behind them, they heard voices calling out: "You're not allowed in that place!", and "Get out of there!" But their curiosity captured them. They waded their way through the files to the platform, as those shouting—people from the audience and the stage—began filing in after them.

Jefferson stepped up and ripped away the drape. At the top of the dais were a computer screen and keyboard, a microphone, and a video screen showing what the audience saw at the rostrum. Frantically entering commands on the keyboard was a short bald man with thin legs and a trim white beard, and clad in boxer shorts and a tank top. The little man was so intent in his work that he hadn't noticed he had been exposed.

The elfish figure was shouting into the microphone: "...For some banks are too big to fail, especially my Bank! And some insurance companies too..." He punched in a command on the computer, and on the video screen appeared the image of money growing on trees.

He suddenly realized his curtain had been pulled back. He turned and glanced at his onlookers with astonishment, while his mouth kept moving and speaking. "…and other politically powerful companies! Some are too big, some of us are, much too big to fail…"

By then, many persons—branch managers of the Federal Reserve, executives of banks from around the nation, and the ChairMan's stage accomplices—had entered the room. They leafed their way through the littered floor on over to the dais, shaken by what they saw, and confronted the would-be wizard of wealth.

"You're a fraud!" shouted the Lyin'Man, speaking the truth for the first time in a while.

"Your paper currency is worthless!" shouted the TinMan, suddenly a fan of the gold standard, or at least sound money.

"You're leading us into bankruptcy!" shouted the StrawMan, stating the simple truth for once.

"How am I supposed to spin such a scandal?!" cried the Wicked Witch of the Western states.

Abigail told the ChairMan: "You should be ashamed of yourself, for lying to the people and debasing their money, their labor, the sweat of their brow."

Ex-President Jefferson, citing one of his successors, told him: "You can't fool all of the people all of the time."

An Abject Confession

Financial leaders from around the country gathered around the wizard.

The chairman of the St. Louis Federal Reserve picked up one of the folders scattered about, and documents spilled out of it. "Why wasn't this place ever audited?!" he demanded.

"I figured there was no need for an audit," said the ChairMan mildly. "No one ever looks into the way we run things. We had carte blanche to do what we want."

A banker from Missouri asked, "Why did you bail out all those big banks, while the smaller ones from my state had to scrape by without support?"

"That's obvious," said the ChairMan. "The big banks give millions in donations to the people in power."

The Minneapolis Federal Reserve chairwoman asked, "Why do you keep printing money, pushing interest rates to near zero?"

"If interest rates went up," said the ChairMan, "the Government's cost of borrowing would soar, and it couldn't pay back its massive borrowing. No can do."

The ChairMan was reduced to a shadow of his once fiery image. Glumly, he offered, "Perhaps it's the Government that's too big to fail."

He turned apologetic. "I admit that I'm all smoke and mirrors. As you can see," he said, pointing to his shorts and tank top, "I'm just a man, and an unimpressive one at that. But all the power and all the slavish attention given me got to my head.

"And I didn't know what to do, frankly. I'm no businessman, no innovator, no engineer. Just a number-crunching wonk, a boring economist. When the economy hit the skids, I hadn't a clue. So I just started pumping money. To buy time until I thought of something else. But I couldn't think of anything, and meanwhile I was being treated as some kind of god, looked up to by everyone. For the first time in my life, I was somebody. My predecessor, you might recall, was universally hailed as some kind of maestro. I figured it would be the same for me, forever. So I just kept the printing presses going!"

Some of the bankers, from the heartland of America, had huddled together in conversation. One from Indiana stepped forward, and addressed the Founders.

"We want to express our gratitude to you three patriotic Americans for exposing this imposter. We've been under his spell for far too long, but now we hope the spell is broken."

The banker paused. "We were wondering if you might have advice for us, for moving forward, and for getting out of the current fiscal mess."

A Frugal Founder's Frank Advice

Franklin, shaken by what he'd seen in the littered room, cleared his throat. "I'll say a few words." He took a Jefferson nickel out of his pocket, and rubbed it in his hands, composing his remarks.

"First off: in this world, nothing can be said to be certain—except death and taxes." His listeners laughed.

The good Doctor continued. "A penny saved is a penny earned. Rather go to bed without dinner than to rise in debt. These aren't clichés, mind you, but truer than ever.

"Beware of little expenses, for a small leak will sink a great ship. If you know how to spend less than you get, you have the philosopher's stone." The financial people were stunned. No one had preached the value of thrift to them in ages.

Franklin went on. "The way to wealth depends on just two words: industry and frugality. Waste neither time nor money, but make the best use of both."

Abigail and Jefferson smiled, recognizing the quotations from a famous Franklin book of their era, *Poor Richard's Almanac*.

The board members and the bankers, for their part, were astonished at the terse wisdom of the old man's words.

"Without industry and frugality," Franklin concluded, "nothing will do, and with them everything."

The financial executives broke into applause. They pledged to spend and borrow much less, to encourage the people's inherent talent and thrift, and to urge the rest of the government to do the same.

The Founders made their farewells, and made their way out of the auditorium.

Back on Constitution Avenue, Franklin remarked, "It's odd that an institution so unconstitutional is placed on Constitution Avenue."

Abigail and Jefferson congratulated Franklin on his brief, persuasive talk. He pensively waved away the praise.

"When the people find that they can vote themselves money," he stated, again quoting himself, "that heralds the end of the republic."

Jefferson, for his part, was humming a tune he'd taken to playing on his violin: "Follow the Yellow Brick Road…"

…Suddenly, he felt a pain on his cheek.

"Thomas, please come to! Are you all right?!"

It was Abigail. And Franklin was drawing back his hand to gently slap him again.

Jefferson lay on his back on a sidewalk on Constitution Ave., his friends bent over him with great concern.

"Thomas, you're awake!" cried Franklin. "After you fainted, you were unconscious for at least a minute. Are you sure you're all right?"

Shaking himself awake, Jefferson propped himself up on his elbows. The wizardly ChairMan, and his entourage, and their strange central bank had seemed so vivid, so real, and not like a dream at all.

"Well," he sleepily told his puzzled companions, as he gazed down Constitution Ave., toward the Federal Reserve's non-descript building, "I guess I'm not in Virginia anymore."

"The Founders Encounter Agricultural Oddities"

Once, while strolling along the National Mall, the Founders chanced on a new farmer's market, set up by the region's orchard growers and dairy farmers. A throwback to the old city marketplace on 7th Street, it was crammed with vendors hawking apples, peaches, cheeses, ciders, wines, and other produce, and eager customers lining up to taste and purchase the goods.

Perfect Pickings

For the trio, who'd run large plantations in Virginia, a family farm in Massachusetts, and published a popular farmer's almanac, respectively, the place was enticing. Jefferson for one was thrilled to see that Virginia wines had become as plentiful and flavorsome as French and Italian vintages.

"Things do seem a bit antiseptic, though," commented Abigail.

Unlike the markets of their day, she pointed out, no live animals, no pigs, sheep, nor cattle roamed about, adding noise, scent, and color to things. Nor their droppings, which she judged a good thing.

The fruit in particular struck the Founders as something manufactured. There were no worm holes in the apples, nor spots, and the different kinds of fruit—whether they were plums or nectarines—had similar sizes, shapes, colors. It seemed almost too perfect.

"The result of intense cultivation and hybridization over two centuries, wouldn't you say?"

asked Franklin, rolling his fingers around a perfect peach.

"And probably," answered Jefferson, "some of the biotech methods that brought us back."

"Except that," replied Franklin, running his somewhat arthritic fingers over his bald pate, "we are far from perfect."

Reap What You Stow

Munching on sweet potato pie, they moved on, to a portion of the Mall downhill from the Washington Monument. This section contained not a farmer's market, but farmers, who'd turned acres of the wide lawn into cultivated land. Parcels of turf were strewn with corn, soybeans, and wheat, although fallow land made up most of the acreage.

"Cultivators of the earth are our most valuable citizens," stated Jefferson, proud of the yeomen farmers he'd often celebrated. "They are the most vigorous, the most independent, the most virtuous, and they are tied to their country and wedded to its liberty by the most lasting bands."

The Founders approached one man in overalls, work boots, and a straw hat, who was lolling on a tractor on the edge of his untilled soil.

"Not the right season for planting?" asked Jefferson.

"No sense in sowing when they pay me to squat," the fellow responded.

Seeing the Founders' puzzlement, the man explained that the Department of Agriculture paid him not to grow anything.

"It was afraid too many crops would depress the price of crops, so it started giving farmers cash to sit on their hands.

"It's worked—prices at the grocery store are higher than ever before."

His lips pursed, the industrious Franklin responded: "There must be very many applicants for 'work' like this."

"Not that many," said the farmer, yawning. "Most of the people getting such swag are wealthy, and very politically connected. And surprisingly few are actually farmers; some are even big-name broadcasters and sports stars. The number's as small as the gross payments are large: billions of bucks a year."

The Founders looked away, scratching their heads, then were amazed to see, on a field in the distance, what appeared to a famous figure from their own era.

A grinning, barefoot youth in ragged overalls, propped up with suspenders latched to a loose, rumpled shirt, was loping from field to field. From a large satchel around his neck, he tossed packets or pieces of paper into the air, or handed them to grateful farmers.

"He looks all the world like Johnny Appleseed!" cried Abigail, of the mythic figure who'd spread fruit seeds throughout the early United States.

Propping up the Produce

She and her friends were about to greet the happy lad, when they heard another farmer cry out from an adjoining corn field.

"I can't believe it!" the farmer shouted, dancing a jig of joy next to his BMW Z4 roadster.

The Founders walked up to him, admiring his sports car, and the finely ripened stalks of corn he'd raised.

Jefferson was impressed at how humble "Indian corn" had become such a major foodstuff in modern America. He asked, "Celebrating a bumper crop?"

The man stopped dancing, wiped away sweat, then began his whirligig anew. "I suppose it's a pretty good harvest," he said, kicking his legs up high. "But the price supports are even better!"

"What's a price 'support'?" asked Jefferson, though he suspected he knew.

"This corn's worth maybe five bucks a bushel," the man answered. "But I hear the Ag Department's gonna give me ten!" He moved his dance to the hood of his auto. "Means another Beemer for me!"

The former president was compelled to ask, "Why would the government pay you twice as much as the crops are worth?"

"It's afraid too low a price would depress the income of farmers, so they started giving us higher prices."

Abigail was confused. "Doesn't that contradict what they've done for your neighbor, paying him not to grow, while paying you more for growing something?"

The farmer took small dance steps, balancing himself on the BMW's quivering hood. "Maybe, who knows? It all washes out in the end. The farm bill costs a total of $500 billion, so any loot I get ain't worth a hill of beans in the scheme of things!"

The man stopped dancing, turning serious for a moment. "I guess I should care about all this cash tossed around, and the debt piled on the next generation." Then he started his little jig again. "But I'll be long gone before all this comes to a head, thank you very kindly!"

Iconic Agronomist

The farmer again stopped his jig, on seeing that his sleepy neighbor on the tractor was wide-awake, his eyes blazing. For Johnny Appleseed was skipping across the fallow field, nearing the tractor, and gleefully tossing out items from his sack. The farmers jumped from their sports car and tractor and ran toward the horticultural legend. The Founders, eager to meet the fellow, followed briskly.

They found Appleseed handing the farmers small pieces of paper. When the Founders arrived, the lad pushed some of the material into their hands.

At first glance, the papers looked like dollar denominations. They had the bleached color of U.S. currency, were valued as "1 Dollar", or "5 Dollars", and featured images of American icons like the Liberty Bell. But instead of "The United States of America" at their top, the materials were inscribed with "U.S. Department of Agriculture" and, in large print, "FOOD COUPON".

Admiring the depiction of the Liberty Bell from his hometown, Franklin asked, "What's a Food Coupon?", though he suspected he knew.

The youthful Appleseed grinned sloppily, his rows of oversized teeth arrayed like stalks of corn, and sparkling with platinum and gold fillings.

"Oh you know—food stamps. For the purchase of stuff at any store. Food mostly, but also liquor, tobacco, or even strip club fees, and lottery tickets if you want. We won't check!"

He paused to pull a handful of coupons from his satchel, and threw them into the air.

"As good as legal tender!"

Abigail coughed uncomfortably, her stubborn New England upbringing, and its moral qualms, coming to the fore.

"Presumably, sir, such vouchers should be assigned to the poorest of the poor, the truly hungry. So I'm compelled to inquire: why are you giving them to these two affluent farmers, as well my two friends, whom I assure you are men of means."

Appleseed handed the grateful farmers more food stamps, and threw more of them into the breeze. He chortled, and recited the Agriculture agency's new ad slogan, "'Food Stamps: Not Only for the Hungry Any More!'

"I've been charged, you know—by the agricultural committees in congress, the farm lobbyists on K Street, presidential campaign staffs, and welfare agency activists—to recruit as many folks to the Supplemental Nutrition Insistence Program—SNIP—as I can.

"And my job, it's a snap! Like handing out free money. I've signed up 50 million Americans, and counting. Polls show I'm the most popular man in the country. There is such a thing as a free lunch!" And Appleseed shoved two big handfuls of stamps into the hands of Franklin and Jefferson.

The latter two turned a deathly white. The coupons dropped from their hands, except for two they held on to with a deathly grip.

Jefferson saw that the $5 dollar food coupon bore his own image! As representing America's most famous farmer, while ignoring his record as a strict keeper of the public accounts.

Franklin saw that the $1 coupon bore his image, and Jefferson's, and John Adams. From the famous painting of them presenting the Declaration of Independence to George Washington. The four of them, on this declaration of—Dependence!

'People wonder', reflected Abigail, 'what the Founding Fathers would think if they returned to America today.

'Now they know'.

Appleseed turned his satchel inside out; no coupons were left. "Not a problem!" he shouted, and pranced back through the fields, fallow and planted alike, mostly fallow. He raced in the direction of the U.S. Mint.

"There's plenty more where these came from!"

The fallow farmer returned to his idle tractor, and to dozing off.

The other farmer returned to his sports car. Taking a hose from a gas pump, he began to fill its tank.

Franklin, curious about any technology, asked the gentleman grower: "Is it gas or diesel?"

The man looked at his crops. "Mostly corn mash in fact. Ethanol. I use a thirty percent mix."

Franklin called up his knowledge of the internal combustible engine, and basic chemistry. "That's a high percentage: Won't it gum up the motor of that fine automobile?"

"I suppose. But the government pays me big bucks to grow corn for ethanol. So I figure I should use up my share of it.

"Besides, diverting corn for ethanol, instead of food, helps prop up the price for my produce as much as the price supports.

"It's a win-win all around!

"At least for me it is: It means higher food prices for the poor. But what the heck—they get food stamps!"

"The Founders Find a School for Political Campaigns"

Scratching their heads over the capital's agricultural scene, the Founders departed the farms of the National Mall. They walked north, through downtown, and into City Hall Plaza, on Pennsylvania Avenue near the Treasury Building. From their time in Washington, D.C., Jefferson and Abigail recognized Treasury, next to the White House, but were familiar with little else. Back when, Pennsylvania Avenue had been an empty dirt track leading from the new White House and Treasury to a Capitol Building then under construction.

Now the avenue was a paved boulevard ringed by stately buildings. City Hall Plaza was itself a wide concrete square on which tourists strolled, government workers lunched, and rollerbladers rolled. Recently it had become a place for al fresco dancing, where coupled swayed to waltzes played on portable radios.

The Plaza was also home at times to outdoor expositions, an unusual one of which the Founders found themselves observing.

A series of booths and open-flap tents occupied much of the place, over which hung a bright banner that read: "School for Political Campaigns".

Undercover Evidence

Intrigued, the Founders entered a large, circus-like tent. There a man stood in an elegant business suit, and his wife in a party dress. A name tag identified the man as the ex-chief executive of a Maryland county on the District's eastern border. Next to the man was a toilet, and next to the woman was a table with an assortment of ladies undergarments. Both persons were holding large bags of cash. Besides them each stood another man and a woman with badges pegging them as contractors from a political consulting firm.

The former county executive took wads of dollar bills out of his sack, piled them into the toilet, and pulled the flusher. He grimaced as water, tinted with the color of money, surged up and over its rim and onto the floor.

"You have to be more patient," advised the male contractor, walking over. He slipped on rubber gloves, took a single wad of cash from the bag, and placed it carefully into the toilet.

"Studies have shown," he advised, "that one can effectively flush just twenty bills at once." He pressed the plunger; the money roared down the hole. "You can pocket a bribe in an instant, but dispensing with the evidence can take time."

Meantime the wife, having taken off her suit jacket and blouse, was having trouble stuffing dollars into her brassiere. The female contractor rushed to her aid.

"It looks rather full," she said. "Could I suggest a bigger size?" She handed over a larger bra from the table, then held a large towel around the wife, who strapped on the undergarment.

"Yes, that's much better," smiled the contractor. "It'll hold more cash, without the tell-tale clumps that tip off police you're sneaking hot dollars out of your house."

As they watched in wonder, the Fathers stood next to the head of the company running the school.

Nodding to the threesome, he told him with a conspiratorial air:

"Sneaking out cash and other sensitive materials, you know, is a venerable Washington tradition. In the 1990s, the National Security Adviser himself—I think his name was Burger or hot dog or something—was caught taking top-secret documents from the National Archives in his Jockey shorts. In the 1980s, a colonel working at the National Security Council got his secretary—I think her name was Dawn or Fawn, something sexy like that—to sneak out Iran-Contra documents in her brassiere. Even back in the Civil War, Confederate spy Rose Greenough had a servant ferret away secret Union Army documents in her pantyhose."

"I appreciate the history lesson," said Abigail, uncomfortable at the unusual methods of transporting materials, and even more uneasy at their illegality. "But aren't you teaching people how to be better criminals?"

"That's not how we see it," the man smoothly replied. "Corruption and vice in government are inevitable—we merely teach pols to manage their illicit behavior more effectively.

Scratching his chin, Jefferson asked, "I'm interested in knowing the background of the officials around here—what did they do before entering politics?"

"I'm not sure I understand," the contractor answered. "They're politicians."

Franklin explained: "My friend is wondering what they did before they ran for office.

"To give you some examples, from the, um, the distant past: Along with his life in public service, President Washington was a noted soldier, planter, surveyor. Abigail Adam's husband was a

257

businessman, a prominent barrister, and with his wife a successful farmer. Abigail Adams, along with being the matriarch of one of America's most influential families, was a noted woman of letters. Thomas Jefferson was a diplomat, architect, and—"

"—And Benjamin Franklin," interjected Jefferson, "was an author, inventor, scientist, among other useful occupations."

"Such a range of experiences," Franklin went on, "gives one a wealth of knowledge for public matters. To finish my point, what jobs did these crooked politicians have before attaching themselves to the 'public teat'?"

With a puzzled look, the contractor answered: "Like I said, they're career politicians: politics is all they've ever known and all they'll ever do.

"Frankly," he added, "to be a politician, I don't think you need the skills of those other professions. The job is very simple actually. Take debating, for instance, critical to any pol's success. It requires no real skill."

Jefferson objected: "Rhetoric? Oratory? Forensic debate?! Why, those are among the most sophisticated of mankind's skills! It takes years of studying the Greek and Roman rhetoricians to master just the rudiments of public discourse."

The contractor, thinking Jefferson a fuddy-duddy, and out of touch, shook his head.

"Nah, it's not rocket science. Let me show you." And the contractor brought the Founders over to a demonstration on how to successfully debate.

Poll Watchers

In a large, open-air meeting space, the Founders watched a public-speaking demo with keen interest. A man in a thousand-dollar suit and a telegenic red silk tie stood at a lectern—and placed what looked like swim goggles over his eyes. Next to the lectern was a large display screen, visible to the Founders. The man faced a reporter at a table in front of him; the lady journalist was leafing through papers and scanning her computer tablet, preparing for the event. Behind the journalist were rows of seats, on which sat 25 adults from various walks of life.

Franklin wondered idly if the audience members were going to throw things at the speaker. "Are those goggles some form of protection for the eyes?" he asked.

"Not protection," replied the contractor, "but enhancement."

The reporter adjusted her hands-free microphone, and stated: "I'd like to welcome the candidate and the audience to this practice debate. I'll start off with the first question.

"Mr. Camelon, jobs are of prime concern to voters. How would you improve the economy?"

Candidate Camelon made an adjustment to his goggles, and the display screen glowed to life. It showed a list of 25 voters, categorized by name, age, income, job, religion, ethnicity, sex, political party, voting record, and other groupings.

The Founders realized with a start they were seeing what the candidate saw in his goggles, namely, detailed data on the audience members.

"How did his eyepieces call up that information?" asked Franklin, ever fascinated by electronics.

"The goggles," said the contractor, "have sensors that collect all the data in the participants' smart phones, including their social networking and political preferences.

Candidate Camelon began to speak.

"Why that's a very good question," he stated confidently, "on an issue of great import." He paused, and the screen, and his goggles, displayed the following:

Tax cuts for affluent—70 percent of audience opposes.

Social Security cuts—80 percent opposes.

National debt—20 percent see it as major issue.

Washington, D.C.—90 percent have negative view.

Jobs—75 percent see it as biggest issue.

The candidate scanned his display, thought a moment, then looked at the audience and replied:

"Well, one way we won't improve our economy is by cutting taxes on the very rich.

"And we mustn't punish our oldest and most vulnerable citizens by gutting Social Security, just to balance the budget.

"Also, isn't it amazing how Washington does nothing about the most important issues?

"When what it should be doing is creating jobs!"

The candidate stopped, and the audience exploded with applause; some listeners sent out texts of approval, which appeared immediately on the screen.

Dr. Franklin remarked: "It's as if Candidate Camelon is able to read their minds!"

As the office seeker soaked up the acclaim, another block of data appeared on his goggles and the screen:

Latest Nation-Wide Insta-Poll!
According to a survey by Phew Research,
Americans remain most concerned about jobs:
in particular high-school and college grads who
are having trouble finding work…

After glancing at the display, the candidate cleared his throat, and stated: "Just let me add I know many of you have children, who are struggling to find work during these hard economic times. So our efforts on job creation should be focused on those struggling to enter the job market!"

The audience rose to a standing ovation, and sent out so many texts that "jobs for youths" became a trending item on Twitter.

The contractor told the Founders: "You see, debating is a lot easier with today's technologies. All a candidate has to do is echo his audience's concerns, based on their demographic data and Internet preferences.

"Eventually, electronic interaction like this will replace elections. Who needs a vote when you know what people think anyway?"

"And, great rhetorical skills are definitely *not* required to become the most popular man in the room, or the nation!"

Jefferson objected: "But this hardly seems sufficient to—"

"—You're right," the contractor agreed. "Look!"

The candidate had waded into the audience to shake the hand of each voter. As he did so, he gave each a brand-new smart phone.

"Candidates today," explained the contractor, "often give away phones and other goodies, to sew up the votes."

Jefferson stared at the brazen handouts. "But this is like ancient Rome's bread and circuses!"

"What do you mean?" asked the contractor.

"Rome's corrupt Emperors," he explained, "would hand out free bread, and stage lavish public spectacles, to win the support of the rabble."

"What a great idea!" the contractor exclaimed. "I wonder how much it would cost to rent Cirque de Soleil?!"

He scribbled down a note about circuses, then told the Founders, "Even more important than pandering are other techniques for electoral success.

"Let me show you."

In a Negative Light

He led Adams, Jefferson, and Franklin to a tent that resembled a school room. Attendees sat at desks placed around a high-definition screen and console. Next to it stood an instructor, who excitedly slapped a pointer into his palm.

The teacher stated: "We going to show all of you would-be candidates for office how to craft hard-hitting TV ads. The best campaign ads are, of course, negative ones—for the easiest way to win an election is to smear your opponent!"

Jefferson's ears picked up. Historians had long regarded the 1800 presidential campaign between him and John Adams as the dirtiest in American history. Vicious attacks had caricatured Jefferson as an atheist and agent of France, while Adams was slandered as a puppet in the pay of the British king. So the Virginian was curious to see how modern politicians slung around the mud.

"To illustrate the power of 'attack ads'," continued the lecturer, "let's take some famous statesmen of the past, to show how commercials can wreck the reputations of even the most revered individuals."

The instructor pressed a button, and the screen played a video of a feeble old man with bad teeth wearing a powdered wig and a tattered military uniform.

The title of the ad rolled across the display:

"George Washington: Collaborator with King George!"

Then the narrator of the ad was heard, in a sneering, insinuating voice:

For five long years, before our war of independence against England, George Washington was a colonel in the British Empire! He fought on the side of our enemies the English against our brave allies the French, not to mention our oppressed Native American tribes. Later, his cronies made up lies he could throw a coin clear across the wide

Potomac, an impossible feat. They even bragged about him chopping down the environmentally sensitive cherry tree!

George Washington: 'The Fibber of his Country'—Too Dangerous to Trust!

The Founders were startled. Jefferson shook his head while Abigail erupted: "But they're smearing President Washington's service during the French and Indian Wars—when the French were our enemies, and the British Army our savior!"

The instructor commented, "Note that George Washington, if a candidate today, might try to deny the charges, but the damage would be done. His 'negative' ratings would fall through the filthy cellar of his Mt. Vernon home!"

As the students nodded their heads and took notes, the teacher pressed the console button.

Another video was played of a doddering geezer with bifocal lenses wearing a tight-fitting ruffled shirt bursting from his potbelly.

The title of ad displayed:

"Ben Franklin: Foreign Spy?"

The Founders were shocked.

The narrator spoke in a menacing voice:

Should old Ben Franklin be at our Constitutional Convention, writing the very rules for our new nation? Let's examine the facts.

During our Revolutionary War, Franklin's own son William—his illegitimate son—was a traitor, acting as Britain's royal governor, of the corrupt state of New Jersey. And Ben Franklin himself had sexual affairs while residing in France, a nation whose intelligence services are known entrap gullible foreigners with alluring femme fatales. The hypocritical elder even set up an anti-slavery society, after owning slaves himself!

Ben Franklin: Unproven, Unreliable, Unpatriotic!

The Founders fell silent, with Dr. Franklin especially pensive. Finally he remarked to his friends:

"Given the demands on the modern statesman—the continuous fundraising, the endless recitation of the same rote speech, the abject pandering to the lowest common denominator, the complete lack of personal privacy, the strong temptations of corruption, and the savage attacks on one's person and pride via the electronic media—I doubt any man of substance would bid for public office today."

"I suspect," agreed Jefferson, "that today's men of highest ability, such as yourself and General Washington, would instead constrain themselves to managing a large enterprise, or an institute of learning, or maintaining a career in the military, instead of exposing themselves to the tedium and vitriol of political affairs."

The contractor, meantime, was glancing at the school's schedule. "Another class on negative campaigning is just starting. On the most recent and innovative campaign technique! Why don't we catch it?!"

An Infernal Revenue Service

The Founders and the contractor next entered a hands-on class, whose students were political candidates. They watched as one participant took a seat at his computer station, where he was joined by three persons in business suits and green eyeshades.

"These new arrivals wouldn't be computer workers, would they?" asked Franklin, the optical innovator. "It's my understanding green glasses can protect eyes that have to stare at a screen all day."

"No," said the contractor. "These three are IRS agents, from the Internal Revenue Service. They're to offer advice about campaign fundraising. "

Jefferson frowned. He'd been disturbed to learn the federal government now had a vast organization to tax and punish those who accumulated wealth, whether it was by working hard, setting up companies, inheriting wealth, saving money, hiring craftsmen, investing wisely, or inventing useful things.

The agency's activities reminded him of the harsh hand of the French King, or of Imperial Spain, whose envoys he'd often treated with, and whose heavy-handed tax and regulatory acts had ruined the commerce of their once-vibrant lands.

But he couldn't imagine why such an institution of the state would be involved in fundraising.

"What does a revenue Agency have to do with electoral donations?" he asked the contractor.

The latter eyed him smugly.

"Perhaps you're looking at this from the wrong angle. Of course, the donations part of a campaign deals mostly with raising money for one's own side.

But nowadays, it also means stifling the fundraising, and the activities, of the opposing side too.

"And the best way to do that is to sic the IRS on them."

Jefferson didn't like what he was hearing, but he was still unclear about the role of the taxing authority.

The contractor raised his eyebrows. "Watch what the agents do. You might learn something."

The IRS workers were sitting at their own computers next to the candidate's. The latter watched intently as they began entering search terms, shown on the display screen above his PC:

Constitution
Bill of Rights
Tea Party
Rule of Law
Christian Groups
Balanced Budget
Jewish Groups
Self-Reliance
Veterans
Patriot

After entering the items, a long list of organizations associated with the terms were displayed.

"The groups listed," said the contractor, "are the ones most likely to raise funds and conduct activities against this particular candidate. Thus they're ones the candidate will use the IRS to harass and suppress.

"The agency will tangle them up with so many forms and inquiries that they'll never even get to the campaign's starting line!"

Abigail flushed. "But based on the 'search terms'," she objected, "these groups seem reputable enough, even admirable. Why, John and I even supported a 'tea party' back in Boston that dumped tea into the harbor—" she stopped abruptly, biting her tongue.

The contractor was incredulous. "There are Tea Parties in New England?! I'd have thought they've been suppressed long ago in such a progressive place!"

Jefferson was steaming. In his day, his followers, against much opposition, had begun to expand the voting franchise, to beyond those possessing large amounts of property. His aim had been to make the nation more democratic, to open up the political system to more of the people. But today, candidates were learning how to restrict the people's participation. 'And with the help of the government,' he thought, 'and its infernal tax agency!'

The candidate's eyes gleamed at the list of organizations to target. If he acted fast to harass these opposing groups, his election was a near-certainty. With great care, he printed out the list of groups, and copied the list to a disk drive, and to a thumb drive, and for good measure sent himself an email with the list in it. "No reason to take a chance," he cried out, "of losing such valuable information!

"Although," he continuing, laughing, "if I ever need another copy, I could look it up at the NSA!"

He jumped up from his PC, and rushed from the class with the IRS agents, all eager to get to work crushing the candidate's foes.

The Founders were too deep in thought to watch the rest of the class, and their guide the contractor, after receiving a text, excused himself as well.

"A high-ranking pol is asking me for advice on the 2024 presidential election," he told them. "One can't start too early—and as today's campaigns are endless one can never stop either! I have to go, but please check out the rest of the classes."

An Elective Course

Though shaking their heads over the conduct of the tax agency, the Founders were curious to learn more about modern politicking. The campaign school was now winding down, and they decided to take in one more exhibit, on the mechanics of holding elections.

Inside a wood hut they watched a dozen students, who sat at desks in front of an instructor standing at a portable whiteboard. On the walls of the class were framed photographs of a Chicago mayor from the mid-twentieth century. The teacher was marking the board up with chalk about controversial elections from history. These included: "Florida 2000", "Illinois 1960", "The Corrupt Bargain of 1824", "The Stolen Presidency of 1876", "Philadelphia and Miami-Dade 2012". The students strained to make out the instructor's scrawl.

Abigail recognized the reference to 1824. In that year, her son John Quincy Adams had been accused, unfairly she thought, of stealing the presidential election from the popular Andrew

Jackson, by making a deal with Jackson's rival, Sen. Henry Clay, to gain the most electoral votes.

The Founders had read of the controversial 2000 federal election in Florida, with its famous "hanging chad" recount.

"Perhaps," Abigail ventured, "this is a class on how to guarantee fair and above-board elections."

"Perhaps," replied Jefferson, sounding skeptical.

The teacher put down the chalk and, turning to the class, announced: "As you know, I asked you to do some research before today's session. Let's now have an oral presentation on what you've learned.

"Miss Flake, let's hear from you."

A woman in a short dress and fishnet stockings, and a Georgetown sweatshirt, though seeming rather old to be student, stood up from her desk.

The teacher folded his hands. "Yes, Sandy, why don't you take us through the steps for running an effective voting operation?"

"Well, Professor," she began, "if you're running for congress, you should pick a district that's been redistricted."

"That's an excellent point!" praised the instructor. "Can you explain why?"

"Well, if you run for and win a seat that's been redistricted, one that congress has rejiggered with the right mix of income and ethnic groups, statistics show you'll win re-election 98 percent of the time. Any future opponent will run into a brick wall, demographically, and lose.

"Why spend years and big bucks running for office just to retire after a failed re-election? You want a sure thing!"

"Exactly correct," said the teacher, nodding. "And what about the mechanics of voting?"

"You need to execute well at every polling place," said the knowledgeable student. "First, outside, you want to station a couple of mean-looking thugs to ward off your opponent's voters. Say it was 1950, and you were running in a district of the old South: you might station several KKK members in Klan robes to scare away voters. Today, if you're running in a poor district, in Philadelphia, say, you might station members of the New Black Panthers Party, garbed in gangsta regalia, to intimidate voters."

"Very good," said the instructor. "Yes, you need to skew the vote in your direction from the start. What about inside the polling place?"

"Well, Professor," continued Flake, "each voting place is supposed to have poll watchers from both parties, to act as a check on each other and to challenge voters who aren't correctly registered.

"Actually, third parties are supposed to be represented as well, but as the Democrat and Republican parties block third parties from debates, and have a stranglehold on fundraising and organization, in practice only volunteers from the two major parties might be on hand.

"But of course," Flake went on, "in the voting booths you only want representatives of one party there—*your party*. So, you should work with the local election boards to impede members of the other party from attending. That way you'll have a free hand in challenging their party's voters, while your own voters, properly registered or fraudulent, get a pass."

"Excellent point again!" cried out the instructor. "And you bring up the vital matter of voter fraud, critical to winning elections these days." The

271

professor flipped over the whiteboard. Its other side had a TV screen, and he pressed a button on its side.

"This is an opportune time, for a teachable moment, on this very matter. And from an expert on the topic!"

The display showed a video from an undercover reporter and an accomplice with a hidden camera. The film was on their interview of the son and campaign manager of a local Virginia congressman.

"Hello, sir!" greeted the reporter, after he and his cameraman had approached the campaign manager in the street. "I really like your dad, and hope he wins the election, but I missed the deadline for voter registration! Is there any way I can still vote for him?"

"Not a problem," answered the congressman's son in a cocksure manner. "Just head to the local polling station with a utility bill from somebody in the district. Say you're that person and, after the poll worker checks that name off the rolls, go ahead and pull the lever."

"Excellent. But will they only accept a utility bill?" prodded the reporter.

"Just about anything will do," the campaign chief smoothly assured. "Utility bill, cable bill, Internet bill, rent bill, phony driver's license, fake Social Security card. In a representative democracy like ours, it's important that *everyone* gets to vote."

"But I'm not from his district," answered the reporter. "Is that a concern?"

"Not at all," said the congressman's son. "We bus in people from all over the country to vote for us.

"Another thing you might do," he continued in a knowing voice, "is to randomly pick two or three people from the online White Pages, and call them up. Tell each person you're with a public opinion poll, and ask him if he's intending to vote. If he says, 'No way,' there's your man. Use his name and address at the polling place. After all, you don't want people showing up to find someone's already voted for them!"

"That's really clever," flattered the reporter.

"I know," preened the campaign manager. "You gotta stay on your toes to win elections.

"And if making a few phone calls is too much work, just look up some names and addresses in the local obituaries. Dead voters aren't officially eligible of course, except in Chicago!", and he laughed loudly, "but it usually takes years for states and cities to take dead people off the voter rolls. Believe me, our campaign carries an overwhelming majority of the 'Zombie Vote'!" He laughed again, and his face, normally very red, perhaps from drinking, became even redder.

"The same goes for people in prison," he went on. "In our state, felons can vote now. Grab some criminal's name from a headline about rape or murder, and pretend you're him. There's zero chance of him showing up," he chortled, "at least 'til he's paroled!"

"Well, I gotta go now," he told the undercover journalists. "I got a meeting with the IRS about the rival candidate."

The professor pressed the button on the display, ending the video.

"As you can see, class, you can boost voter turnout in many ways. In a Jeffersonian democracy such as ours, poor voter participation just won't do. We must aim for 'one man, one vote', actually, 'multiple men, one vote'! Ha hah!

"So thank you, Sandy Flake, for your enlightening presentation. And I want to thank every student for attending this class. I hope to see all of you on the campaign trail, and in the voting booth, or booths, that is, if you're voting more than once!"

The Founders left the school fascinated by what they'd learned, although rather determined to never run for public office.

"The Founders Witness a Great Storm"

The Founders had taken to spending time in the nearby town of Alexandria, Virginia, ten miles down the Potomac from D.C. The place had hundreds of buildings dating from the colonial and Revolutionary War eras, and could make them almost feel like they were back in their own time. It was a genteel and quiet place, away from the bustle—and prying eyes—of the Capital, and often visited by tourists seeking a quiet day of historic sightseeing and shopping after "doing the museums" of the National Mall.

Memories of Ancient Broils

Early one very rainy morning, the Founders themselves played tourist, and strolled about Alexandria's Old Town. At a graveyard in a narrow alley of the Old Presbyterian Meeting House, they came upon the little-known Tomb of the Unknown Revolutionary War Soldier. The inscription on the burial slate of the slain patriot was faded, but not the memory of the onlookers.

"I'll never forget the horror, and the pride," said Abigail, "of the battles near my hometown." She placed on the tomb one of the roses she'd bought at the town market.

"How many did we lose in all, Doctor?" asked Jefferson, always gloomy in recalling the bitter British invasions of his Commonwealth state, and America generally.

"If you made the numbers proportional to the population today," murmured Franklin, wiping drops of rain off his bald pate, "which is some 320 million souls, it would come out to a veritable holocaust—six million dead and missing."

Walking down the small alley to the street, still named Royal after the British king, they noticed the elegant St. Mary's Catholic Church, dating from 1793, standing next to the venerable Presbyterian one.

"I recall word of its founding," said Jefferson, "while in Paris as Secretary of State for President Washington. Ironic that it was built during the French Revolution's Terror, when Catholic prelates were being imprisoned and killed by the score." Jefferson thought of his good friend Thomas Paine, author of "Common Sense," who'd been jailed and almost executed in Paris around that time.

"The locals here must have been shocked," said Abigail, "at a gaudy Papist cathedral taking root next to a trim, modest Puritan one."

"Alexandria was always a seaport," replied Jefferson, "and always open to diverse influences, including the Catholics down the Chesapeake in their saint Mary Land colony." He pointed out the pineapple sculpture at the entrance to a house built during their time. "Did you have these in Boston, in Philadelphia?" he asked his friends. "No? Serving pineapple, imported from the bustling Asia trade, was a mark of hospitality here in Virginia's seaport towns."

Raising umbrellas to shield themselves from the rain, they moved on, and came across the boyhood home of Robert E. Lee, the Confederate general, and son of Gen. "Light Horse" Harry Lee. Jefferson had known the latter, a fellow Virginian and staunch patriot, at the Continental Congress, and

Franklin knew him from the Constitutional Convention that led to the Constitution.

The Lee house was a block down from Washington Street which, they were pleased to see, had not kept its old name of King George Street. Yet there they encountered disturbing evidence of old American discord: Confederate graves under the shrubs of Christ Church; and, further down the boulevard, a defiant Confederate statue, of a soldier with his back, and backside, deliberately turned on the Washington Monument visible far in the distance.

The thought of Americans fighting fellow Americans put the Founders in an even greater gloom than at the Tomb of the Unknown.

"Faced with a dire outside threat," said Franklin, "we managed to get past our regional differences, and unite, during the Revolution."

"But we ever had the 'wolf at our throat'," replied Jefferson, speaking of slavery, "and the fissures from that unfortunate institution became overwhelming."

"'Unfortunate' is hardly strong enough a word for it," said Abigail, recalling her searing exposure to forced labor during her time as First Lady in Washington, where the slave trade was legal. "Perhaps, if your Southern states had outlawed the practice, as we in New England did—"

"—I tried to outlaw it in the territories, North or South," replied Jefferson quickly, turning more downcast, "as a legislator during the Articles of Confederation period, after the Revolution and before the Constitution. But," he stated, his heart falling, "my proposed law lost by one vote."

"It might not have been properly enforced in any case," noted Franklin, "given the bungling government we have—we had, under the Articles. But

277

it does show how every vote does matter. I wonder what ever happened to the pro-slavery lawmaker who cast the decisive vote?"

An Old Town Ramble

The Founders' spirits rose just off King Street—still unfortunately named in honor of British royals—on encountering General Washington's old town house. Moderns Alexandrians had restored the two-story, brick-and-stone place, Washington's home away from his Mt. Vernon home.

"It's just as I remember!" cried Jefferson, casting his architect's eyes over the foundation, then gazing across Cameron Street to the manse of Lord Fairfax, the British magnate sympathetic to the Revolution.

"Sometimes," he told his friends, "General Washington would entertain us at his home, after services at Christ Church, on some cold winter morning, after servants had placed hot coals in the metal pew boxes to warm us, and later Washington would offer us beverages warmed on the Franklin stove of his home."

Jefferson smiled. "The central heating of today makes all that sound rather quaint."

Franklin, the noted optician, was intrigued by the home's unusual, and wary, means of greeting a visitor. A series of reflective mirrors outside the entrance door allowed the owner, while sitting in the comfort of his parlor, to identify who was outside, and to decide whether or not to answer the door.

"I wager," smiled Franklin, "that Washington often left you two and Mr. Adams out here in the cold after some bitter political dispute." The three laughed.

In the rain, they walked up King St. to the edge of Old Town, whose boundary was marked by two unusually named, parallel streets, "Patrick" and "Henry", after the Virginia governor and firebrand of the Revolution.

"Because of his 'Give me liberty or give me death' speech," remarked Jefferson, "most people today would be surprised to learn that Governor Henry opposed the Constitution and the federal government it established."

"You're right," said Abigail. "He had an ally in that regard in my own state, with Sam Adams."

"Some said at the time, Thomas," commented Franklin, "that your own sympathies lay against the Constitution."

"I supported the compromises you and the other delegates worked out in Philadelphia," replied Jefferson. "But I feared the Central Authority would grow bloated, ruinously expensive, engage in open-ended foreign wars, and be destructive of the people's liberties.

"Not that any of that," he smiled wanly, "has come about."

They then headed back down King St., a road actually surveyed and laid out by a young George Washington, Jefferson noted, and not King George, and strolled in the rain to the town's broad waterfront.

As a respite from the downpours, they stopped at one of their favorite haunts, the Torpedo Factory, a munitions plant from the Second World War, long converted to an artist colony where sculptors, painters, and other craftsmen worked in studio offices open to the gazing public. Jefferson enjoyed how the designers had preserved the original architecture of an arms factory while transforming it into a cultural center. Abigail admired the handmade dresses, scholarly books, and jewelry on sale, while Franklin was fascinated by several cutting-edge artists engaged in multi-media work, melding graphics, text, and Internet news into social media apps.

On arriving, they split up to pursue their separate interests. About a half hour later, Jefferson saw Abigail in the main floor's crowded gift shop, awkwardly carrying several bags of purchases. She approached Jefferson, and dropped one of the parcels. When the latter reached down to pick it up, he noticed that the floor of the lobby was covered with a thin film of water. He looked up to the entrance facing the harbor, and saw water pouring in.

Jefferson spotted Franklin on the second floor, standing in the studio of a multi-media artist. "Ben!" he shouted. "There's a flood!"

The trio rushed outside the Factory to the city docks, and all were soaked by a drenching gale. Just in front of them, the mighty and muddy Potomac, as it often did, had overflowed its banks, and was steadily rising, and covering the waterfront. Alarmed, they hiked briskly with many town residents and tourists to King St., which had a steady incline up from the river, and afforded a place to collect themselves away from the deluge.

From their roadside perch, they saw the waters spill into the main intersection of King St. and Union St. And they watched the denizens of Alexandria act quickly to protect their historic town. Before every threatened store front, owners and employees wielded shovels to fill up large sand bags, and laid them against the entrances. Up King St., workers in overalls slipped into manholes to check water and electrical lines. A private bus arrived bearing a church group, which dispensed sandwiches and coffees to the workers. The surge was nearing a condo complex, and a town cab company offered free rides to get residents out of harm's way. Inside their homes, some locals got on their amateur ham radios to keep their neighbors informed of weather and tidal updates.

Heroes to the Rescue

Dr. Franklin pulled out the collapsible telescope he carried in his waistcoat, and surveyed the river flowing over the shore. Four or five feet of rising water now filled the intersection. He zoomed in on a pier at the water's edge—and dropped his scope.

"Follow me!" he bellowed, and charged down King St towards the Potomac. Jefferson squinted at where Franklin had been peering, and dimly made out a woman with two infants clinging to the pier, and struggling in the surf.

He and Abigail took off after their gray-haired friend, who bounded with surprising speed down the street's decline. Just as they caught up, Franklin neared the intersection, took two quick steps into the water, and leapt into the air with an arching dive into the waves.

Jefferson well knew Franklin's ability as a swimmer. He dove in right behind, then desperately stroked behind Franklin's swift-moving draft, trying to keep up. Abigail did the same behind the former President, thankful of the funnel-shaped wake his large frame created.

Heart pounding, Franklin made it first to the pier; the mother was battling to keep her head and her infants above the churning water. He grabbed one of the babies; Jefferson, just behind him, and gasping from swallowed surge, took the other. Abigail, reaching the mother, urged the woman to grab onto her.

The three Founders turned on their backs, life-guard style, letting their charges rest on their chests. With one arm clutching a victim and the other paddling toward shore, sheets of rain and gusts of wind sweeping them, they began inching toward dry land.

Then, to their horror, they found themselves pulled by the currents away from the town and out onto the surging, flotsam-filled Potomac.

The two babies wailed horribly, their mother screamed in distress. Jefferson turned his neck to spot the other Founders, and a large log smashed into his forehead, stunning him, almost knocking him unconscious, nearly causing him to lose the baby.

"Try to hold on!" yelled Franklin. "Perhaps we'll reach calmer water!"

Abigail saw the new danger first. A 60-foot yacht—which the surging water had ripped from its mooring—rushed toward the swimmers, threatening to crush them.

"Watch out!" cried the former First Lady. Involuntarily, the three Founders suddenly stopped stroking, in awful expectation, as the yacht loomed over them.

And, for a horrifying eternity, it kept looming over them. Frozen, as if by an invisible hand. Struggling to keep the mother and infants on their chests, the Founders looked up at the yacht's bow, and awaited their doom. But the vessel, miraculously, stayed where it was, a few feet from swamping them.

Through the driving rain, they watched the starboard and port sides of the yacht waver, and creak and groan. Slowly, other craft became dimly visible in the near distance. Crew members aboard other boats were throwing ropes and hooks onto the rails of the yacht. Franklin tried to make the vessels out but his bifocals, though somehow still on his face, were hopelessly befogged. Abigail, with the sharpest vision of the three, saw that they were sail boats, emblazoned with the marking, "Old Dominion River Club". Seeing the marauding yacht, members of the waterfront club had taken their sailing boats out in the storm, and corralled the errant ship.

A measure of Franklin's hoped-for calm arrived. The rain, and the tide, tempered a bit, and the Founders slowly backstroked with their charges toward the southern end of the town's swollen waterfront. They made shore near some old warehouses and new condos, and deposited the woman and her children with some of the many volunteers along the shore from the Salvation Army, Chamber of Commerce, and local civic organizations that were helping townspeople cope.

The same Good Samaritans provided the Founders with dry clothing and hot drinks. Word of their own good deed spread quickly, and a TV van from the local station of a national network nosed in their direction. They waved off the reporters, with Jefferson stating, "Anyone would have done what we did," worried that a camera might air footage of them that reConstitution Biotek might see. "It would be unfortunate to be found out," Abigail told her companions, "for simply doing what good citizens should do: help one's fellow citizens."

They walked along Lee Street, well above the flooded area. Franklin's gout, which the biotech engineers had neglected to cure in his "new edition," was acting up, his big toe inflamed from the mad dash to the river, and the hard kicking of his swim. They wended their way to King St. and to Pat Troy's pub, and further revived themselves there with hot grub and, for Franklin and Jefferson, coffees and Irish whiskey; the tee-totaling Abigail stuck to hot tea. When their meal was done, they headed out straight for the waterfront, curious to see the effects of the storm.

The waters had quickly receded, leaving little mark of the flood but for puddles near the shoreline. They returned briefly to the Torpedo Factory to retrieve Franklin's day pack, which he had left on the floor of a dry, upper-story studio.

At King and Union streets, the volunteers, policemen, workmen, shopkeepers, and others were restoring the town to normalcy. At the intersection, the Founders noticed a tall post marking and dating the high-water marks of previous floods. The highest crease was 24 feet in 1913, the lowest was 2 feet in 1874, with other flood years likewise marked.

"They forgot about 1779," Jefferson told the others. "That was a bad one—another worry on top of the war. But I recall, in the governor's office, receiving dispatches of countless acts of voluntary assistance, just like today."

"Yes," remarked Franklin proudly, "many Americans here certainly haven't lost their individual initiative, and sense of civic pride."

A Jaunt up the Potomac

They noticed that, despite the storm, the Independence, a tourist ship plying regularly from Alexandria to Georgetown, was still operating. Too excited by the morning's events to rest, Franklin, Adams, and Jefferson determined to take the boat upriver, to see how the Capital City was itself handling the tempest.

Soon the Independence chugged against the downstream current, its hull banged by floating logs, its prow shaken by waves. Despite occasional squalls, Jefferson and Adams spent most of the journey on the top deck, which afforded a wide view of the river basin. Franklin went below to take a look at modern engines.

"It uses a diesel apparatus," he said on returning, "a sort of advanced James Watt steam engine, but with a petroleum distillate for fuel."

"I still can't get over the fact that these heavy things can float," commented Abigail.

"It's all physics, and ballast," said Franklin, "if the latter sufficiently exceeds the mass of the ship." As the rain picked up again, he looked over Abigail, whose dress and long dark hair were soaked, and Jefferson, whose forehead had a welt where the log had struck him.

"Are you two feeling all right?" asked Franklin, his ponytail dripping rain water.

Jefferson nodded stoically while Abigail said, "This journey is placid compared to the voyages John and I took across the Atlantic, when he traveled to serve as envoy in Paris. We feared capture by the Royal Navy, which would have hanged my husband for treason. On other occasions, storms almost sank and drowned us."

The Independence approached its berth on the Georgetown waterfront. To the left was a large wooded island close to the river's Virginia side.

"My friend George Mason owned that peninsula," said Jefferson, "It was sodden and mosquito-ridden, a font for the plague. He sold it off."

"A bad real estate move," remarked the canny Franklin, "given what it'd be worth today." He glanced at the smart phone he'd reprogrammed with added functions. "It's a wildlife refuge now."

As persons of the 18th century, Franklin and Abigail were still getting accustomed to the notion of having to *protect* wildlife, as opposed to protecting themselves from the beasts of the wild. Jefferson, who'd himself set aside some wild lands for preservation in the 1700s, was pleased by the now-common practice.

"It's called Teddy Roosevelt Island," Franklin added, "after that energetic president of the early twentieth century."

"He was a hunter, an equestrian, and, what is the term, a 'cow boy', right?" asked Jefferson. "As well as an author, historian, city police chief, and diplomat, among other duties and chosen pursuits."

"A true Renaissance Man, like you two," said Abigail.

Recalling the campaign school they'd observed, she added: "It seems the statesmen of today are more narrowly cut."

"They spend their lives politicking, or lawyering, or lobbying, or campaigning, or talking, and little else."

On their right, running for half a mile near a narrow river road, were two sprawling concrete structures they recognized from their sporting event.

"What horrific urban design!" declaimed Jefferson. "Those hideous buildings cut off the city center from its natural resting point along the Potomac!"

Franklin displayed on his phone the images of the Watergate complex and the Kennedy Center.

"The authorities," continued Jefferson, thinking of the stately structures he designed, "would do well to demolish those buildings, and open up their fair town to the river. Think of the waterside parks one could design with all that space!"

"The structure over there," said Franklin, pointing a bit upriver, "is the Watergate hotel and condominiums." He shrugged at the latter term. The Founders were puzzled why anyone would pay a steep monthly upkeep for a domicile they in theory owned, as opposed to maintaining it themselves and owning it outright.

Franklin glanced through a wiki on the subject. "It was the site, some forty years ago, of a break-in, by operatives of one political faction into the offices of the other faction. It resulted, during a time of protracted foreign war, economic crisis, and cultural turmoil, in the threatened impeachment, and forced resignation, of the Chief Magistrate, for failing to fully disclose his knowledge of the burglary."

"It's odd," said Jefferson, "that so severe a penalty was imposed for so seemingly minor an offense. In my presidency, for instance, we reserved court action for such things as high treason by Vice President Burr, for trying to steal away half of the country as a personal preserve. That's what I call an impeachable crime—and Burr never served a day!"

"I observe that's a burr," winked Franklin, "that still gets under your skin."

The rain had stopped, and some sunlight began peeking through the roiling clouds. Abigail toweled some of the remaining water from her hair. "Refresh my memory. What again is that squat, ugly edifice just downriver?"

The concrete and steel-rod construction looked like three layers of a giant wedding cake that someone had squashed together and pushed to the water's edge. The Founders could see holes where chunks of stone had dropped from the building's overhang onto the roadway underneath.

"It's the Kennedy Center." Franklin consulted his app. "The Kennedys were a large and influential family whose members included the president, an attorney general, and the longest-serving senator in American history."

The Founders remembered Jefferson's hellish vision about President Kennedy's assassin. "Yes," said Jefferson of the president, "like Hamilton, he died tragically and before his time, from the gunshot wounds of a villain."

Abigail stated: "I know about the senator, who was from my Commonwealth. At the start of his career, he drove a motor carriage off a bridge in Massachusetts, with a young female acquaintance. He fled the scene, before returning much later, after the woman had drowned."

"And went on to be the longest-serving senator?" wondered Franklin.

"These moderns have a strange sense of what constitutes a serious crime and what doesn't."

A Riverbank Banquet

The Independence reached its berth at Georgetown's riverfront, and the Founders disembarked, their limbs stiff from the journey and their prior heroics.

They alighted at a scenic waterfront park extending a thousand yards up to the Key Bridge. Offshore, teams of rowers in sculls, eager to get in a workout during a break in the weather, braved the perilous currents, and labored against the river's flow.

"This sort of park is exactly," said Jefferson, "what should replace those Watergate and Kennedy monstrosities."

Observing the Potomac, Abigail swallowed hard. "I pray we won't have to make another riverine rescue. Look—the water is rising again."

It was true. Though the local downpour had paused, a surge of water, from torrential rains upstream, was pushing downriver.

The Founders drifted from the park to the adjoining wharf of outdoor restaurants and bars. Normally crowded, the establishments had been abandoned during the tempest. But with the pause in the rain, they'd begun to regain their usual clientele. A horde of workers and managers from lobbying firms, congress, the White House, city government agencies, and federal departments, given the day off due to the storm, were filling up the tables and stools, drinking liquor and eating heartily, placing the considerable expenses on charge cards.

Here the idlers, and the Founders, were disappointed to find their river view cut off—by a thin, rusty metal curtain, about 12 feet high, that ran along the restaurant portion of the shore.

Franklin stated, "It's a levee of sorts. To keep floodwaters out." He skimmed a wiki. "The local authorities, with an assist from the Army Corps of Engineers, built this thing back in the 1960s."

"It looks like it couldn't withstand a gentle breeze," said Abigail, "much less a savage storm."

"There've been calls for its reconstruction and strengthening for decades," replied Franklin. "But the authorities," and he looked at the government employees and lobbyists celebrating at the tables, "said there were more pressing priorities."

"What could be a greater priority for any government," asked Jefferson, "than a reliable means to protect its citizens' safety?"

Jefferson, to his dismay, then noticed the second leakage of the day.

"Look!" he called out. "Water's seeping under the metal curtain."

"Not only there," cried the sharp-eyed Abigail, "but there!" Looking like Diana, the huntress of the woods, she pointed like an arrow downriver, where cracks had appeared in sections of the curtain, through which filthy river water was dripping. The Founders' concern soared to alarm when the leaks turned into spurting jets of water.

Continuing their feast were those in the bistros—senators, advocates, hangers-on, presidential aides, pressure-group lawyers, bribe takers, agency wonks, bribe givers, congressmen, disappointed office seekers, policy geeks, solicitors, party hacks, committee staffers, influence peddlers, interns, PR flacks, miscreants, legislative assistants, community agitators, appropriation chasers, and more lawyers.

The loudest group was a tabletop of three older men, in reverends' guise, two from Chicago, and one from Brooklyn, named Jeremiah, Louis, and Al. Their ample bellies tumbled over their Armani belts. The rain began to pick up again, but they little noticed, intent on their chomping and chatting, as flacks and family looked on.

Abigail observed that the reverends gave the impression of non-stop motion with their collective mouths, either eating, drinking, burping, speaking, or opinionating every moment, often all at the same time. She wondered how any were able to comprehend what the others were saying.

'And if these men are really reverends," she reflected, "then I'm the Pope.'

At another table, a film crew from a local network television station was recording an interview with a former congressman, the ex-head of the Joint Ethics Committee, who'd resigned after continuously tweeting photos of his affair with a prostitute. The legislator, who'd recently returned to public view via an anchorman slot on cable TV, was hoping to further his comeback that day with announcement of a run for governor.

"If anyone was offended by my past transgressions," he told the reporter, "then I sincerely regret it. If they were not offended, then I welcome their support."

An Irreverent Reckoning

The Founders heard a rumbling from the riverside. They thought it might be thunder, but thought again as the sections of the curtain with the leaks shuddered, then collapsed.

Just feet from the breach, Jefferson was knocked down by a stream of onrushing water, and knocked into the shorter Abigail, who fell into Franklin, who toppled like a soggy bowling pin.

The level of the water was quickly dissipated throughout the broad harbor front, and they scrambled to their feet in river sludge up to their thighs.

But then other sections of the curtain collapsed, and the rushing water, a swift, boiling current, reached their waists, and higher. Struggling, they lurched away from the river.

This second collapse seized the attention of the diners, who paused all at once, wine glasses, scotch tumblers, money proffered, money accepted, forks, and butter knives frozen in mid-air, eyes fixed on the missing sections of metal curtain and the onrushing water.

In a panic, the three reverends started to, or tried to, run, slowly, given their bulk, and habitual lack of exertion, below the neck, or above the eyes. Then, after trotting a few steps, they stopped cold, despite their peril, on seeing the television crew.

Suddenly able to move with great speed, the sharply dressed preacher Al from Brooklyn rushed over to the reporter. Once a schemer behind a murderous arson in New York, he was now a radio host and White House Counselor to Underserved Communities.

"A catastrophe like this disproportionately affects the disadvantaged," he bellowed into a microphone, digging into his gold teeth with a silver toothpick.

"I demand a faster response from the government, and more financial aid that my organization could funnel to the needy, after taking its share for administrative costs."

A waiter rushed up to him with several hundred dollars, stating, "Sir, the change from your meal." This reverend Al, who usually saved his Sunday sermons for talk shows, stored away the cash in supersized pockets.

He was pushed from the camera by another of the preachers, a fellow nattily dressed in a silk suit and bow tie, who spoke in a slow, sing-song, almost-calypso-like way.

"This flood, is a *conspiracy*," he inveighed. "I know I saw a U.S. Navy ship, that's the U.S. *Navy*, plant a depth charge, *underwater!* Near the metal curtain *levee*, just an hour ago! That's right, *I did!*"

"How could you see the river," asked the puzzled reporter, "when the metal curtain was still intact?"

"Oh, I remember *now!*" said the preacher, in a halting, angry way that seemed aimed at pulling at and piling up the raw emotions of his listeners. "I saw them plant it, plant the *bomb*, just *minutes ago*—when a panel of the curtain gave way, as if blown inward, by a *powerful bomb!* That's it, I *do remember!*

This preacher was shoved aside by another reverend, also a Windy City resident, with a scowl on his face and rainbow-colored vestments draped over slanted shoulders.

"This bomb plot," he screamed, "is proof of the evil design behind America! God has damned America, and its chickens are coming home to roost!" And he accepted the oversized doggy bag his waiter had brought him.

The water was by then lapping near the reverends and the TV crew. The latter hurriedly packed up its gear and hastened up a set of steps behind the restaurants. The former began to haul their heavyset physiques up the stairs, when a speed boat from another network rushed up to the waterfront. Its outboard engines strained to keep the vessel in place, to let its camera crew shoot footage of the flooding harbor.

The reverends couldn't help themselves. Their only path to salvation lay in quickly mounting the steps. But the camera was only 70 yards away, and beckoned to them like the irresistible siren sound of a whirlpool luring sailors to their deaths.

The New York rabble rouser, like before, acted first, taking a step down, the water at his shins, then another step, the water at his chest. The two Chicago agitators followed. All three were stunned by the force of the current and, losing their footing, were swept into the torrent. They emerged far from the stairs, gasping, swallowing buckets of river filth, their swollen bodies like giant buoys swirling in the waves. Still, their main concern was not their safety, but the attention of the camera, which steadily recorded their desperate flailing to gain its angry-eyed attention.

They got their wish, sort of. An undertow took hold, pulling them to within feet of the boat, whose reporters tried to grab the reverends' arms, which were stretched out waving at the camera. The journalists managed to grab the greasy palms of two of the preachers, but the hands slipped from their grasp.

Then the undertow swirled them past the boat into the open river, and sent them hurtling downstream in the raging current.

Hightailing It to High Ground

On the waterfront, the waters kept rising. The surge undermined the remaining portions of the curtain, which fell with a mighty whoosh. Water poured into the land as in a tsunami.

The fleeing Founders mounted the broad steps above the restaurants, and bumped into the television crew attempting the same. They looked behind them, and realized with dread the surge would consume them before they reached the top of the stairs. They all stopped, expecting their demise.

'Such a contrast to my previous death,' thought Jefferson philosophically. 'I was very ill, but home at Monticello, made comfortable by family and servants, awaiting the end for days. This, though, so violent and quick.'

Franklin wondered, 'Will they revive us again in some other time and place? I rather hope so—there's so much to learn and experience about the novelties and innovations of future times.'

Abigail was more practical, and vocal.

"Everyone, look! Run to that entrance!" The perceptive Adams had spotted the back door of a high-rise condominium behind the restaurants. The door was propped open, and the group ran for its lives, entering seconds before the waters surged past.

They fled up the staircase, the rising water trailing behind. The Founders helped the crew carry its heavy TV gear up six flights of steps. Lungs pounding, they emerged on a rooftop that afforded a sweeping view of the ongoing drama below.

Downriver, the circular shape of the three drowned, heavyset reverends, like receding buoys, could still be glimpsed, but growing smaller, as they floated steadily south. Directly below, the flood had shattered the chairs and counters of the eateries into a thousand chunks and splinters, flotsam in the tide.

The would-be governor, his interview interrupted, was now clinging to a piece of floating tabletop, and paddling madly away from his thrashing mistress, who threatened to swamp his skimpy raft. In his panic, he paddled into the undertow, and was carried into the river, his mistress right behind, trying to reach him, both rushing to their doom.

The Founders and the camera crew crossed to the northern side of the roof, and were horrified at the sight. In minutes, the water had flooded many low-lying city blocks, with water rushing into scores of businesses and houses. They spotted hundreds of people milling on the roofs of their homes, after bolting from flooded basements and ground floors.

However, the angry Potomac had left the higher ground of M Street untouched, leaving a dry escape route to Foggy Bottom, one mile to the east.

The Founders moved to the rooftop's eastern edge, which afforded a view of both the harbor and the destruction inland. The TV reporter and her workmates set up their satellite dish, camera, and monitors. One monitor provided a live feed from their studio, which was broadcasting footage of the city mayor, the Honorable Gray Noggin, attending a fundraiser.

"His Honor," announced the onscreen reporter, "has for now put off issuing an Evacuation Order for affected areas of the city, as he is overwhelmed with the responsibilities of raising money for his re-election, and redistributing the funds to dummy campaigns."

"What's a dummy campaign?" Franklin asked the camerawoman. "Is he referring to his own campaign?" He figured that likely.

"No," she replied. "To draw off support from his main opponent, the Mayor gives funds to opponents who pose no threat of winning. It's illegal, but it worked in the last campaign, so he figures, 'Why not again'?"

The camerawoman began filming the dramatic scenes below her, as the reporter prepared notes for a voiceover. The Founders were starting to get used to this kind of situation, where women were in control of the group of workers. Not to mention the technology that let the media inform the public almost instantly of a major event.

Emergency Response

Abigail pointed across the river to an expanse of open land between a riverside highway and Arlington National Cemetery. She told the reporter, "I think you're missing something."

Scores of tractor-trailers, and trucks with refrigeration units, had been driving slowly along the parkway. Now they pulled off the road and motored into the broad meadow, pulling to a stop. The drivers unhooked the trailers, and drove off. Jefferson asked the purpose of all the vehicles and equipment.

"That's the work of FEMA," shrugged the reporter.

"A thigh bone?" asked Franklin. "A femur?"

"*FEMA*," stressed the reporter. "The Federal Emergency Management Administration."

"The federal government has a department to 'manage' disasters?" asked Jefferson skeptically.

"It believes so," said the reporter, who was styling her blonde locks for the next camera shoot. "After every emergency, it brings along a great many trailer homes, as temporary housing for the dispossessed, as well as refrigerated trucks, to store food and medicine, at a spot far away from the calamity."

"Well," said Franklin, "it does show concern to move into position such useful materials. When will FEMA move it into Georgetown?"

"I doubt it will," the reporter stated blandly. "It typically leaves the stuff sitting unused for months. That's certainly what it did after Hurricane Katrina. And its provisions for Hurricane Sandy were skimpy, and delayed. After a disaster passes, it moves the material back into storage, or throws it away."

"Then what good is the material?!" demanded Jefferson.

"Well," surmised the reporter, "it is a major expense item, and greatly boosts the agency's budget…So I suppose FEMA thinks it's good for something."

"More like it's good for nothing!" replied Jefferson.

"Well," said the reporter, "the government *will* compensate the store owners in the harbor for damage, though not the homeowners further back from the waterline."

"Why not?" asked Franklin. "The flood affected both equally."

The journalist explained, "It's the practice of the government to compensate those who live or do business in the most dangerous areas, such as flood zones, or along rivers with faulty levees."

"But doesn't that perversely encourage people to build, work, and live in risky areas?" queried Jefferson.

"Of course," answered the reporter. The tall fellow seemed an intelligent man, with an air of authority, but she was surprised at his naivety.

"It means the government's budget for emergency response grows greater over time, because there're more people in more disaster-prone areas."

She added: "Isn't that the purpose of any agency—to grow its budget? Or of any manager within it to 'grow his empire,' adding as much funding and personnel as possible?"

The journalist continued. "Above all, no agency can permit itself to actually solve the problem it was set up to handle. That might put it out of business. But it's real business is to stay in business, by finding new reasons for its existence."

Jefferson was thunderstruck, and not by the lightning flashing in the distance.

Staring across the river through his telescope, Franklin pointed out a man on a horse who'd appeared in the midst of the trailers. Trotting his mount along the vehicles, he seemed to be inspecting them.

"That's the head of FEMA," the reporter informed.

Borrowing his friend's scope Jefferson, a skilled equestrian, admired the horse, a thoroughbred. "Although I like this magistrate's choice of antiquated transport," he told the reporter, "I wonder why he doesn't use a mechanized conveyance."

The woman was amused at the man's odd phrasing. 'He's kind of cute,' she thought. 'Though I'm probably too young for him. He seems kind of old school, and a little stodgy. I bet he has deep pockets though; I'll tell him later to look me up on Facebook.'

"His background," the reporter explained, "was in horse breeding. And fundraising."

"But that's hardly the background for a job of this sort," said Jefferson.

"Exactly," said the reporter.

For a few moments, Jefferson and the others stood frustrated and silent.

Then the camerawoman, who'd moved back to the north side of the roof, started waving her arms excitedly. "Over here!" she shouted, peering at the streets below.

Down below, the tide in the flooded neighborhoods had retreated somewhat, to knee-high level. This allowed people who dared to wade through the streets.

"Let's pray things return to normal soon," said Abigail.

Flash Larceny

The camerawoman zoomed in on a grocery store at one of the nearer intersections.

"Looks like things are about to get very abnormal!" she grinned, happy at the chance to record a breaking story. "It's crowd of 'youths'."

Franklin was looking through his collapsible telescope at the approaching group of 20 swaggering young adults.

"'Youths'," he told Abigail and Jefferson, "is the modern term for physically able young adults who, in our era, would have been working on the family farm for their parents, or toiling in town as an workman's

300

apprentice, but who today largely sit around idle, when they're not out creating mischief."

Everyone looked at the drama below. The youths had stopped a half block from the grocery, and were talking and texting excitedly with their smart phones.

"Surely they can't be indigent," said Abigail, "if they can afford the monthly rates of modern cell phones."

As if in response to the phone messages, other youths were sloshing in from every direction to join the swelling crowd.

Eagle-eyed Abigail noticed many of the youngsters wore loose-fitting pants that hung down their derrieres, exposing their thick-cotton underwear.

"Have belts gone out of fashion?" she asked.

Franklin said in a low voice, "'Youths', 'kids': perhaps when expectations and terminology are set to the level of children, churlish and childish behavior results."

The kids, listening to their phones or keying in messages, started sloshing toward the store.

"Ten to one it's a 'flash mob'," said the camerawoman.

"A 'flash mob'," mouthed Franklin, grasping the concept instantly. "A roving gang of thugs, their prey identified and their movement aided by lightning-quick group communications."

"What are you, a lexicographer?" asked the reporter.

"I am, in fact," answered the veteran Philadelphia printer.

The youths, kids, children, adolescents, and young adults swarmed into the store like hornets. Many soon swaggered outside, toting sacks of packaged foods and alcoholic drinks, as others elbowed by them to enter.

"Is there nothing we can do?!" urged Jefferson.

"Our job is to report the news, not make it," said the journalist.

Franklin was tapping on his smart phone. "Unfortunately, cell coverage is spotty from the storm...Up here, that is. Reception seems fine down there."

"Look!" shouted the camerawoman, swiveling her camera to a new spot outside the store. "Help appears to be on the way."

They stared down, and spied three adult men, with belts around their pants, step onto the street from a side exit of the store. Apparently the proprietors, they were carrying rifles. They came around the corner of the store to confront the youths.

At the same time, five police cars, sirens flashing and whooping, and pushing out waves of water, roared up to the establishment. Ten policemen, also carrying rifles, got out of their vehicles.

"Those weapons have repeating parts, right?" asked Jefferson, as the reporter shot him a quizzical look.

"Yes," said Franklin quietly, so that the journalist couldn't hear. "Our old breech loaders are as dead as the dragons of yore. Now, a mechanism inserts the bullets automatically and rapidly into the gun chamber, greatly speeding rates of fire."

"If we had some of those at Breed's Hill," whispered Abigail, "we in Boston would have beaten the British outright."

The youths bustling about the store entrance, however, seemed not to care about either the armed store owners or the rifle-wielding cops, and kept entering and leaving the store with bundles of appropriated goods.

Then the police moved toward them.

"I pray there's no violence," said Abigail. "This is so unreal, and unnecessary."

The officers moved past the youths—and up to the store owners, and pointed their guns at them. The owners dropped their weapons. The police handcuffed them, walked them into the rear seats of their cars, and drove away.

The Founders were grim-faced.

The reporter saw their expressions, again surprised at the naivety.

"Possession of guns by citizens is practically illegal in D.C.," she lectured, "unless you spend months filling out the paperwork. And powerful weapons like rifles are strictly *verboten*."

"B—, b—, but," stammered Abigail. "They're not the ones committing the crime."

"Of course they are," corrected the journalist. "And a far more serious crime. Possession of rifles is a felony, while taking a carton of milk or a case of beer is a misdemeanor at worst." She moved off to speak with the camerawoman.

Jefferson exclaimed, "This approach turns the law on its head!"

Franklin stated: "Not even the right to bear arms, but the basic right to self-defense, is infringed upon here!"

"Infringed?" commented Abigail. "Destroyed!"

Franklin, a rare scowl on his face, took out his laptop, thankful to see its moisture-proof case had stood up to the flood. Grateful at finding a connection, he tapped rapidly on the keyboard. Within minutes, the baggy-pants flash-mobbers were running out of the store, and splashing and dashing fast towards the edge of town.

Abigail and Jefferson looked quizzically at Franklin. The Doctor told them: "Well, I hacked into some of their cell phones, and texted a phony message about a nearby spirits store abandoned by its owners." Franklin smiled. "I was tempted to give them a fake GPS location in the middle of the Potomac. Perhaps they deserved that. But they are just 'youths', after all. So I merely directed them to a deserted, Occupy D.C. encampment."

Wake of the Flood

As the sky had cleared, and the waters had dropped some, the Founders left the TV team on the roof, and descended the stairs to street level. Franklin and Jefferson rolled up their pants and Abigail took off a pair of one of her very favorite inventions of the modern world: nylons.

Curious about the flood's effect, they sloshed through streets of dirty, foul-smelling water. They came across hundreds of people sitting on the stoops of their homes or gazing vacantly out their windows. The power was still out, but they knew there was a dry, safe passage of a mile or so to the refuge of Foggy Bottom. There—Franklin had learned from scanning newscasts—many businesses, the local university, and private charities had set up air-conditioned shelters as well as portable kitchens serving hot food.

The Founders paused at various homes, and explained the way out to the residents. In so doing, they noticed, not for the first time, how lethargic so many Americans seemed. Not one person budged from his residence. When they asked why, they were inevitably told: "A mile?! That's too far. We'll wait right here: FEMA will rescue us."

Dejected, the Founders turned back to the waterfront. A sad scene met them.

At Georgetown Harbor, the tide had fallen to normal levels. Shattered pieces of wood, plastic, and metal lay scattered outdoors, and the ground floors of the restaurants were now dim caverns of wrecked equipment and sodden carpeting. A stench of decay permeated the moist air.

The trio stood at the spot where they first noticed the metal curtain leaking. There was no longer any obstacle to viewing the Potomac. Across the river, more trailers and trucks filled the agency's staging area. Near it, around a fountain dedicated to the sea god Poseidon, the agency's head was trotting his horse.

Then, glancing downriver, they were struck to see an approaching flotilla. Despite the strong flow from the storm's discharge, a mass of vessels moved steadily upriver against the current.

Normally resolute, Abigail felt fearful, for the sight reminded her of the British Fleet launching long boats filled with soldiers to occupy Boston's Revolutionary War environs. Jefferson was reminded of the dispiriting accounts he'd read in 1814, while in retirement at Monticello, of British ships sailing unopposed up the Potomac to burn down Washington.

As the fleet passed the Kennedy Center and drew closer, the Founders' discomfort turned to puzzlement. Franklin thought the vessels a mix of boats from both their own generation and contemporary times. On the one hand, there were sailboats, and long wooden shells with rowing crews, and even some row boats. On the other, there were power boats, luxury yachts, fire department boats with powerful engines and, they were surprised to see, large excursion ships, including the Independence.

The craft, large and small, modern and retro, sidled alongside the shattered harbor, its crews laying anchor or mooring their vessels to the remaining piers.

A Citizen Army

Then hundreds of people began disembarking, pushing past Franklin, Jefferson, and Adams with eager, determined expressions.

They carried tools, buckets, portable power generators, cartons of bottled water, packets of canned goods, gas stoves, and many other useful things. Many went straight to work cleaning up the debris. Others searched the wrecked restaurants for people stranded or injured by the deluge and, finding some, helped them to waiting physicians. The more mechanically inclined inspected the plumbing and wiring in the upper floors of the establishments, and strove to get the utilities back on.

Many in the influx wore shirts identifying their organization. The Founders watched members of countless groups—the Kiwanis Club, Alexandria Baptist Church, Arlington Chamber of Commerce, Church of Latter-Day Saints, Habitat for Humanity, Catholic Charities, the Alexandria town council, the United Way, the D.C. Triathlon Club, the Air Force Association, among others—disembark and get to work. Franklin noted with pleasure that municipal and volunteer fire departments, of the kind he'd founded in Philadelphia, were in the vanguard of those lending aid.

Feeling slothful and uncharitable for simply observing, the Founders pitched in. Franklin went over to the condominium where they'd taken shelter, and got its lights back on. Abigail organized a committee to identify missing children and reunite them with their parents. Jefferson led of team of inspectors to determine whether damaged shops should be restored or demolished.

The inspectors' work was slowed when an official from the government arrived, and demanded they fill out a host of forms before continuing. Then Jefferson showed the man his document identifying himself as a former Secretary of State. After apologizing profusely, the official, fearful of losing perks, pension, and pay, slinked away.

In short order, the badly injured were taken to hospitals, much of the debris was cleared out, and power was restored to many places.

As the sun began setting, the Founders, weary from their long and active day and, indeed, from the eventful months in their new lives, found themselves on the broad set of steps where they'd run into the television crew at the height of the flood. There they were surprised to see the broadcast team again, setting up its gear for another televised spot.

The Fate of the Republic

At the top of the stairs, city mayor Gray Noggin, returned at last from campaigning, raising funds, and distributing them to straw-man candidates, stood at a makeshift podium. The head of FEMA had finally appeared, and he and his horse were at the mayor's side. Camera crews from the national and international media joined the local crew.

Rocking back and forth on the wing tips of his tasseled shoes, the Mayor launched into his main theme.

"For decades, the nation ignored our pleas for help in rebuilding the vital Curtain of Safety, the noble breakwater that protected our citizens from the ravages of the Potomac. The result was today's disaster..."

A congressman from the Subcommittee on Public Works stepped by the city's chief magistrate, and slipped a bulging envelope into his jacket pocket.

"...So I demand a massive new federal effort for rebuilding our country's dams and breakwaters..."

A lobbyist for the region's largest construction unions passed by the Mayor, and popped tickets for a Cayman Island vacation into his pants.

"...And a minimum allotment of $25 billion for this fiscal year..."

Franklin, Jefferson, and Adams looked across the river at the idle FEMA trucks, then at the swarms of private citizens busily putting the town in order, and then at the verbose, demanding Mayor, and those flittering about him, seeking a piece of the public pie.

"God helps those," commented Abigail, "who help themselves."

"Yes," replied Franklin, "but some of those 'helping themselves' are not very godly."

Jefferson wondered aloud, "What kind of society do the American people have anymore?"

Franklin quoted himself in reply:

"'A Republic—if they can keep it!'"

The End of the Beginning

A few wrecked stores away, three hard-faced men stood intently watching, not the press and politicians, but the Founders.

"Well, we finally found them," said a man of Afghani descent, holding valuable thumb drives pilfered from a destroyed government building.

"They've been hiding in plain sight," stated a man whose retro clothes and hair style resembled Jefferson's. "Right here in the city of Washington!"

A third man, tousle-haired and mustachioed, twirled the Derringer for which he'd become infamous.

"It'd be an easy shot from here," he stated, peering at Jefferson. "What a dramatic act—to eliminate another president!"

"No, not now," Abdullah told John Wilkes Booth. "We may want to capture them first, before disposing of them as we wish."

"For now, I concur," said Aaron Burr arrogantly, fingering his own weapon, a .56 caliber dueling pistol. "But I have scores to settle with that vile Virginian, and with the wife of the noxious Mr. Adams."

Abdullah smiled darkly. He'd mastered reConstitution Biotek's technology: his clones were perfect! He was bringing back not heroes from the past, but villains—he would use their skills to extort and loot and wreak mayhem.

"In time," he stated, "you two can have your way with the President and the First Lady. But I'll spare Franklin's life, and force the old man to invent powerful new weapons for us."

Then he led away the killers from America's past, eager to take on the Founders in the future.

Made in the USA
Charleston, SC
17 April 2015